Addicts and Those Who Love Them
Behind every addict is someone traumatised by loving them

Antonia Rolls

First Published in Great Britain in 2025 by Drawn to a Story.

978-1-7384222-4-1

Designed by Cath Brew, www.drawntoastory.com
Paintings and words by Antonia Rolls

This book is dedicated to all the brave people who took part in the Addicts and Those Who Love Them exhibition. Behind every addict is someone traumatised by loving them, and yet, still we love. I also dedicate this to my sons Costya and Dimitri who died from addictions.

For all those suffering from this dark and painful thing, addiction, my boys showed me not only the power of a love that is tough and enduring, but that you are not your addictions. You are a soul and a person and we see you.

And still we love.

Acknowledgements

My dear friend Cath Brew created this book. Thank you Cath, and her wife, Angie who always supports. Both Cath and Angie help at the exhibitions with grace and kindness.

My dear cousin Maddy has been with me and my work for the last fifteen years. She helps with humour, dedication and love.

My daughter Lexi is always a wonderful support. She is so good at knowing what to do, as are my other great helpers Hannah Clough and Marcus Megastar.

Thank you to Ian who is on the poster and is the face of the Addicts exhibition.

Thank you to Costya who started me on this journey, and Dimitri who helped me move to the next exhibition, Beloved.

And finally thank you to all who took part in and attended the exhibitions. I acknowledge you all with gratitude.

- THE EXHIBITION -

Addicts and Those Who Love Them
Behind every addict is someone traumatised by loving them.

Portraits and words from, with, and alongside addiction.

My sons suffered dark and relentless drink and drug addictions. When they felt all hope was gone, they left this world a year apart to escape the pain.

They were 27 and 29.

I have painted portraits of those in addiction, out of addiction, those caught up in the crazy lonely, frightening world living with an addict, and those working with addicts to try and help. Onto each portrait I have painted the words, the story, of the sitter.

I am shining a light on addiction.
And still we love.

- Antonia

Table of Contents

The Paintings, The People and Their Words

"So moving, took the time to read and just absorb everyone's stories. Thank you for taking the time to share their stories and for sharing yours too. Teared up multiple time, thank you for allowing me to feel so deeply."
- Exhibition attendee

Marie 'before' words -

*Total insanity. Wild, exciting, dangerous. Lines of Coke lined up on the toilet
cistern.*

*Alcohol with cocaine
like rocket fuel.
Talking shit. Everyone
loves you.*

*All bollocks.
Not real.*

*It's not being addicted
to the drugs it's addicted
to the person you become
when on drugs.*

*Outspoken, crazy,
everyone loves me.*

Marie 'after' words -

Extreme. I think I am extreme.

*Lines of coke, then Vipassana
meditation. Not just a bit of
mindfulness but 10 days of
silence and not moving.*

*Scanning my body, from head
to toe recognising the
blockages*

I am still coming out of this.

*I'm present
I'm here.*

Marie 'before'

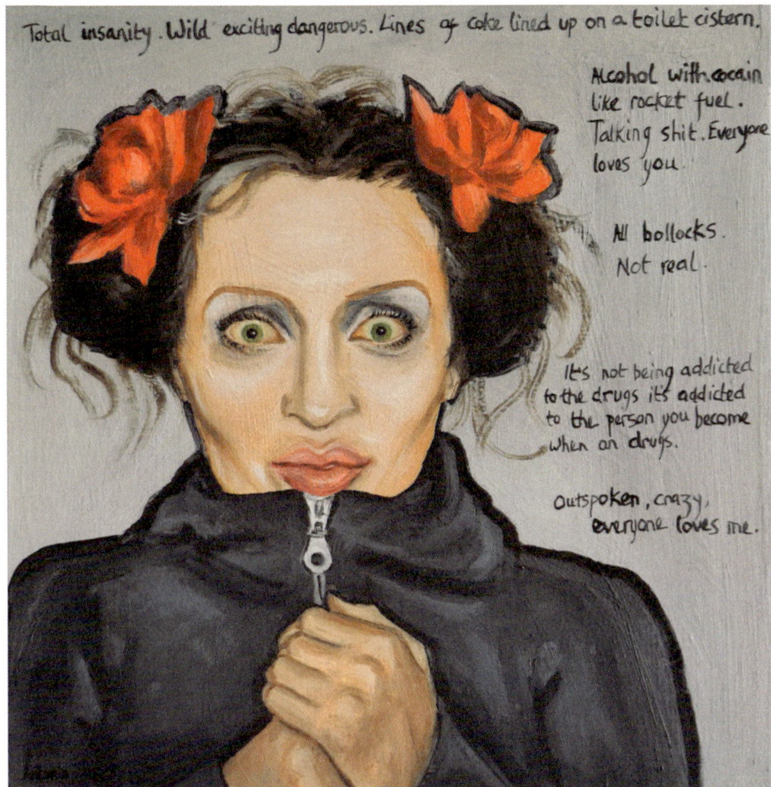

Marie, a dear friend and colleague showed her own work in the exhibition.

I didn't know her at her craziest, but I've heard the stories.

Marie 'after'

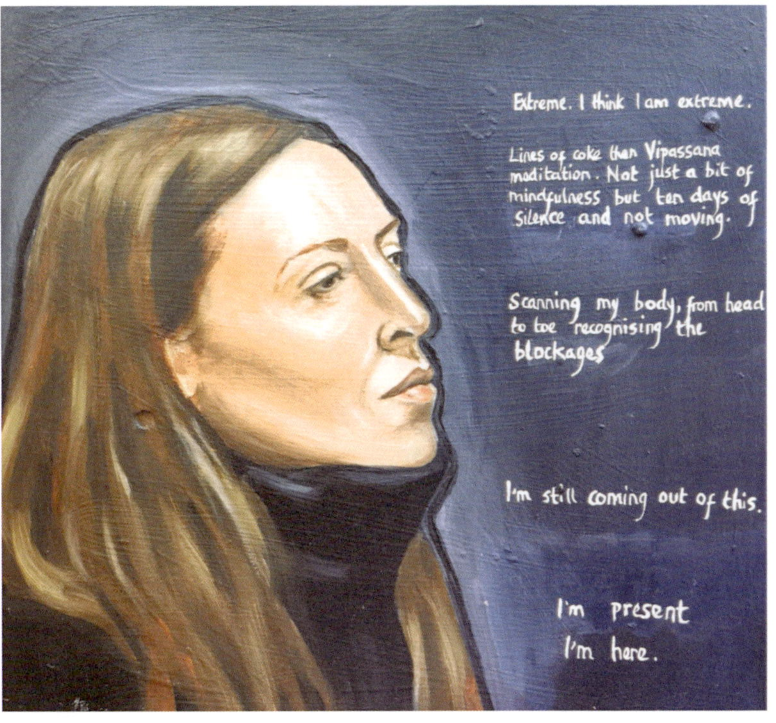

Despite a long, mindful and difficult journey into health and recovery, the crazy has not gone away. This is good. It gives her n edge on life.

Marie is a strong lady.

James | words -

It is not nice to wake up and find out you were threatening or fighting with strangers, let alone friends.

I started to realize I was frightening people.

All the intimate relationships I had ended due to my drinking.

Ever since I started. It was always to get as drunk as possible.

As extreme as possible.

After taking Valium very heavily, my brain would switch off, but my body would still function.

So I would be operating without any sense of reason. I had always drunk too much, but now I was bigger and stronger, my behaviour became more of a danger to myself and others.

The painting with my face smashed in is just what happens when you push your luck so far in the world so far, the world pushes back... I was wearing a jumper I got from a police station because I was walking in the rain in nothing but jeans. One minute. I'm okay. Next minute I'm running riot.

James 1, 2, 3

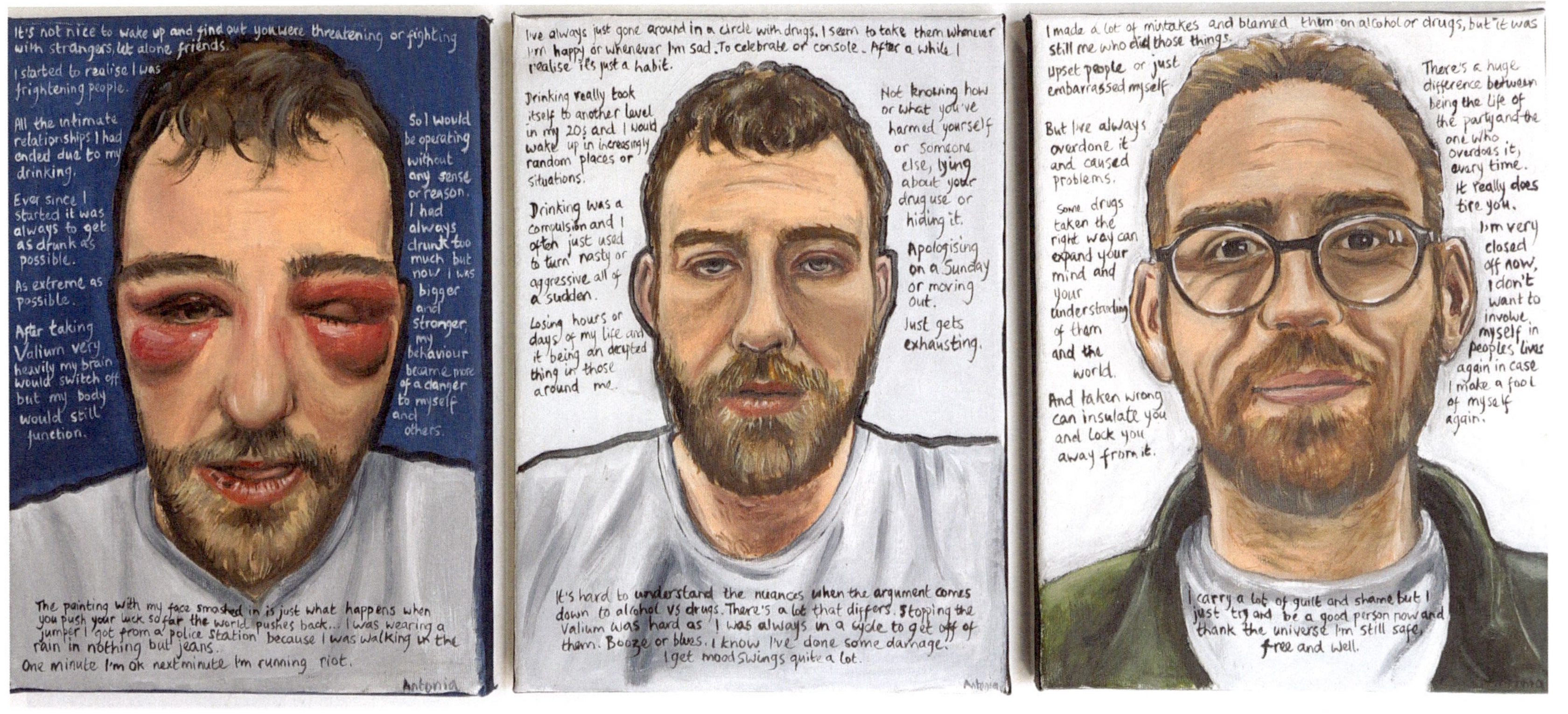

James 1   James 2   James 3

James has crazy energy. Intelligent, interesting, clever. James used to wake after fights, not remembering anything. The beaten face (James 2) is the day he went into rehab. James 3 is him today. James still struggles but he wins.

James 2 words -

I've always just gone around in a circle with drugs. I seem to take them whenever I'm happy or whenever I'm sad. To celebrate or console. After a while, I realise it's just a habit.

Drinking really took itself to another level in my 20s, and I would wake up in increasingly random places or situations.

Not knowing how or that you've harmed yourself or someone else, lying about your drug use or hiding it.

Drinking was a compulsion and I often just used to turn nasty or aggressive, all of a sudden.

Apologising on a Sunday or moving out.

Losing hours or days of my life and it being an accepted thing in those around me.

Just gets exhausting.

It's hard to understand the nuances when the argument comes down to alcohol vs drugs. There's a lot that differs. Stopping the Valium was hard as I was always in a cycle to get off of them. Booze or blues. I know I've done some damage. I get mood swings quite a lot.

James 3 words -

I made a lot of mistakes and blamed them on alcohol or drugs, but it was still me who did those things,
upset people or just
embarrassed myself.

But I've always
overdone it
and caused
problems.

Some drugs
taken the
right way, can
expand your
mind and
your
understanding
of them
and the world.

And taken wrong,
can insulate you
and lock you
away from it.

There's a huge
difference between
being the life of
the party and the
one who
overdoes it
every time.
It really does
tire you.
I'm very
closed
off now.
I don't
want to
involve
myself in
people's lives
again in case
I make a fool
of myself
again.

I carry a lot of guilt and shame, but I
just try and be a good person now and
thank the universe. I'm still safe,
free, and well.

Night Mummy

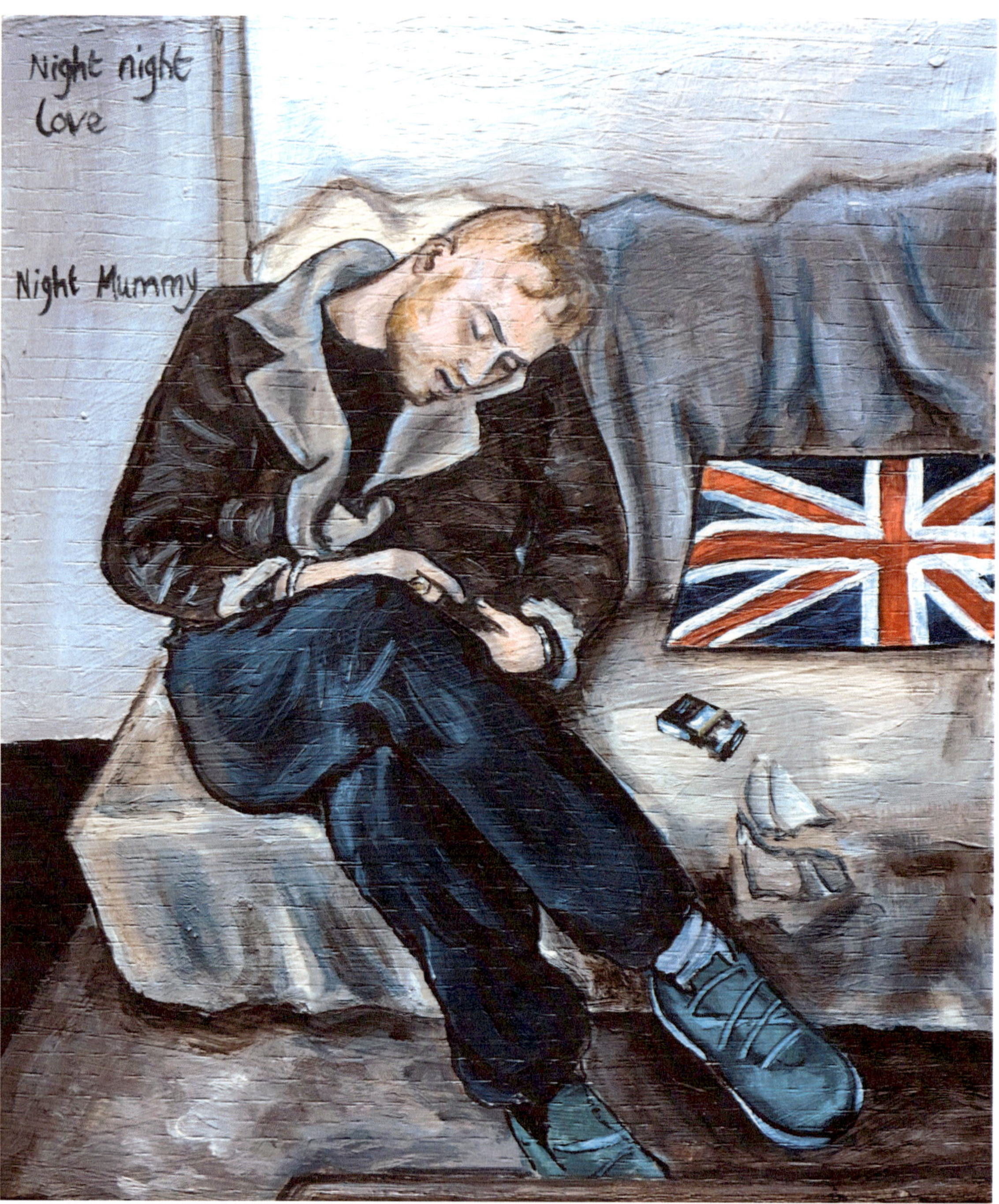

Whatever he has taken, it has made him fall into himself. The sofa is torn, and his cigarettes are beside him. I have to go now.

'Night night love', I say, and remembering when he was a little boy, he'd reply, 'Night Mummy.'

Addict's Room

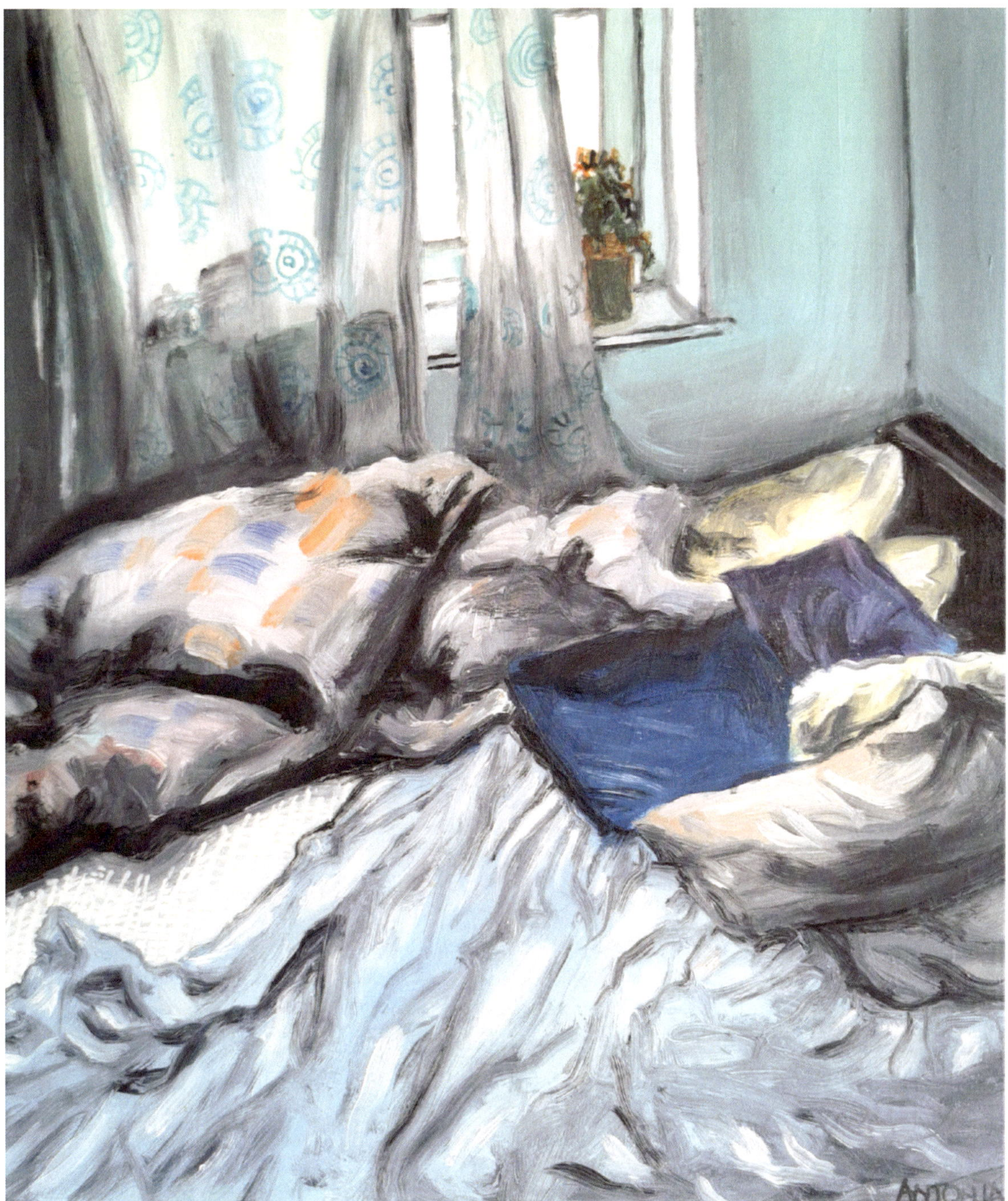

The loneliness of the unmade, unkempt bed, a dead plant on the window sill and the light coming through the windows.

We can't stop the light coming in.

Towards the Light

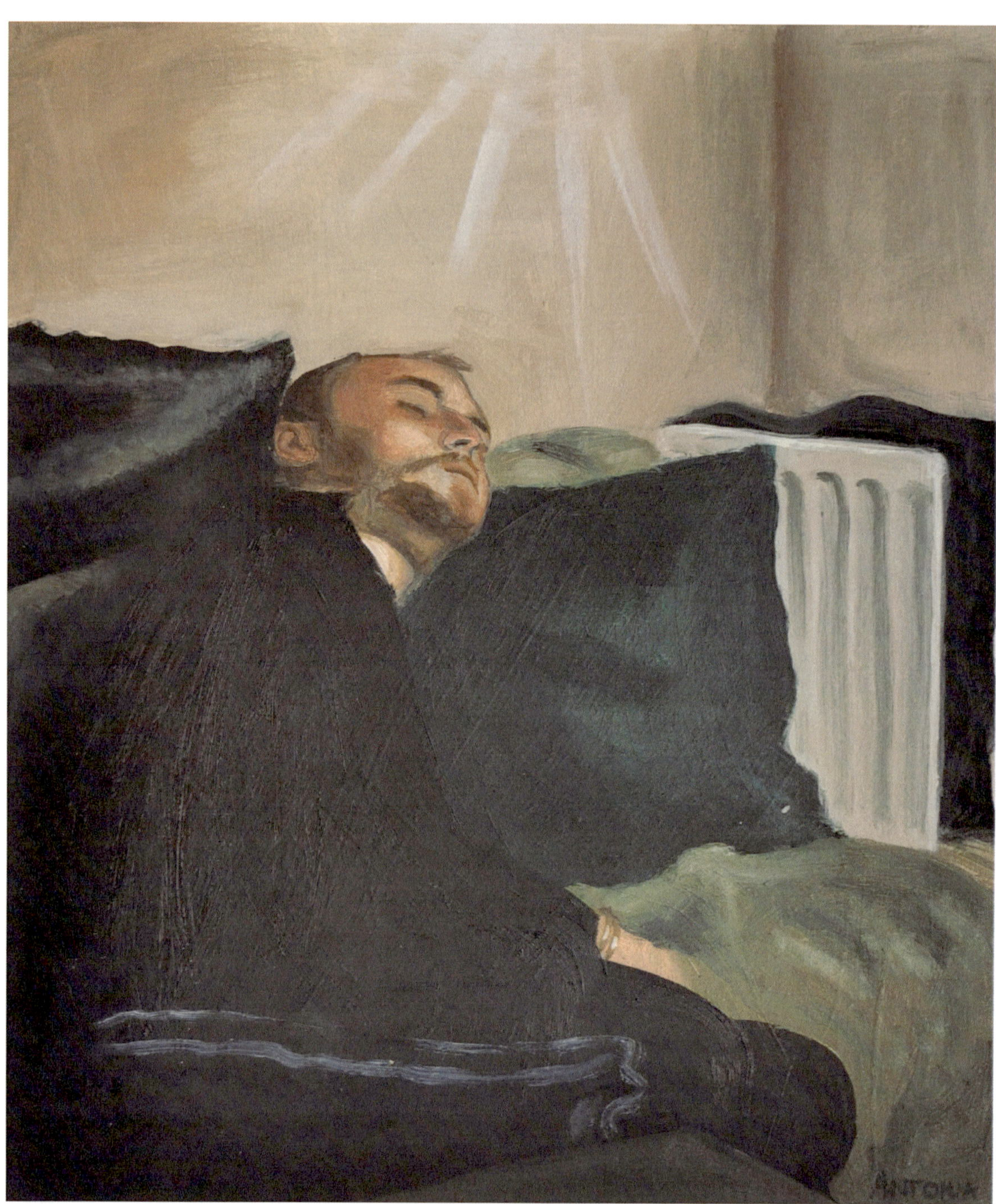

This could be a painting of an intimate interior along the lines of Rembrandt or Sickert. He has overmedicated and sits slumped on the sofa in his dark flat. The colours are warm, he looks asleep. He is sleeping but can't be woken. Why did I paint the beams of light? Perhaps there was no help, no answer, from anywhere else.

Every Addict

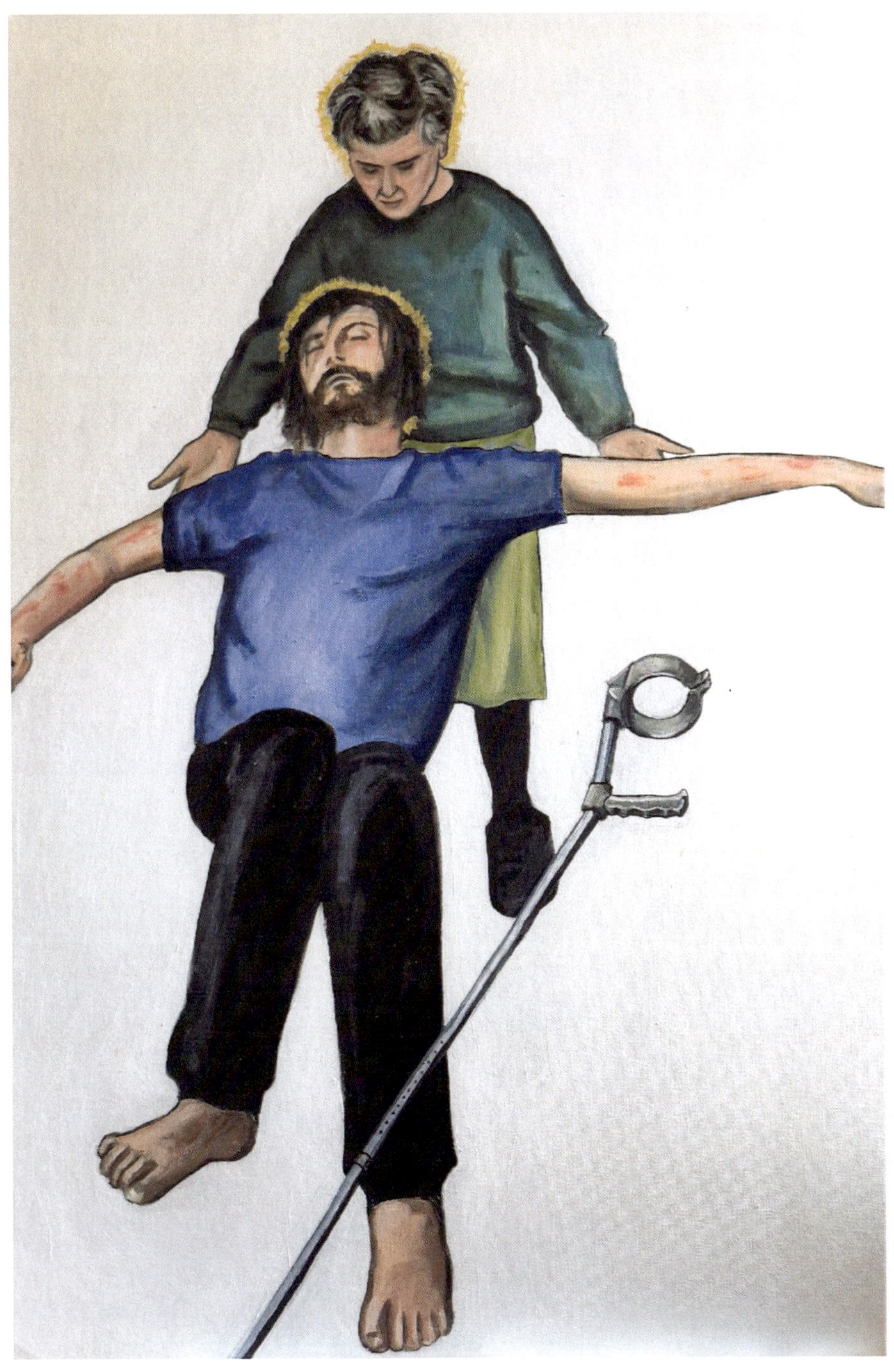

Everyman and Everywoman represent all humankind. 'Everyaddict' represents all addicts. I have painted the addict as a divine figure, desperate and flawed and held - or supported by a figure of love, and compassion. Both figures are ordinary, as we all are, but represent something bigger - love.

Dan Carden's words -

Growing up LGBT with the cumulative effect of the daily denials, the constant fear of being found out and the internalized shame, causes a deep trauma.

It took me a long time to admit that I was struggling with my mental health and alcohol addiction. It took repeated interventions from the people who really love me. I did not know, or I denied, that I had a problem. I suppressed my emotions as I had learned to do so as a kid.

I told myself things were fine. Only looking back now have I been able to accept that in my 20s I twice nearly lost my life to alcohol. I was only saved by the actions of others.

Drinking was destroying my body. It was damaging to me, to my relationships, and in so many other ways.

Alcohol addiction is not just about drinking every day or drunkenness. For me, it was about losing who I was over a long period of time. It was desperate isolation.

It was shutting down my personal life using a drug, alcohol, to feel better, but ultimately to escape and give up on living.

I now know that it has blighted most of my adult life. Fortunately, I have a mother who would protect me at all costs, a father who is the most generous, selfless man I have ever known, a brother who supported me through all this without judgment, and friends who quite literally saved my life.

I'm in recovery and I'm proud of it. Like so many in the recovery community, I'm happy. I'm healthy. I love my life. I have a wonderful, loving partner, and I appreciate everything I have. To stay here takes commitment and daily determination.

Addiction is killing more people and ruining more lives than ever. I am in a privileged position. I'm all too aware that not everyone makes it. Addiction is fatal, if not treated.

I have gone from not recognizing addiction in myself for so long to seeing it everywhere, and doing its worst damage in the most deprived communities. I hope that my openness can help challenge the stigma that stops so many people asking for help.

Nothing would mean more to me than turning the pain I have been through, and that I have put my family and loved ones through into meaningful change. In the end, it is a simple choice. Choose to hide or choose to live.

My advice is to choose to live.

Dan Carden (MP Liverpool, Labour)

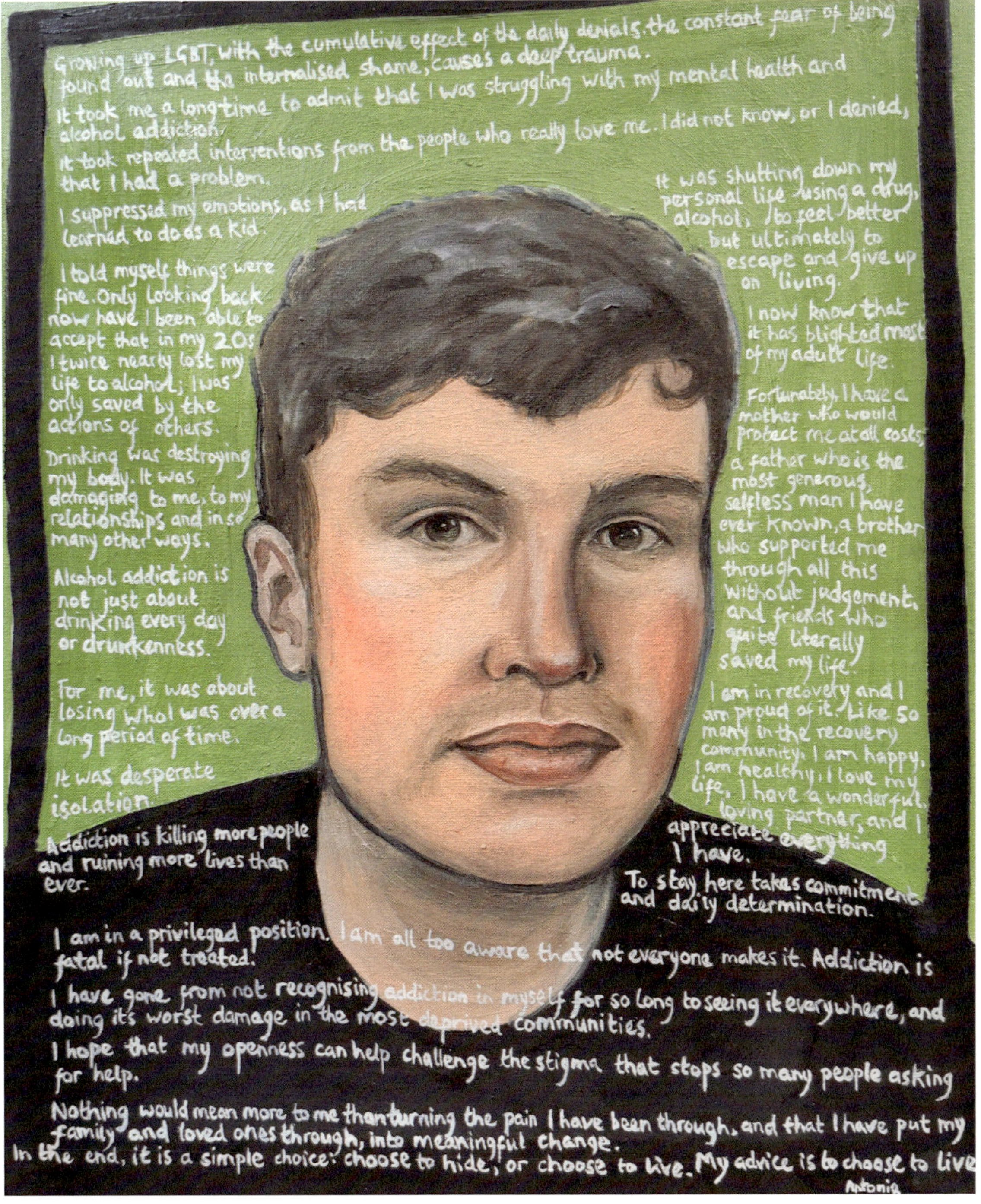

Dan gave a speech in the House of Commons about his alcoholism. Now sober he has set up AA meetings there as he says, so many MPs struggle with alcohol. He has made a big difference.

Passport Portrait

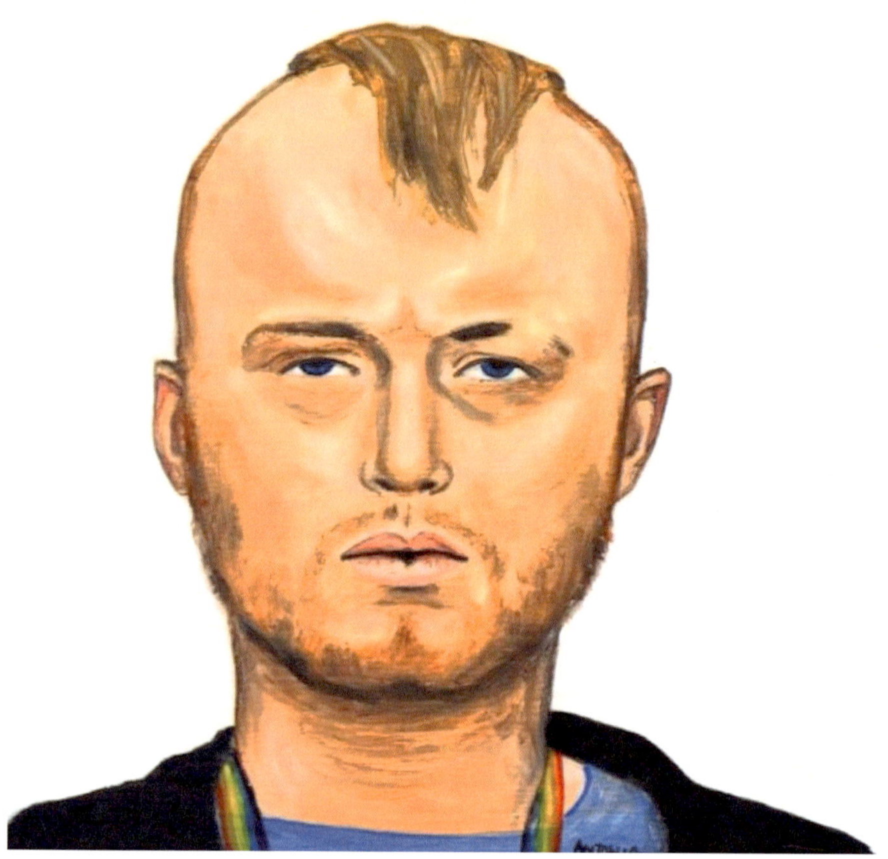

Trying to get a passport photo for him to go to South Africa. There was treatment set up for him there. No passport. So we got this photo done. This is it.

"It's a good one," he said, "I like it."
It's full of pain, I thought. It has captured the darkness.

Karpman Triangle

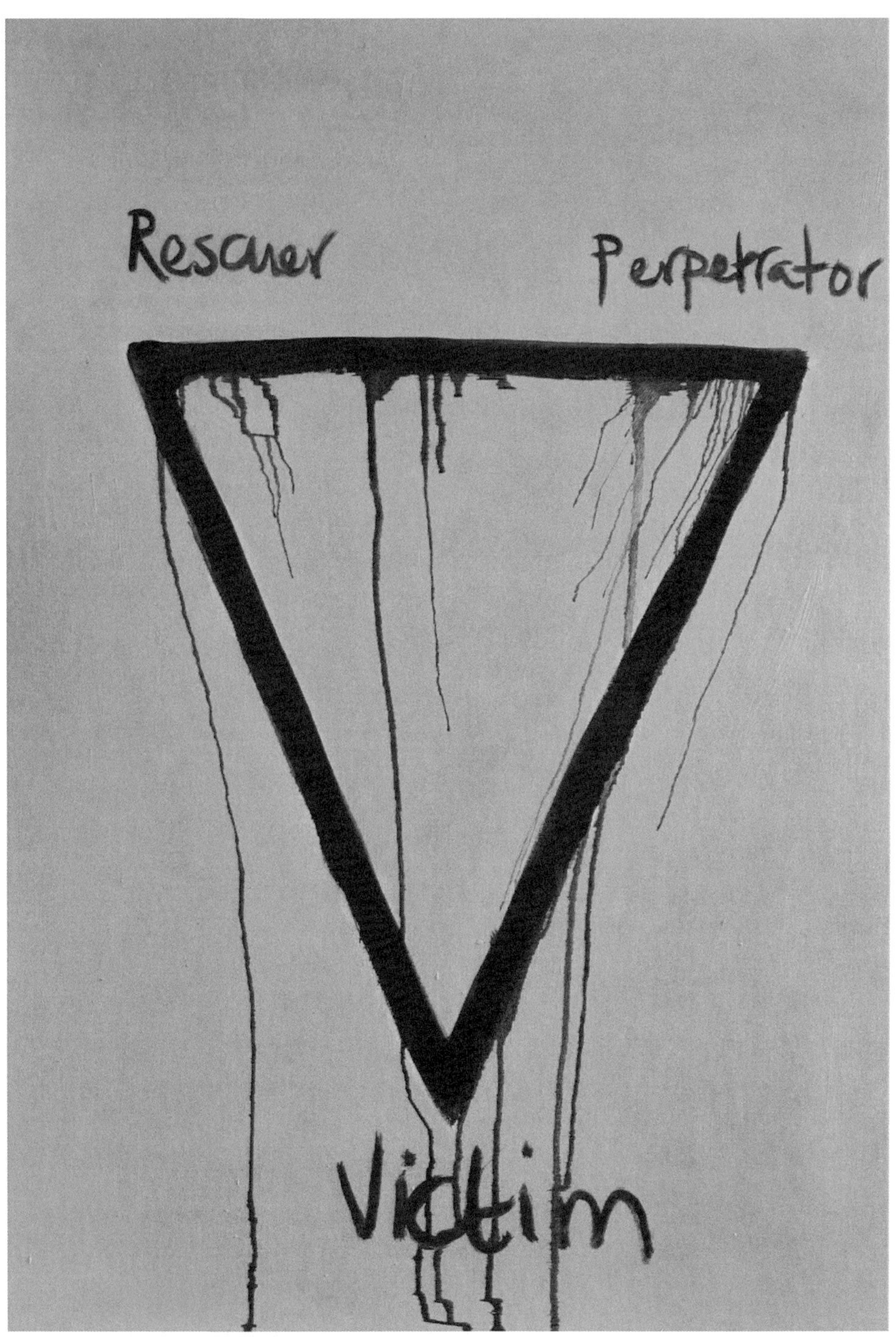

The Karpman Drama Triangle. Oh how I related, and still need, this. "Not meant to encompass healthy arguments or disagreements. Only excessive, disruptive, destructive behaviour, harmful to both participants." For me, this is a classic description of a relationship with an addict. I have to remember to step out of it.

Overdose Triptych

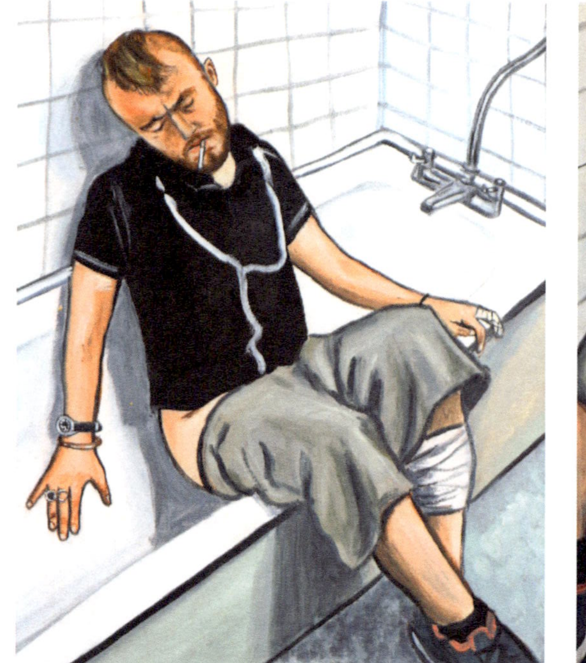 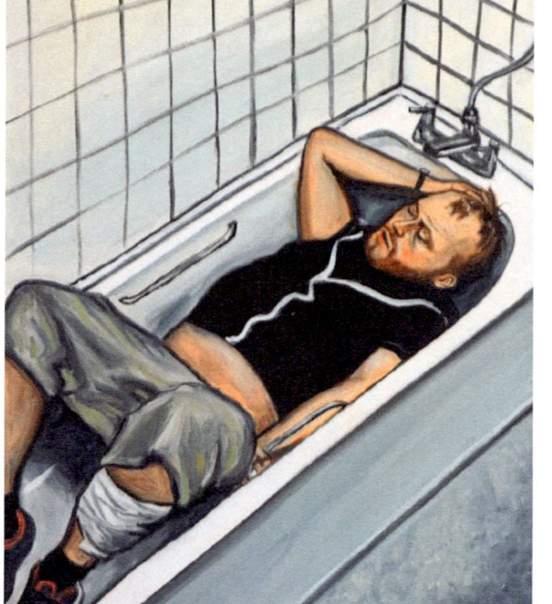 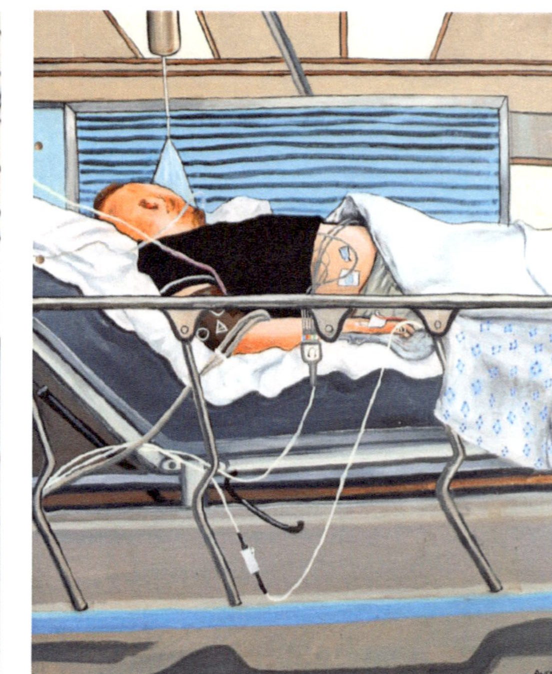

I didn't know what was happening. He had taken something and was losing consciousness. When he slid into the bath and was struggling to talk and to breathe I called the ambulance. There was a burn on his leg and finger that had been neglected.

"You can go now", they said to me later as he lay on the trolley with monitors and tubes. We will call you. Simple as that. Just one more drug problem.

When he comes round he can go, staggering out of the hospital desperate to find his next medication. He didn't even know I was there.

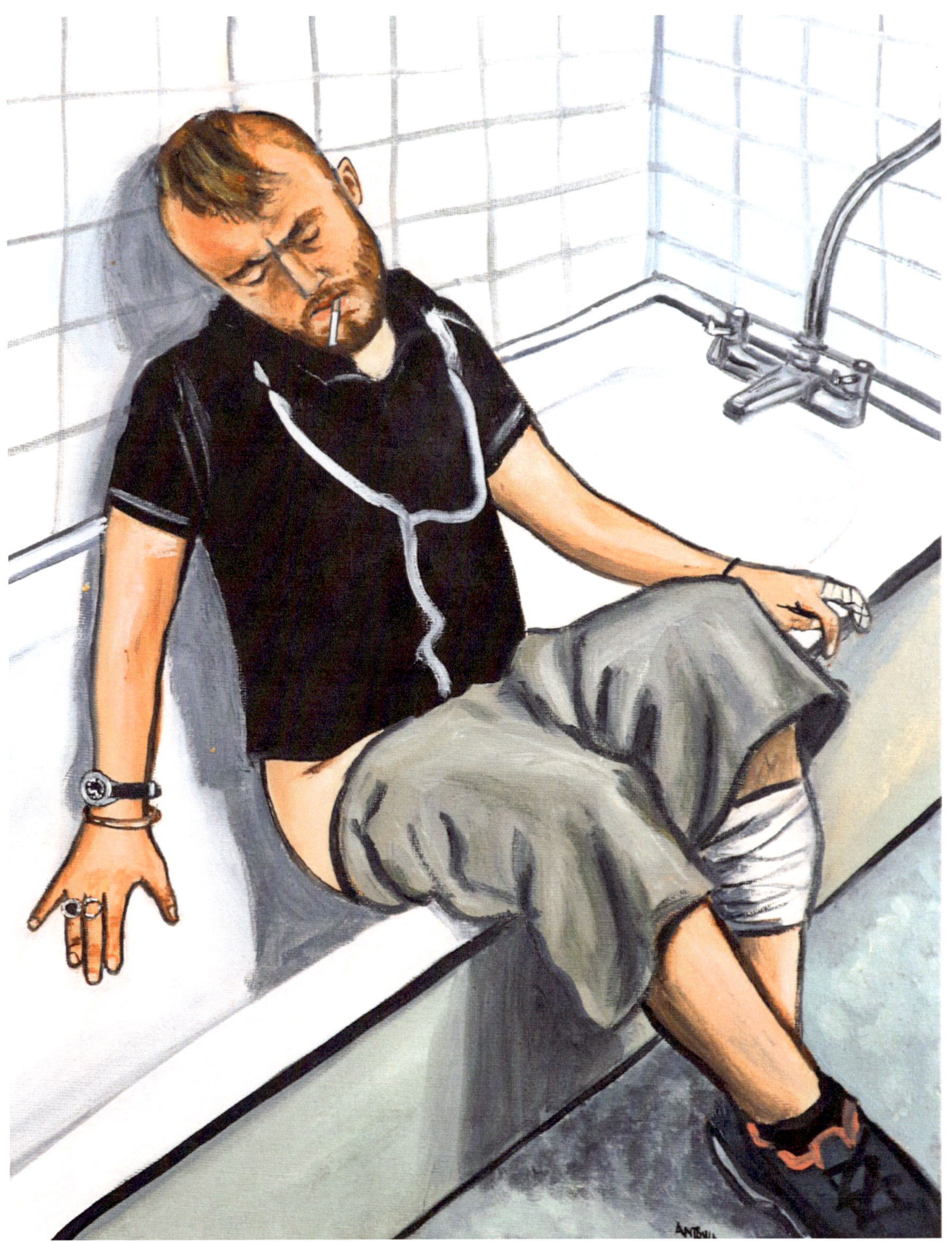

Overdose I

Party

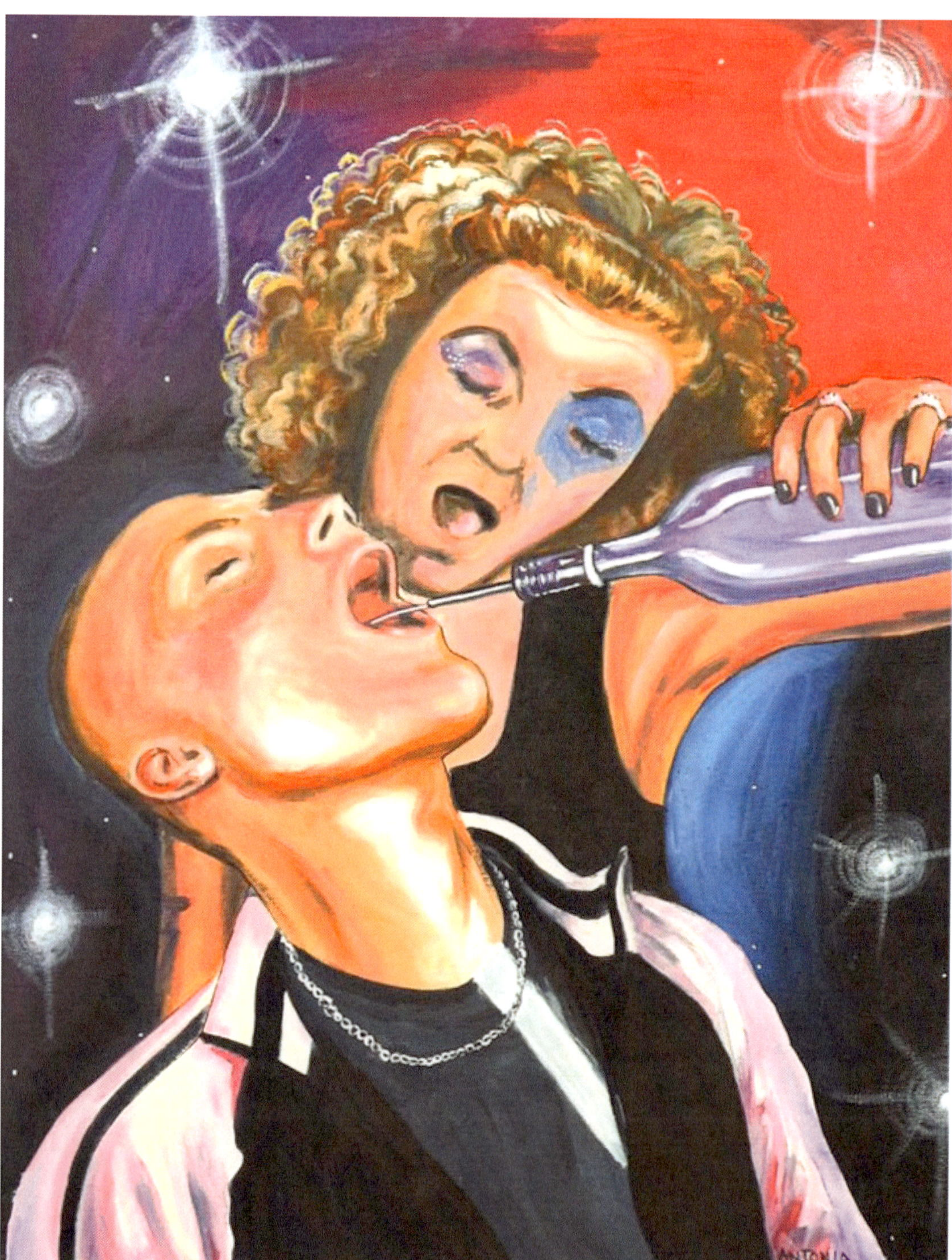

"You must show the partying," my son said. "I was not addicted when I was partying." I found this image, I thought it must have been one hell of a party, but suspect it was just one of many.

Gypsy Boy

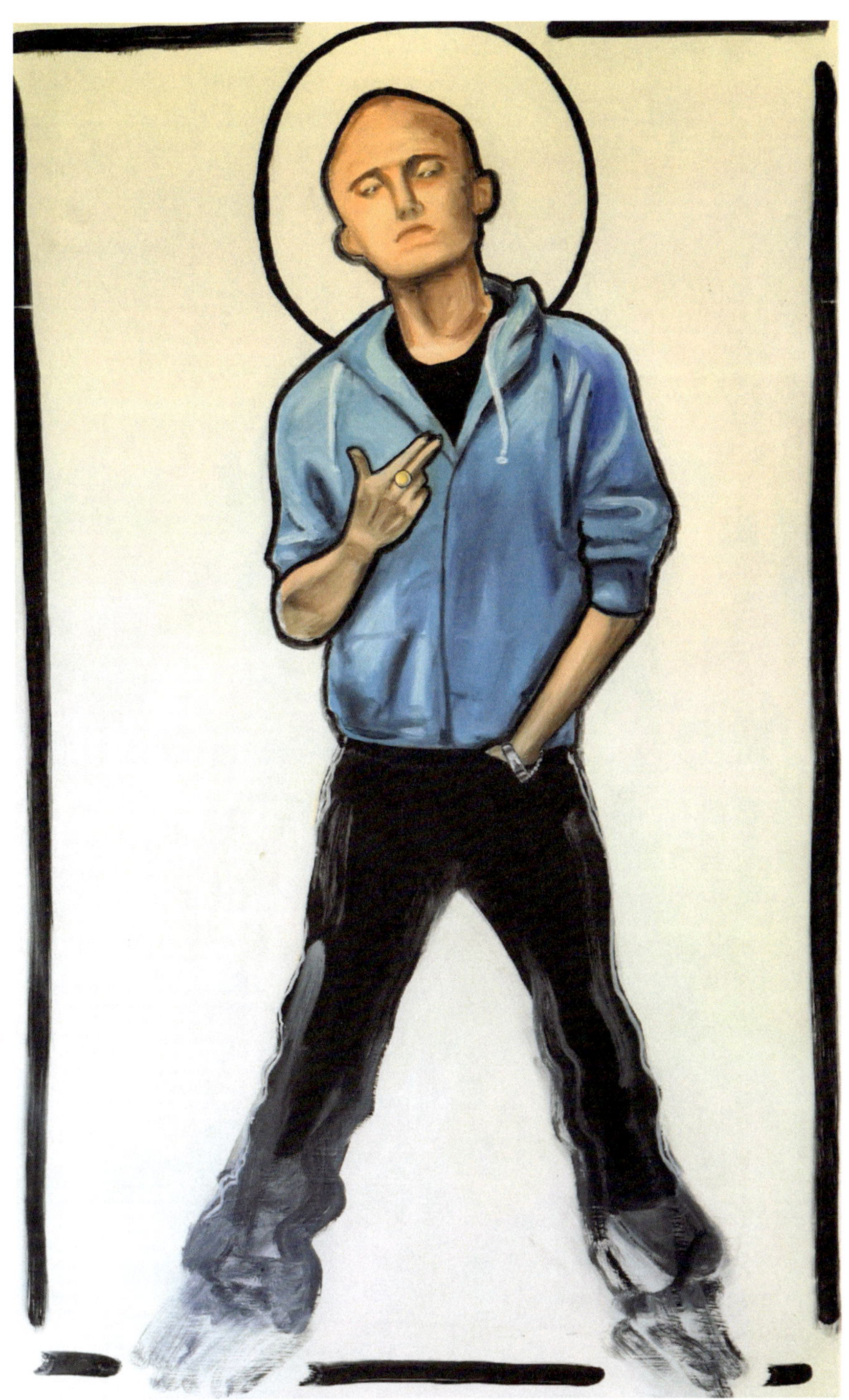

I wanted to paint the beginning of Costya's partying, drug taking journey. Much younger here, he stands posing "Like a Gypsy" he said. His eyes are unfocussed, there is challenge and confidence. I have given him a halo, as in a religious painting of an icon.

Neil's words -

LEAP is an international movement "Law Enforcement Action Partnership" Growing movement of police and law enforcement to seek alternative to failing punitive drugs laws.

Reality of drugs laws - brutal response to health problem. It can't win.

Criminalised supply - empowering the worst elements of our society to exploit the most vulnerable.

Public facing advocacy. I talk to people and win them over. I'm asked, why don't politicians change things?

Politicians and police, to tell the public the system is working. Police remind public they have something to fear.

Current system, not working. Our duty to tell the truth.

I speak at lots of events, addressing the public, worldwide. Grassroots. Big ripples in the pond, social justice issue. Change comes through social movement.

Interventions needed because drug users criminalised.

I have chronic PTSD. Crushing depression. Sense of guilt, harm to so many people. Because I pushed doubts aside. Ethical thinking. Ends justifies means.

I don't regret anything. At least I use my knowledge and experience for good. Helps manage my condition that I can do something to help.

People use drugs problematically - childhood trauma. Other people struggle with mental illness, not trauma. All have common problem that drugs are illegal and they are vulnerable to the wrong person.

Political divide between recovery and harm reduction. Not for us to judge when someone needs help or in a position to get better.

Doctors with prescription pads, not gangsters are the answer.

Caring for people, not criminalising them.

Moral judgment At the heart of all this, I completely reversed my opinion. Personal liberty, important.

Champion, individual liberty, agency, and control over own, mind and body, not other people attempting to take it over.

"Drug Free World Convention" in 1988 said, 'We will achieve a drug-free world by these drugs laws'. A drug-free fantasy.

90% of people have no problem with drugs. 10% have a problem.

Made a lot of sacrifices. Volunteer at LEAP. I can't hold work down with PTSD. Activist. Define myself that way.

Got a mission.

Neil

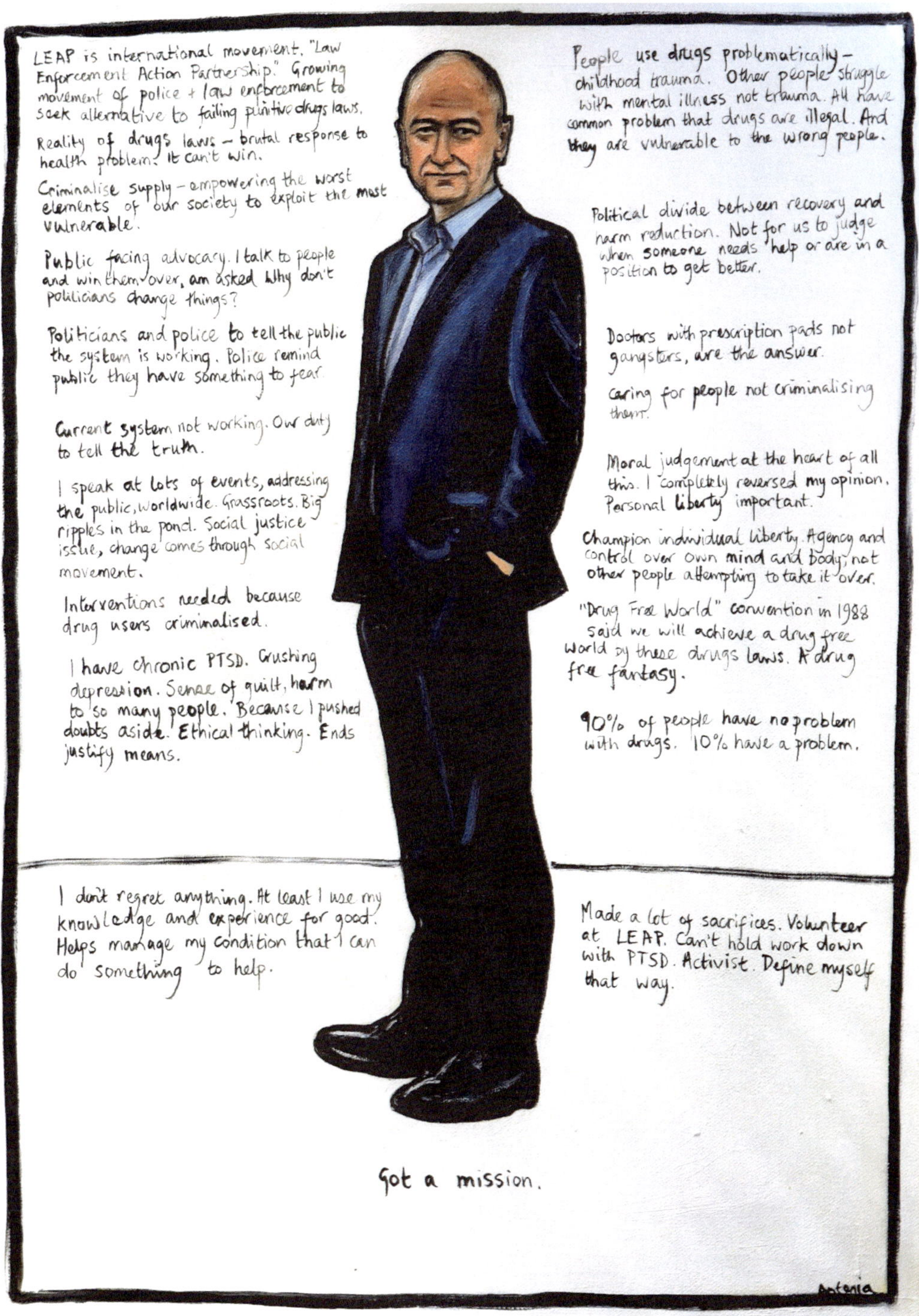

Neil is an author, speaker and former UK police undercover drugs operative. He campaigns, writes and speaks tirelessly now for the reform of international and UK drugs laws. His book, Good Cop Bad War was a huge influence on my thinking. It is well worth a read.

Lou's words -

*I was not addicted to
drugs. I was addicted to
the escape.*

*I just want people to
know there is a light at the
other end. Recovery is
achievable.*

*Helping others gives me joy.
Communication with others gives
me joy, even though it's hard
sometimes.*

*I woke
in the
morning
I
wanted
to
escape
from
my
mind.*

*I've wanted to
kill myself often,
but a little
voice in the
back of my
head kept
saying it's
not worth it*

*Speed, ketamine, MDMA, weed, alcohol,
cocaine, abuse*

Lou

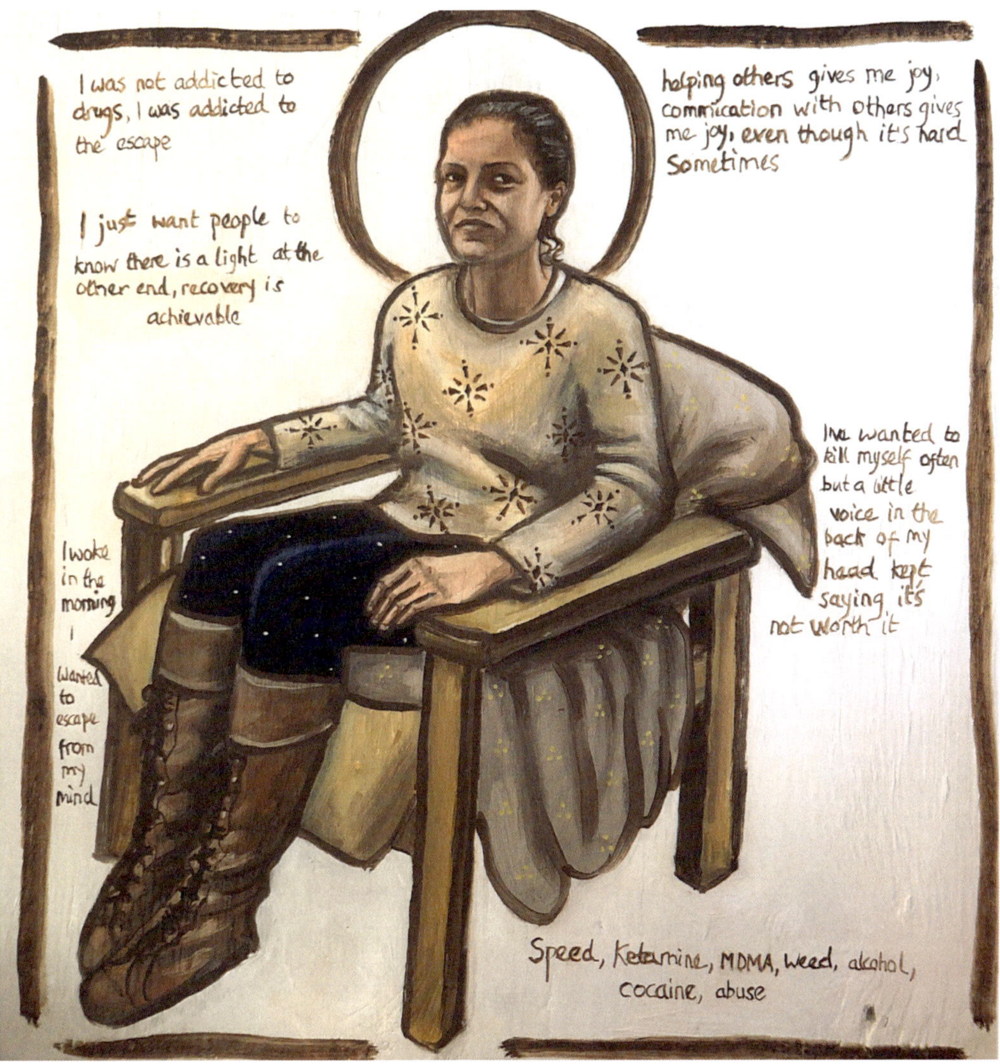

I met Lou at Arun Exact where she helps Ian (also painted here) run a relapse prevention service in Littlehampton.

Lou's story is full of hope. She is expecting her first baby soon, which is a cause for huge celebration.

Mum

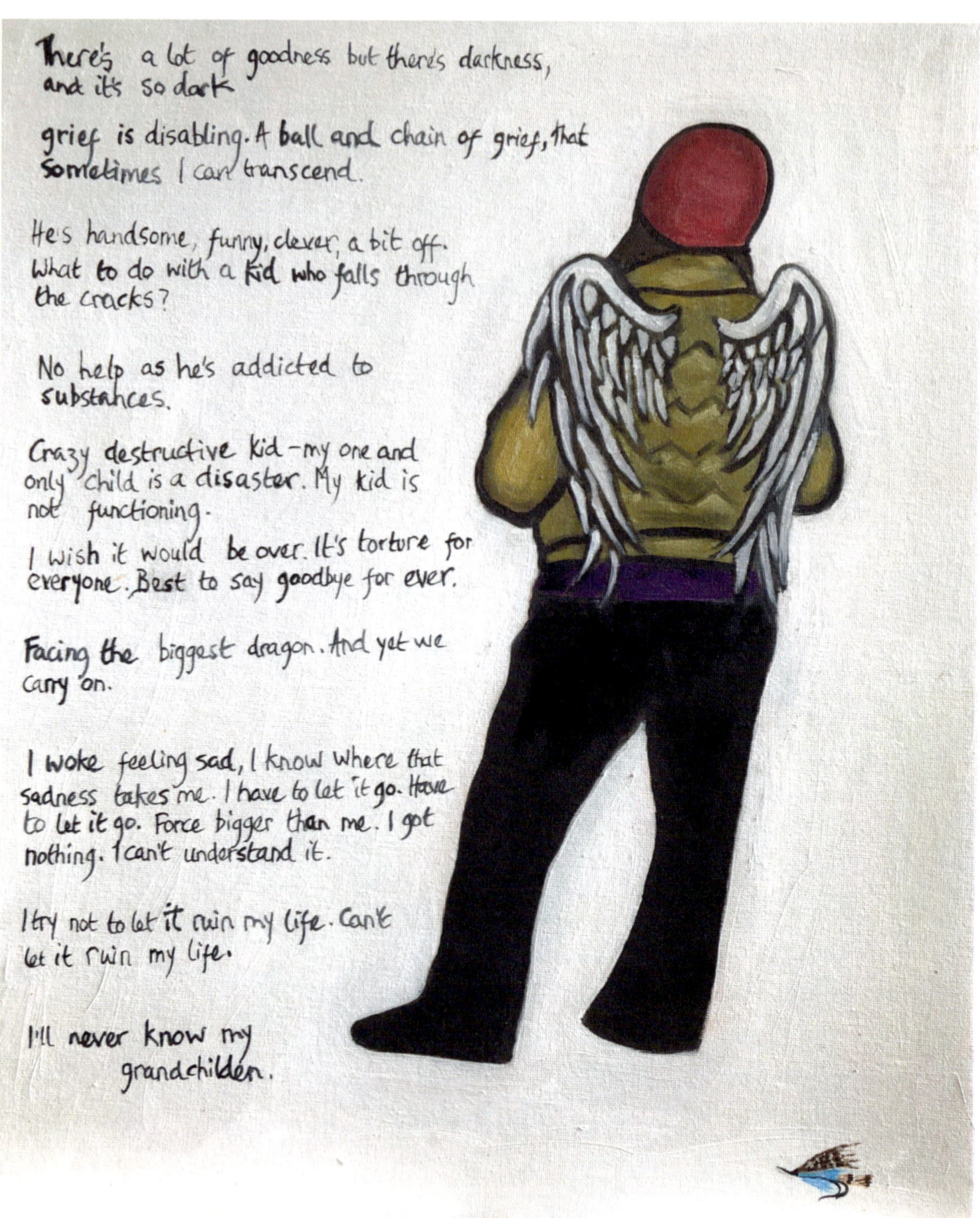

This lady remains anonymous. She can't be known for professional reasons. But her story is the same as so many of us. Her son feels lost to her forever in his addictions. The most poignant thing she says is "I'll never know my grandchildren." This is her only child.

Costya Angel

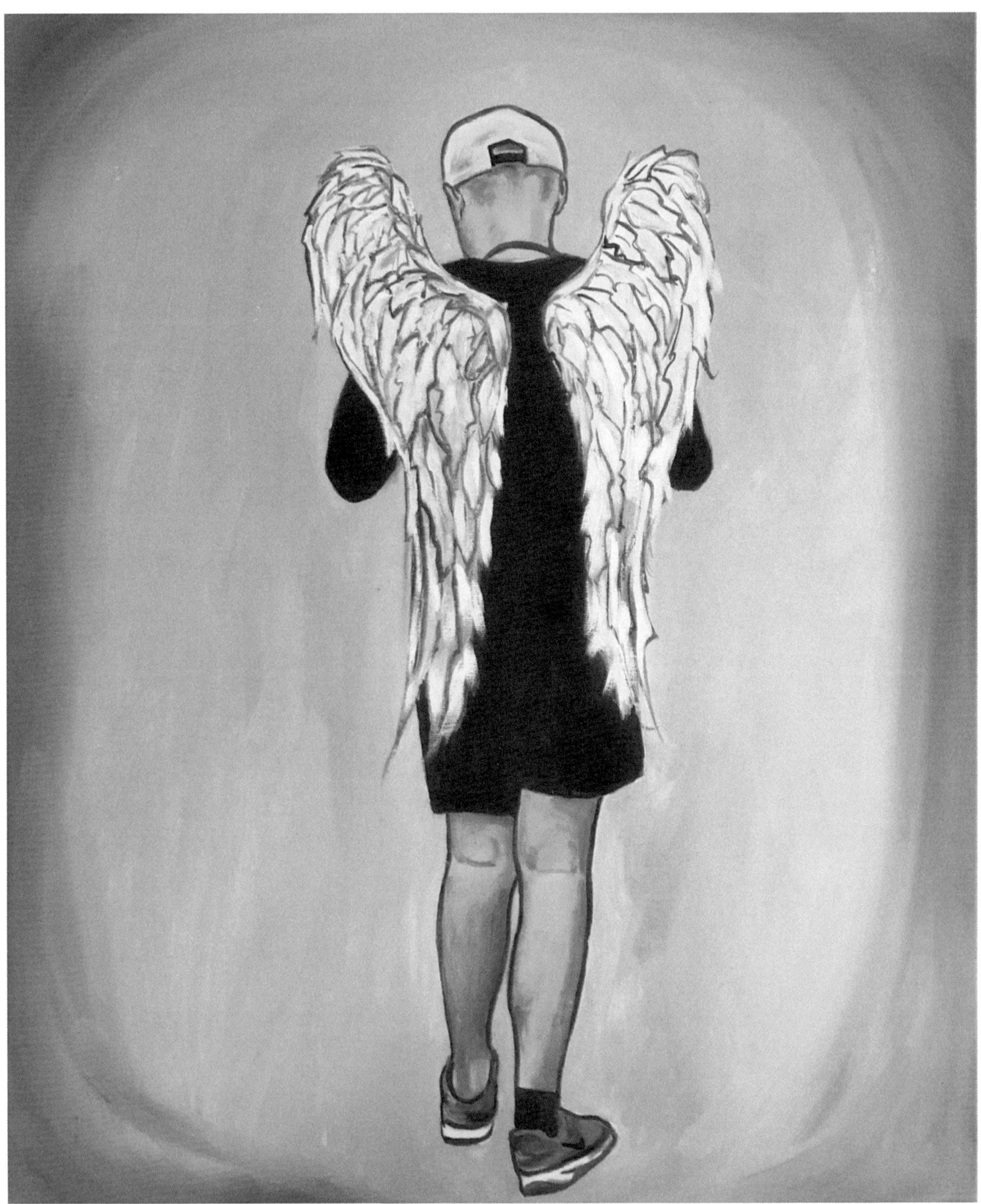

In London, I followed Costya as he walked too fast, his shoes not fitting, not connecting with anything.

I thought, all you need are wings. When I painted this, I gave him wings.

I don't speak of it. I don't say it out loud. I don't let
the expression on my face show the truth as you tell me
the cute details of the amazing love your mum gives your
children, but I feel it deep down in the darkness I keep covered
every day. There's always a longing, too painful to even allow
in for a second...

What would life be like if you were still here?

I'd take off the brave mask sometimes, I'd let myself have
a bad day, my shoulders to relax, I'd let you in and I'd
be the little girl for a while you swoop them up and tell
me it's alright. I'd watch you spoil my children with
sweets that were too sweet and sniff them up as you
squeeze them too tight. You'd be ridiculous, so funny
they'd be belly laugh at your dancing, and go to bed way
too late. You'd tell them stories of little me, and say how
we were alike, and laugh at how you love to see them
messing me around like I did you.

I miss making you proud, I miss having that unconditional
love, I miss everything about you without the drink...

But it was always about the drink, and now you'll always be gone,
every sip you took, took you one step away from me, and now I fear
one day I'll leave them. Irrational. I know, but living without my mum
has been the hardest thing, I don't ever want them to go through it
young, and now living as a mum without a mum, I can't even begin
to think about, so I just accept it, and enjoy them, and be the best I
can keeping you alive through them.

My life is amazing. I really couldn't wish for more... but don't ever think
it doesn't hurt. I will never stop missing or needing you, I wonder if
you'd known what it would do to me, and what you would miss, would
you have tried just that little bit harder, because I wish I wasn't a mum
without a mum!

A huge shout out to NacoaUK for helping me
find my tribe, to embrace being a COA and
realising I'm not alone in my struggles
as a child and my healing as an adult.

Ceri

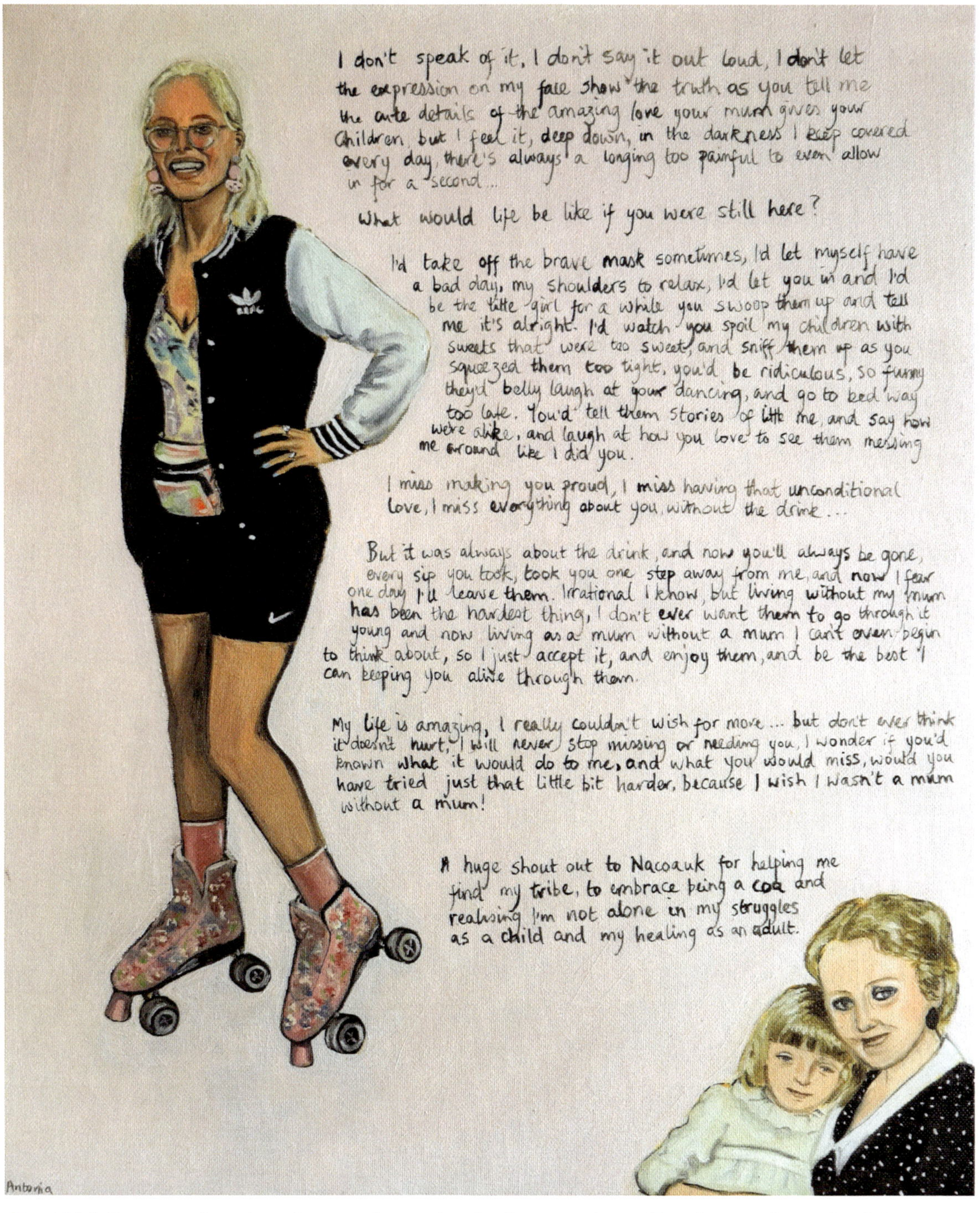

Ceri Walker is the daughter of an alcoholic mother. Ceri's mother died from her alcoholism and Ceri has spent years understanding and recovering from this experience. She loved her mother very much. Now a mother herself, Ceri works to help others in addiction.

Shaun Bailey words -

I have personal links to drugs. My brother drank himself to death four and a half years ago. Four and a half years of loss is nothing to the 12 years of war before that. Mum's youngest son. Pain, selfishness, false bravado and high intelligence. He was clever, charismatic, sharper, and better than me. Our outcomes are so different. Alcohol, was determining our outcomes.

I lost a companion, a contemporary, a sounding board, but for my mum, he was a subtraction a hole, and she is tough as old boots. A strong Jamaican lady. It fundamentally changed us. We have a large family. Near the end I felt separate and different to my brother. It was amazing to watch my huge family be wonderful. I couldn't fix my own brother, but I helped others avoid addiction. I have helped people.

I got into a lift with two high achievers once, in nice suits. One said like a joke. "I was obviously fucked last night". Then, "I probably drank too much." A micro appeal for help.

I'm a Christian, a father, son, parent, youth worker, partner, policymaker, politician. That all means I have tools and experience. I worked with people who grow, sell, and take drugs. I worked with a drug dealer who never took drugs. He said, "those people are fucking idiots. Dunno why they do it."

He makes things possible. He never has happened to himself. People who want to legalise drugs don't deal with alcohol, do they?

I was an athlete. So was my brother. He was better than me. To see what he became, we ran around the Srubs once and I caught him up. He said I only caught him up because I was his brother. Fast forward to my mum finding dead on the bathroom floor.

I tried to go into the house. The police tried to stop me. The young officer was afraid of the dead body. I saw him. It was the <u>worst</u>, the <u>worst</u> thing. Mum had tried to move him. He was so heavy, but she moved him.

I see kids who don't know they steal for weed. I ask, "what did you do with that money?" They say this and they say, "I need puff." I say, "that is what you stole, the money for weed."

I said, "Do a day, a week without weed." Some do and they have the money. At the end, one kid, I said, "Look, you have money. 50% more money." Kid didn't know what to do with his money. No life. I encouraged him to do something. After three months, he got a bike, - life changing decision to stop.

Shaun Bailey, Lord Bailey of Paddington

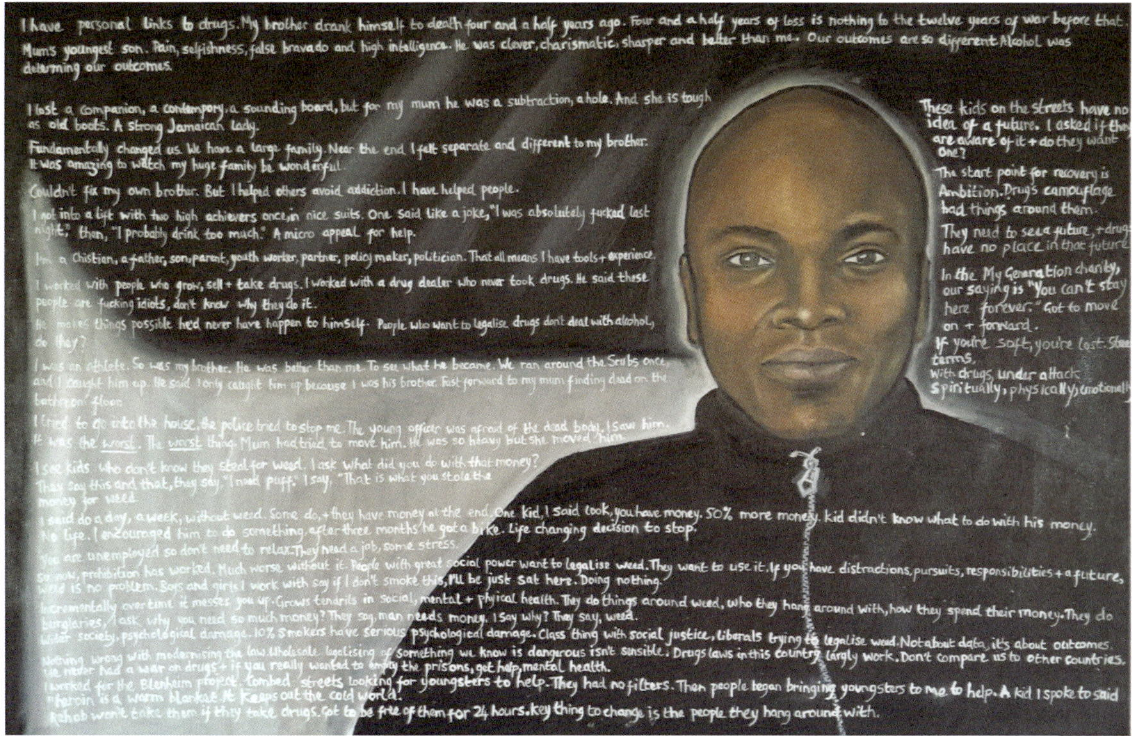

I asked Shaun to join the exhibition after hearing him speak with passion and love for the youth he has supported. He believes our drugs laws are working and I wanted to hear more. Shaun lost his brother to alcohol. He lost a good friend.

Shaun's words continued…

You are unemployed, so don't need to relax. They need a job, some stress.

So now prohibition has worked. It's much worse without it. People with great social power want to legalise weed. They want to use it. If you have distractions, pursuits, responsibilities, and a future weed is no problem. Boys and girls, I work with say, "If I don't smoke this I'd just be sat here. Doing nothing."

Incrementally, over time, it messes you up, grows tendrils in social, mental and physical health. They do things around weed. Who they hang around with, how they spend their money. They do burglaries. I ask, "Why do you need so much money?" They say, "Man needs money." I say, "why?" They say, "Weed."

Wider society psychological damage. 10% smokers have serious psychological damage. Class thing with social justice. Liberals trying to legalise weed. Not about data. It's about outcomes.

Shaun's words continued...

There's nothing wrong with modernising the law. Wholesale legalising of something we know is dangerous isn't sensible. Drugs, laws in this country largely work. Don't compare us to other countries. We never had a war on drugs, and if you really wanted to empty the prisons, get help. Mental health.

I worked for the Bleinham Project, combed streets looking for youngsters to help. They had no filters. Then people began bringing youngsters to me to help. A kid I spoke to said, "Heroin is a warm blanket. It keeps out the cold world."

Rehab won't take them if they take drugs. Gotta be free of them for at least 24 hours. Key thing is change. Key thing to change is the people they hang around with.

These kids on the streets have no idea of a future. I asked if they are aware of it, and do they want one?

The start point for recovery is ambition. Drugs, camouflage bad things around them.

They need to see a future and drugs have no place in that future.

In the My Generation charity, our saying is, "You can't stay here forever." Got to move on and forward.

'If you're soft, you're lost.' Street terms.

With drugs under attack, spiritually, physically, emotionally.

Angel in the Wheelchair

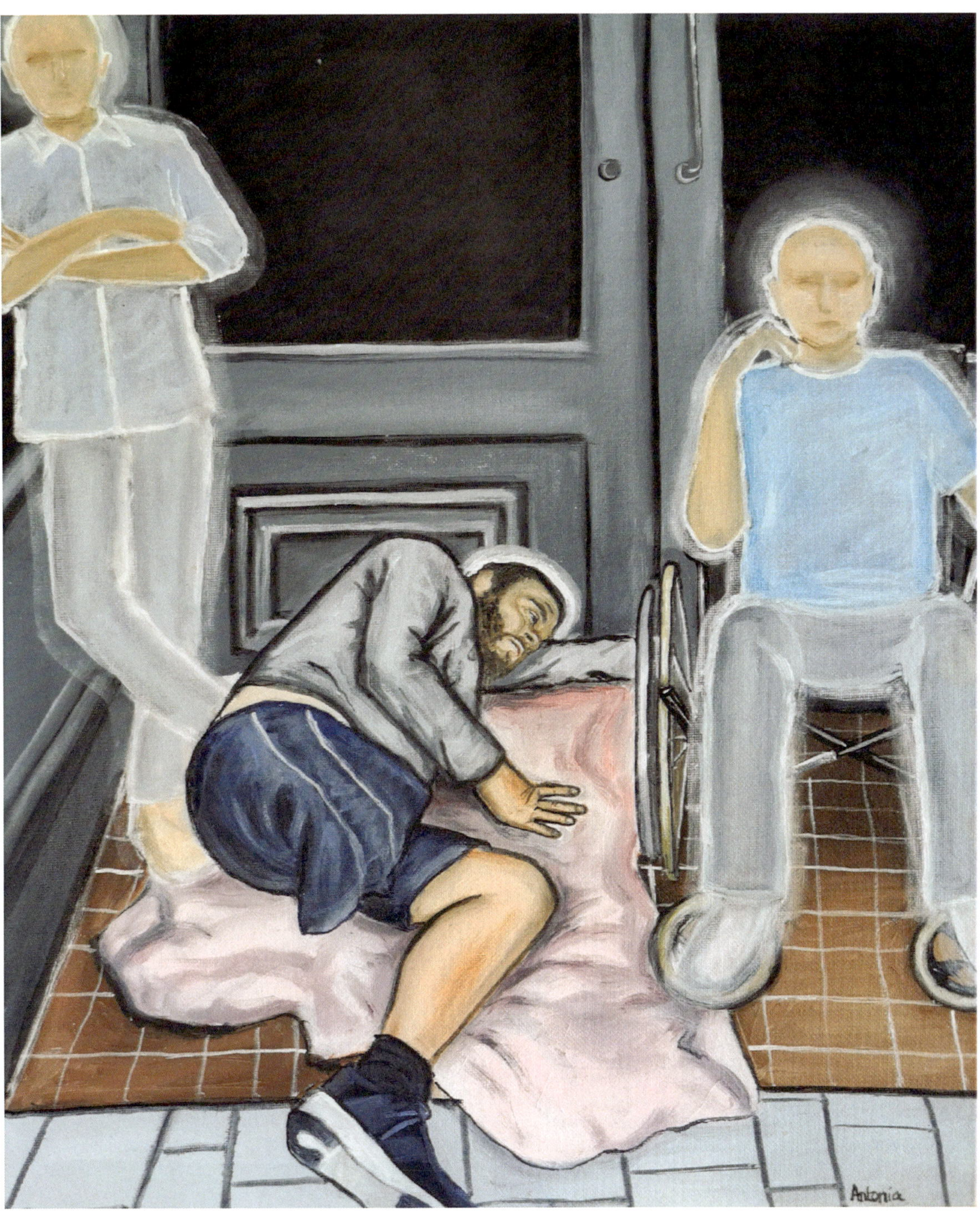

I thought, what if angels guard addicts and never actually leave them?
I saw this man and imagined his angels accompanying him, just being there, and
while he slept, one sits in his chair.

Ian's words -

*Alcoholic parents, 50% genetics
50% environment. Grew up with both.*

*No school, no one could touch me.
No examples. No connections.*

*Age 15, knew Scotland's
problem - drinking, smoking,
taking anything.*

*Things don't run we,
we run things.*

*It takes all sorts of
flowers to make
a garden.*

*vita nova - new life.
Important to recreate
yourself. Make a new
you.*

*Addiction is not a fucking
disease it's an illness.*

*Boxing saved me for a while.
Anger management. Had a
temper. Went inside myself
then outside Borstal.
Bullying.*

*Giving is the most
important part of
recovery. Turning
it around. Learning
to give.*

*Victim - blame on past
survival - out of lifeboat
Warrior - I came back,
had to help
others.*

Only now I feel life is thriving.

Ian

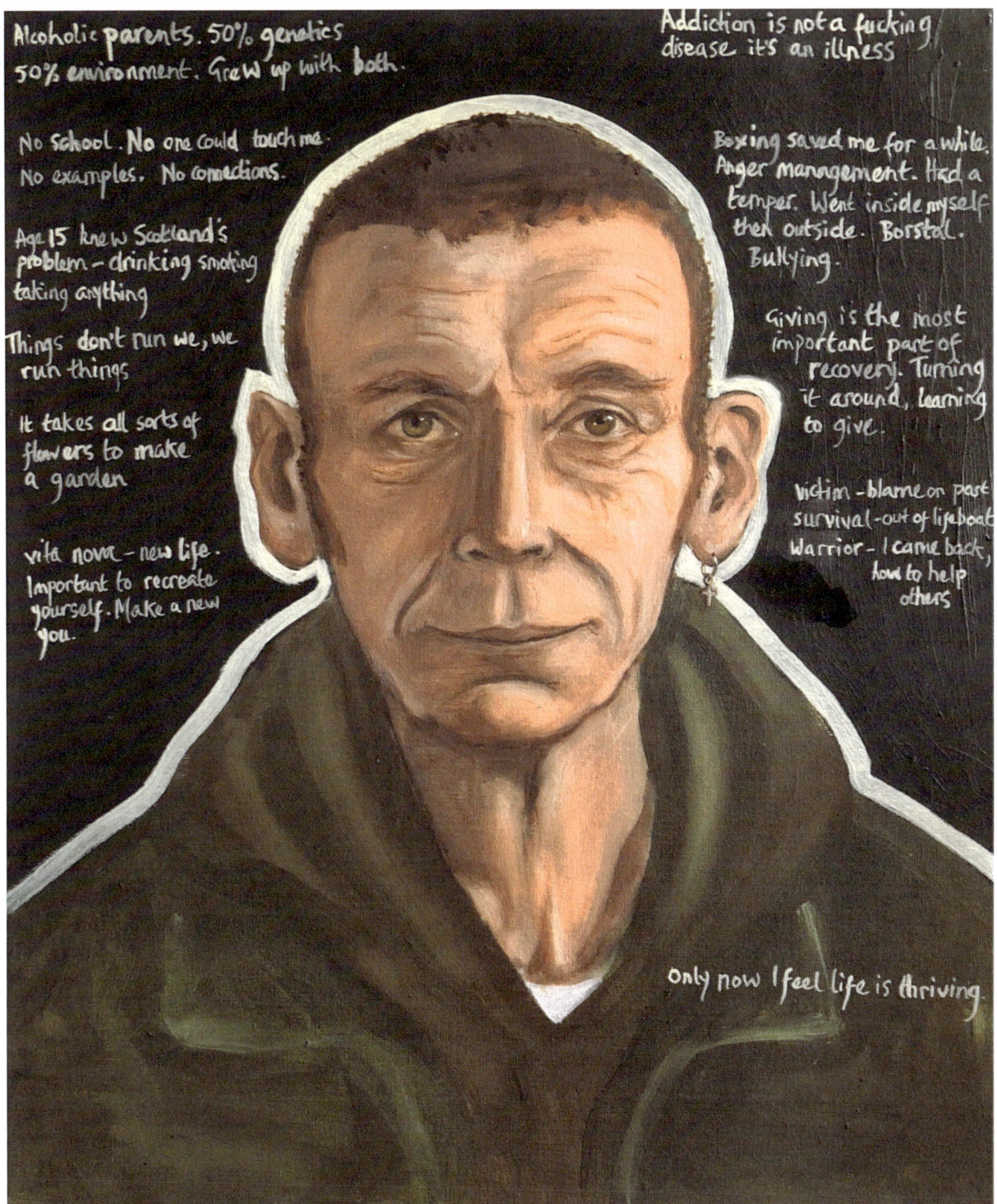

Ian runs the relapse prevention project in Littlehampton, called Arun Exact. Ian has lived through party years of addiction including time in prison. "That was then," says Ian. This is now. Ian has a degree and helps other people in his old situation. "Victim, Survivor, Warrior," says Ian. "I am Warrior."

Marcus' words -

People take drugs for confidence, + I was one of them, hooking up on social media like Grindr or Scruff. Designer sex drugs infiltrated the scene.
I didn't really take drugs. My fragile state made me press the 'fuck it' button. On Grindr, a man invited me to a house. I tried everything. Miaow miao, Meow. GHB, Gina, GTina, crystal meth, ketamine.

I partied, had sex with random people and fell into a lifestyle that spiralled.
I'd be a liar to say I didn't have happy moments.

The feeling of being in love induced by GHB. False happiness. Synthetic. Meet same person or crowd off the drug, and sober, you'd run a mile.

The hell of coming down and your demons hitting you.

All good looking gay men horny + high. Adult porn stars, do adult work. A massive culture.

Having amazing sex brilliant, but not at 3am with no money, at a cash point for electrics or food.

If you have any problems, you're not telling them while sharing gear, they don't want to know.

I met a boyfriend under CHEMS. An addict, 6 days of total love and lust at first sight. It was drug induced. I wanted to save him. We both came off drugs, but the cycle started again. It was such a nasty ending.

He went off with someone richer. I was totally lost.

The betrayal of someone. I ended up loving. Previous dramas all too much. Lost my prided, bodybuilding body. Handcuffed to the bed with two security guards in the room.

The come down and pain so unbearable. My mum + sister came to London when I told the mess I got myself in. Feeling dark for weeks. No counselling or medicine could fix this.

I scored some G + drank whole bottle knowing it would kill me with my mother there in another room.

I remember seeing flames dropping to the floor. Eleven days later I woke in St. George's Hospital. In and out of dream state for days. Horrible reality dream states, including my mother + sister being held captive and raped in a cell next door.

I slowly realised the enormity of what happened. No joy being held in hospital room like a convict. I realised I must never let that happen to me again.

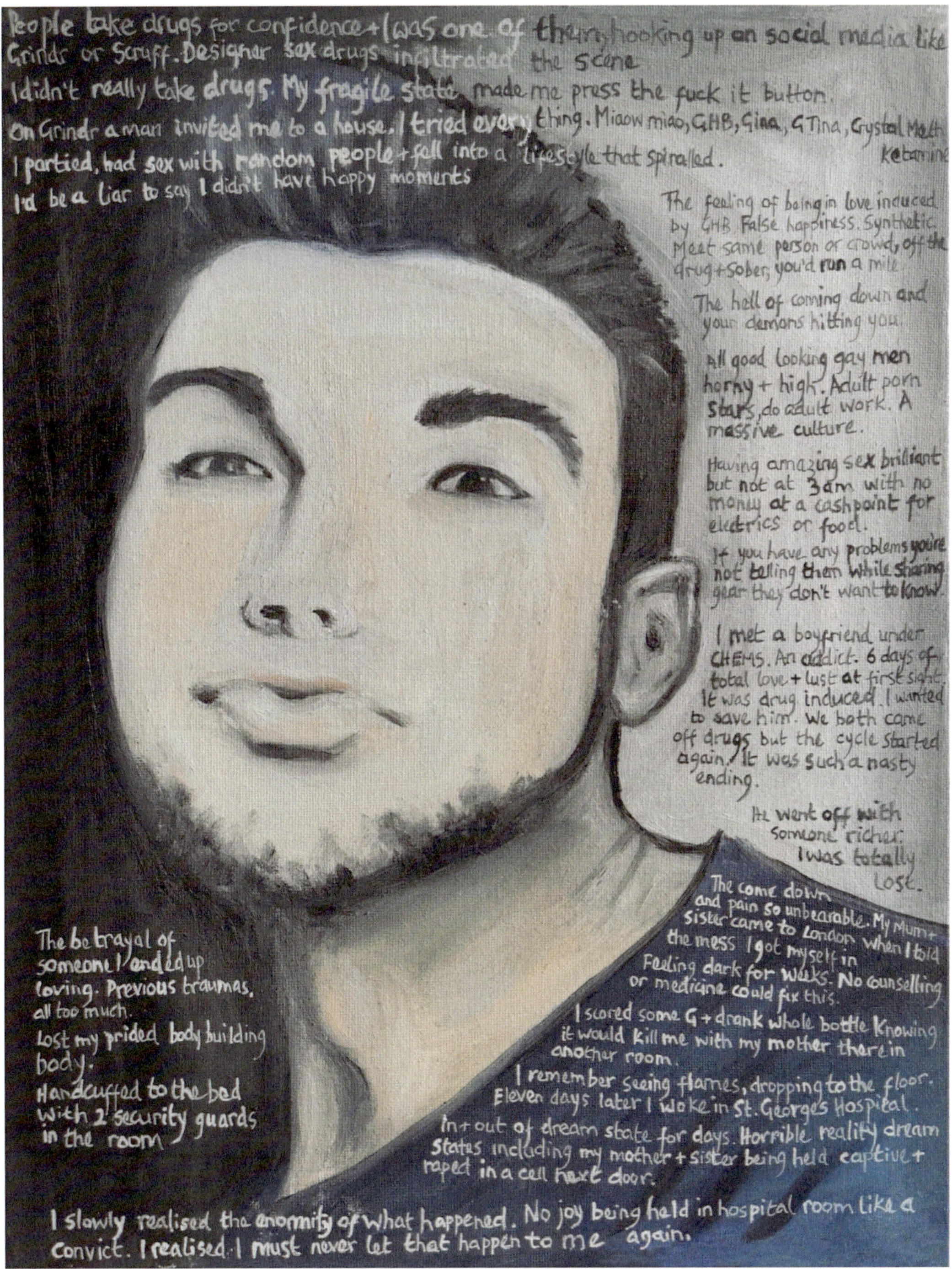

Marcus was at a low point in his life. He found himself in the CHEMS scene, and became lost in the gay CHEMS sex lifestyle until, after 10 years, he tried to end it all.

Marcus' words -

And will I make mega-global stardom my ultimate dream? You watch this space, you bet damn well I will!

I wanted to part of this incredible exhibition for the greater good. CHEMS particularly prevalent in the gay community.

At the bottom everything is so helpless and hopeless. It's very easy to continue chasing the high.

Ten years on I am back in control and the person the six-year-old me always wished to grow up to be. I was halfway through and Osteopathy degree. The establishment were very snooty, I thought this is what society wanted me to be.

I was becoming more and more unhappy and away from the Pop Star I always wanted to grow up to be.

I lacked confidence, tampering with my nose at a young age, left with one nostril half the size of the other which looked peculiar. Can be lonely as a single mature gay man. There's an appeal to go out and join a party.

6 week trick. Take a substance, think how addictive the high is, you will want more of that high. Think what your life will be like if you fast forward 6 weeks.

I had to rehabilitate myself. I had chronic high anxiety and panic after what happened.

I had to live with mum and dad. My brain was churning like a factory of endless song lyrics and concepts. I couldn't keep up with them.

Having to write it all down, waking in the night and scribbling frantically. I started researching song writing.

I got a guitar for my birthday.

My dream was always to be a megastar. As big as Madonna. A world megastar.

I found a song writing academy, met kindred spirits I loved it, it became my focus. Suddenly I was being my authentic self.

I got into prosthetic make up. I never wanted to be a boring artist. I wanted to grasp people's attention and keep them entertained.

I continue to save, go on writing retreats. Mentored by and worked with writers to Christina Aguilera, JLO, Justin Timberlake. Work with a choreographer, I won grants, play at festivals.

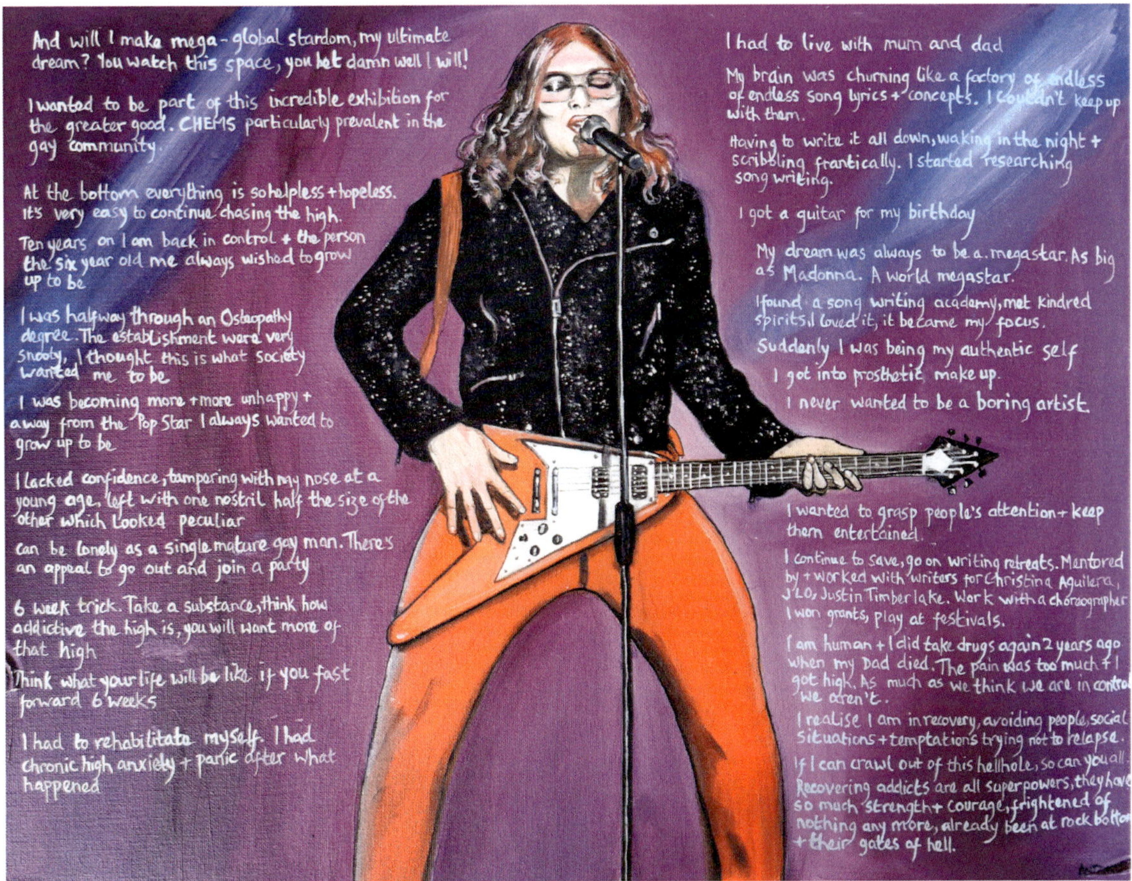

It took determination and time for Marcus to come back. Becoming his childhood dream, a superstar, a megastar is the answer. Marcus changed his name, became a singer songwriter performer and is a megastar.

Marcus' words continued...

I am human and I did take drugs again 2 years ago when my Dad died. The pain was too much and I got high. As much as we think we are in control we aren't.

I realise I am in recovery, avoiding people, social situations and temptations trying not to relapse. If I can crawl out of this hell-hole so can you all. Recovering addicts are all superpowers, they have so much strength and courage, frightened of nothing anymore, already been at rock bottom and their gates of hell.

Thomas' words -

Addiction is fucking grim.
Being an addict is vile,
horrible, lonely, dark.
Imagine someone comes along
and says you have a disease.
Disease means death.

Loads of people die from
addiction. To me, you don't
get better from a disease,
so you need to expect
death when it's a disease.

How does that inspire you
to recover?

Spiritual malady.

Internal disposition, you have
no other choice. Don't want to
address issues, seek pleasure
instead, seek solace in pleasure.

"You're not a proper junkie.
Ketamine isn't a proper drug."

Some of my best times were when
I was an addict, some of my worst
times was when I was a child
and not an addict.

Pinpoint where I, where it went
wrong, talking to people who come
in and out of rehab. I like to talk to
people to find out where it
went wrong.

Need to address the real
issues, hard work, not address
them with drugs, alcohol and
gambling.

I believe recovery is abstinence.

"What's a kethead?"
"Mentally, physically, and
Spiritually Fucked."

"Rehab isn't a safe space, but it
provided the opportunity
for me to build a
new
life."

Thomas I

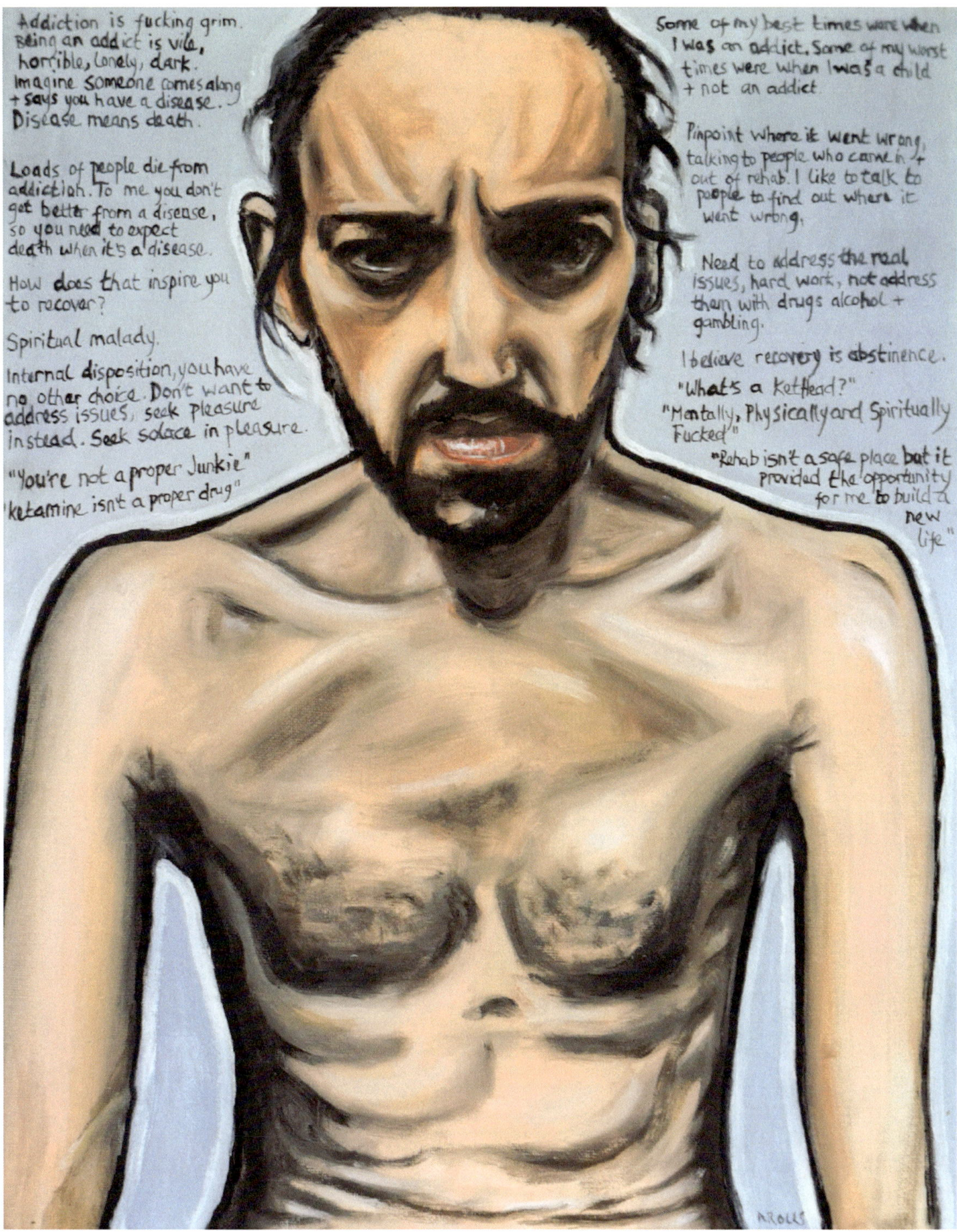

Thomas eventually went into rehab with 'just' a ketamin addiction. He was 6 stone. He said he felt they took heroin, crack, alcohol more seriously but this is what an addiction to ketamin can do. He needed help.

Thomas' words -

I like talking to people who aren't addicts to hear what they say about it. Don't have to be an addict to be conniving and badly behaved. People can't believe I was an addict even when they see the photos. I was only that six stone addict for six months of 14 years of ketamine. People think they can identify addicts.

(I mean, you can't. I was highly functional as a ketamine user.) I tried doing peer support after, but too distressing + exhausting. I stopped doing it, didn't get any better.

Need a cultural shift in how we see addicts. People have narrow idea of addiction. Some highly functioning addicts, doing very well challenging stereotypes.

I look so well now. Hierarchy of addicts in rehab not spoken about in. Glasgow, my rehab categorised heroin and crack at the top, alcohol next, than others. Weird classification. Poorest in the hierarchy was ketamine. I was a ket head.

They couldn't talk to me about ketamine as they were used to heroin + crack.

I felt I'd never qualified to be an addict, annoyed because I looked worse than any of them. So ill, nearly dead, but with no place on the hierarchy because of "only" ketamine, but I was a total addict. 6 stone. So ill.

Junkie, because my life was just junk. Life. Relationships, finances, junk.

Junkie, addict. Use your own words. Say anything and someone will take offence. I wrote about it in a paper, everyone up in arms about the title "Druggie".

Now it's Alcoholics = problematic drinkers. Drug addict = Substance user. When a drug addict, the last thing people care about is what they're called, how they're described.

What do you mean you believe it's not a disease?

People who don't understand, don't have experience, feel they need to change the language around it. Addicts don't. Let's really deal with the issues, not the language.

Do you think a ket head, minds being called a ket head? It was, what it was. It was the underlying stuff that needed dealing with.

I didn't like being called a service user at rehab. Upgraded from addict to service user. People get paid lots of money to have debates around this. Semantics.

Ket head. Junkie. Addict.

Society dangerous when focuses on language. Most addicts have adverse childhood experiences and choose drugs because going through trauma fundamentally

Thomas 2

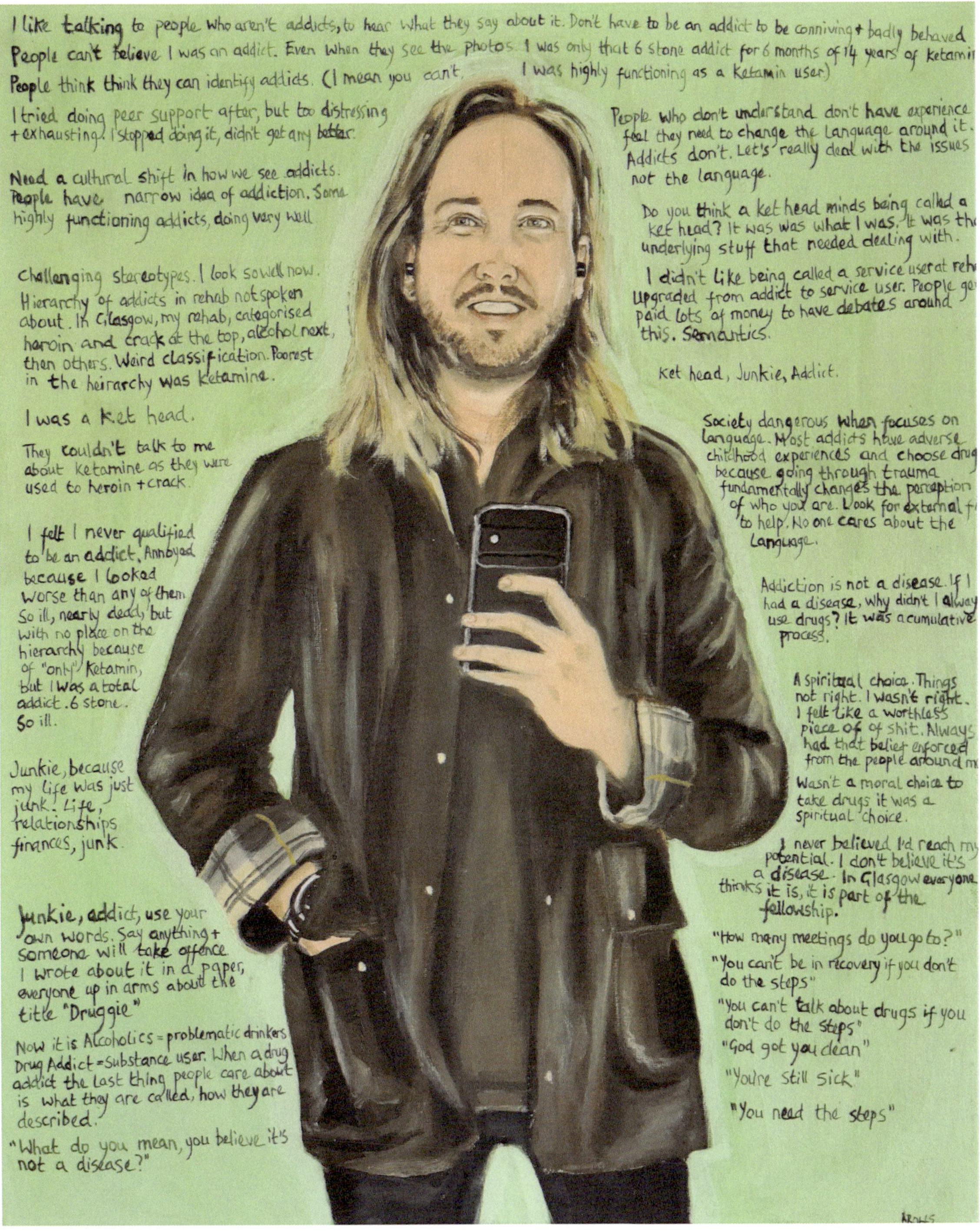

Thomas is a powerful advocate for addiction recovery. He speaks on both mainstream and online media about his story. He now studies for a degree and has recently become a father. Thomas believes in abstinence and is a good example of mindful recovery.

changes the perception of who you are. Look for external fix to help. No one cares about the language.

Addiction is not a disease. If I had a disease, why wouldn't I always use drugs?

Why didn't I always use drugs? It was a cumulative process. A spiritual choice. Things not right. I wasn't right. I felt like a worthless piece of shit. Always had that belief enforced from the people around me. Wasn't a moral choice to take drugs, it was a spiritual choice.

I never believed I'd reach my potential. I don't believe it's a disease.

In Glasgow everyone thinks it is, it is part of the fellowship.

"How many meetings do you do?"

"You can't be in recovery if you don't do the steps."

"You can't talk about drugs if you don't do the steps."

"God got you clean."

"You're still sick."

"You need the steps."

Once a Drunken Hoe

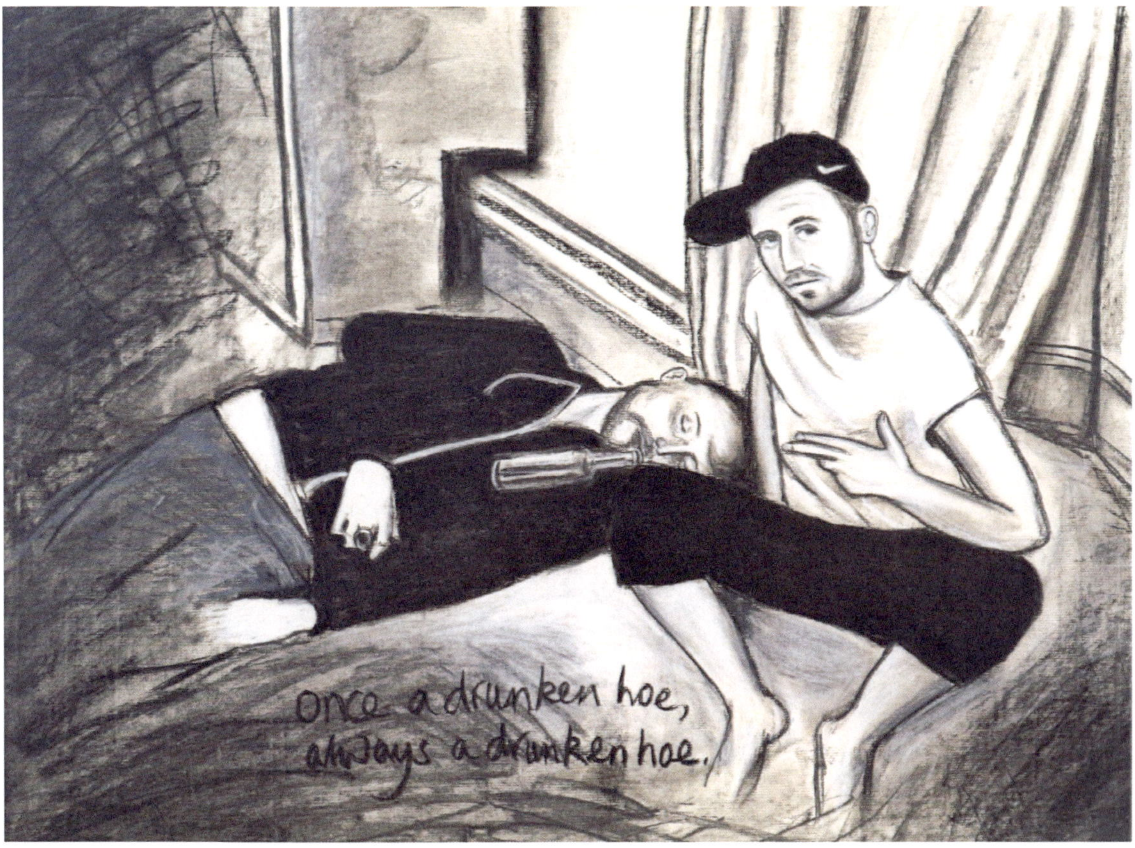

This is about the partying. I used charcoal for this, the smudgy blackness suited the late night party in somewhere not very nice. I don't know where this was. I wasn't there but I'm struck again by the helpless hand.

The title is taken from a comment made on the original photo, 'Once a drunken hoe, always a drunken hoe.'

Fiona's words -

Music and dancing have been a part of the human experience back to cave dwellers and psychoactive drugs have been a part of almost every tribe, society and nation around the world. Whether it's for medicinal purposes, pain relief, spiritual enlightenment, socialising or pure hedonism, we are all drug users.

People say I'm stubborn. I'd say I'm determined! The LOOP co-director says he's never met anyone less likely to take no for an answer than me. I also have a (healthy) disregard for authority.

So maybe I'm stubborn about the things I care about: social justice, equality and education. To make the world a better place. Education is the common theme. It's the springboard to opportunity, empowerment and escape. I've worked in higher education for over 3 decades, worked in prison education and with the LOOP, that's about giving information to people to help them make safer choices.

I love a challenge, to push for something people say isn't possible. The catalyst to trying to get drug checking in the UK because a door was ajar, I pushed it open.

People say there isn't the evidence for drug checking in the UK, my job as a researcher is to say OK, let's collect the evidence. How to deliver pilots to create the UK evidence base, harness research as a driver for change? So the LOOP was created as a university action research project in order to progress its service delivering harm reduction interventions.

Such amazing people coalesce around the LOOP, it's an honour and inspiration to be involved. Over 500 UK volunteers all trained, qualified and experienced, professionals in their field. Another 500 on the waiting list to become LOOP volunteers. The LOOP Australia also has talented volunteers. I'm not sure how that happened but it's awesome.

I was adopted then brought up by a single mother on a low income, which has given me a strong core of independence, self-reliance and inclination to outsider perspectives. I've never had any expectations that anyone would catch me if I fell.

Life is short, time speeds by and I want to make the most of every day.

Fiona Measham

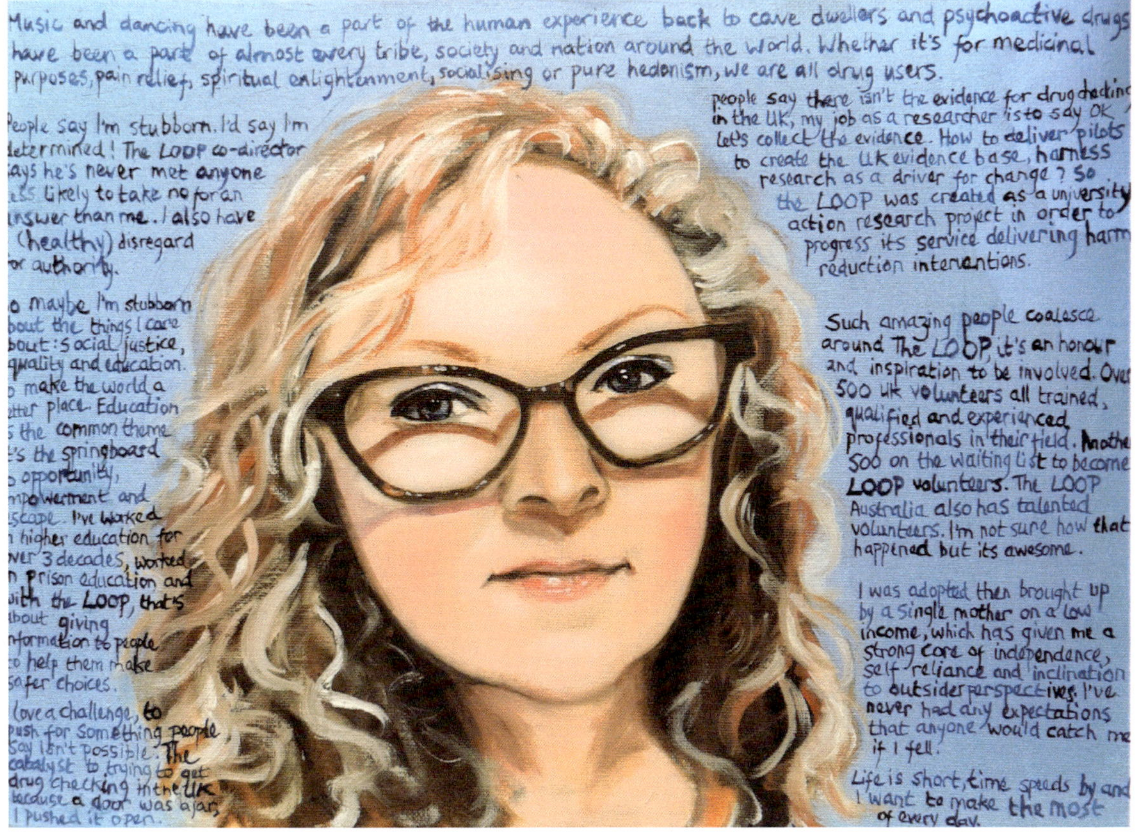

Fiona is a professor of Criminology and Social Policy. Amongst her many achievements is her founding of LOOP, a charity that travels to night clubs and festivals testing the drugs there and offering help, advice and information as well as testing and harm reduction.

Michael and Martin's words -

Over 10 years since my last miserably,
pathetic intoxication and the horror and
terror is still vivid.

Whatever it was that finally enabled
me to finally let go - I'm truly and
humbly grateful.

I felt helpless and confused -
that hold over, Michael.
Every time he stopped was "for
the last time."

So frustrating
and upsetting

Baffling and insane behaviour

Michael, you need to grow a thick skin.

Michael and Martin

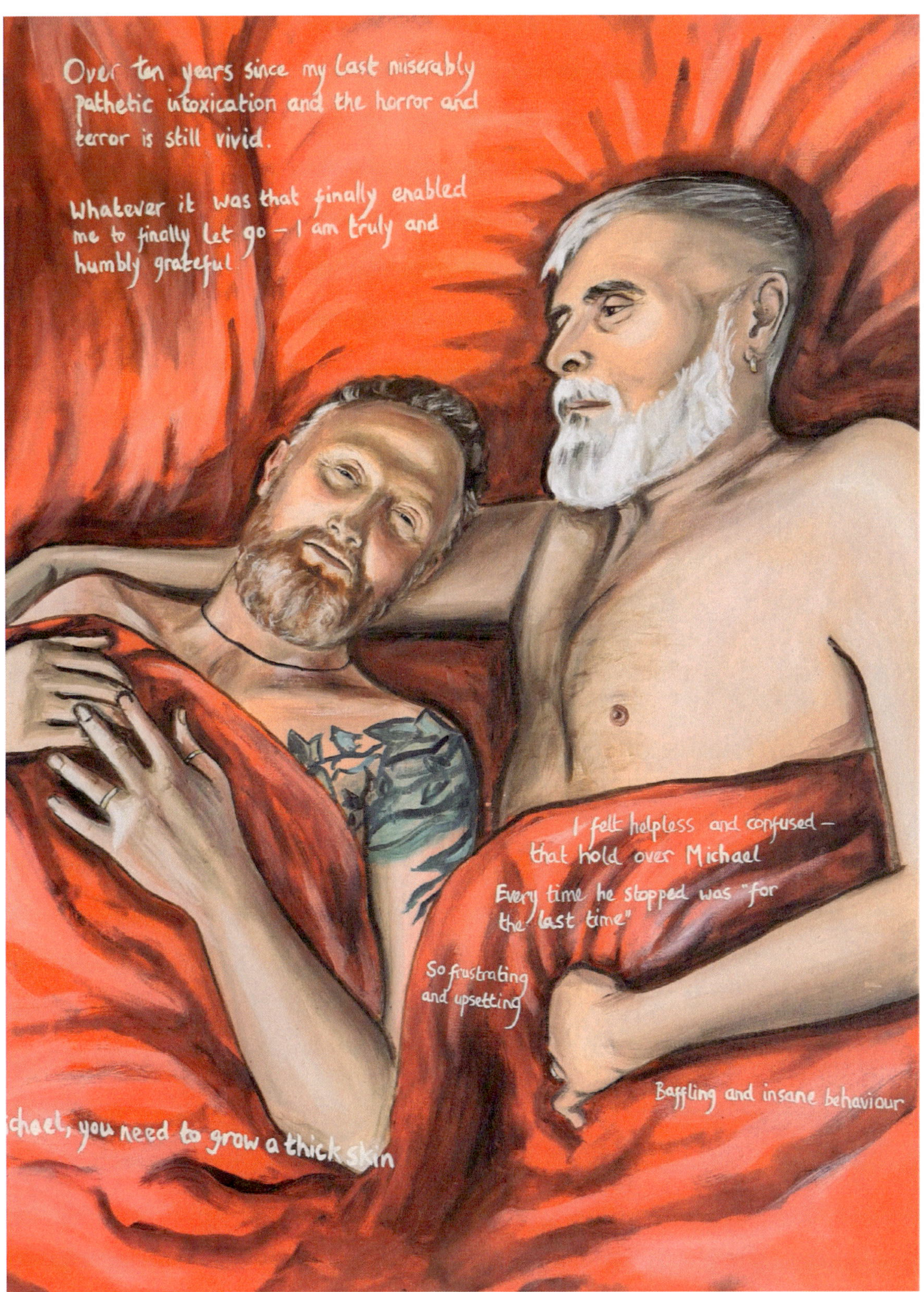

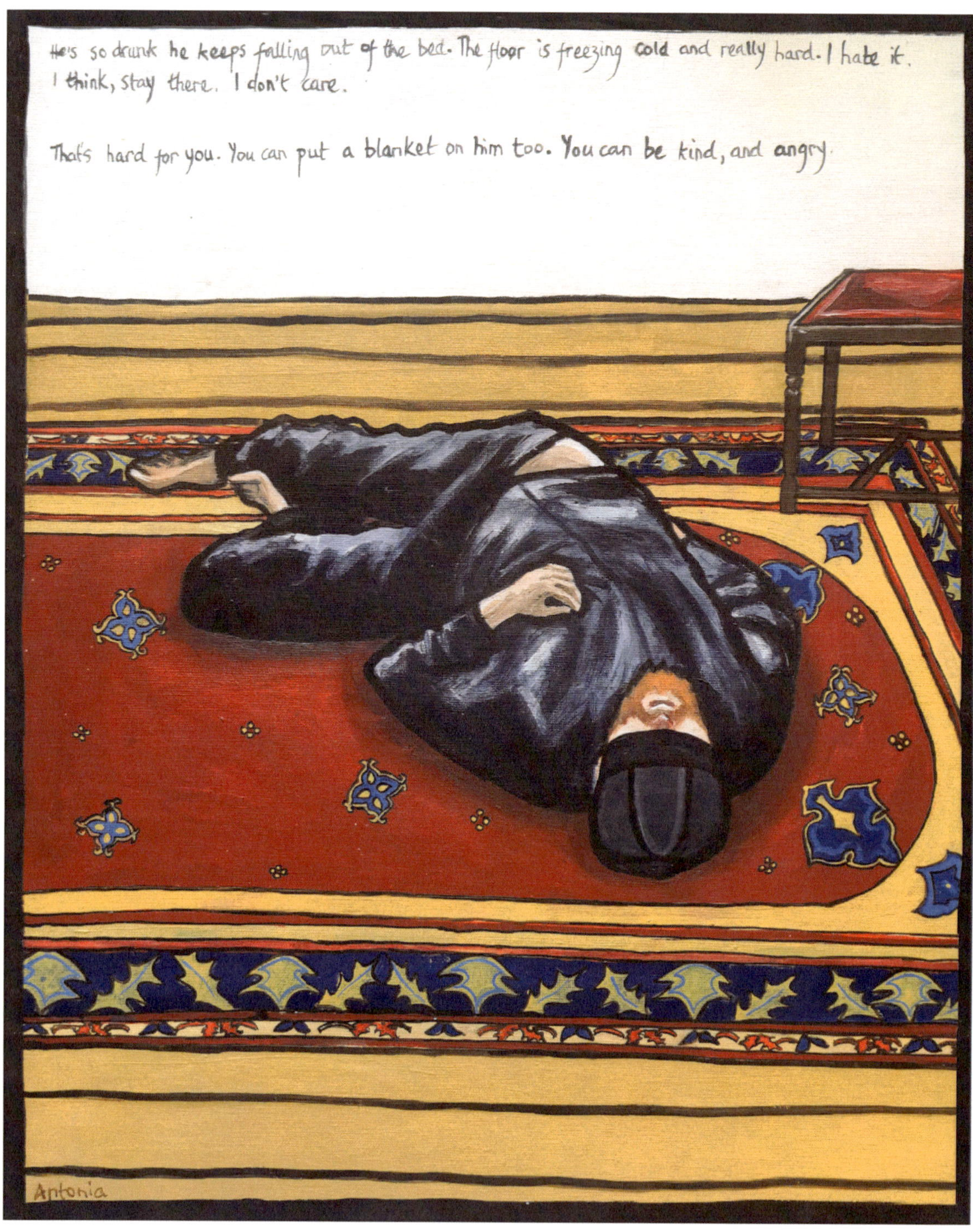

You can be angry and kind. I have been to so many support groups. They help me so much. Hearing other stories makes me realise I'm not alone. At one group, was a lady who was in despair over her husband's alcoholism...

Be Kind 2

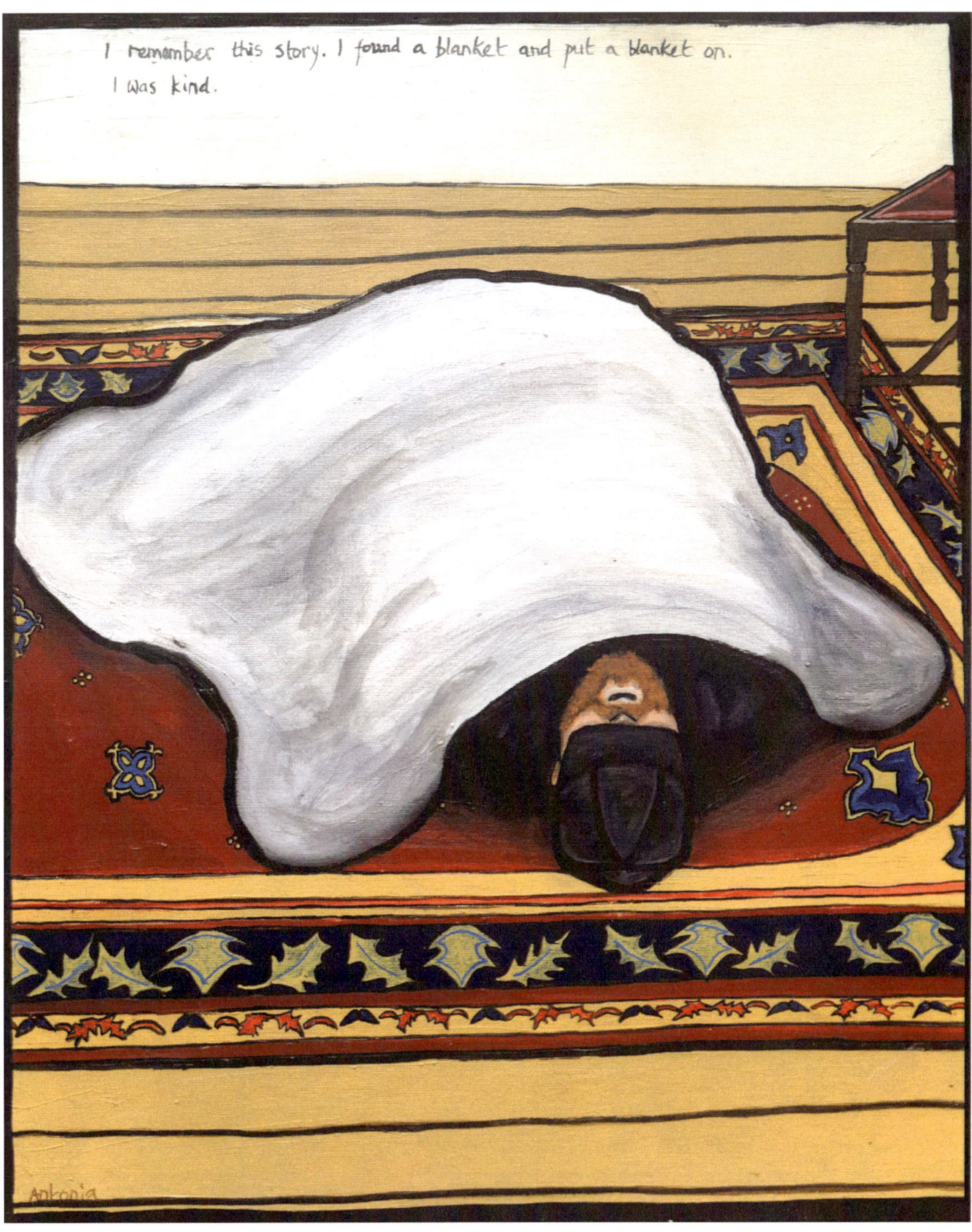

...When she said she left him on a cold hard floor to sleep off his drink, our group leader said she could be kind as well as angry. She said the lady could put a blanket on her husband and leave him there. I remembered this later, in my own family. It's OK to be kind too.

Owl and Pussycat

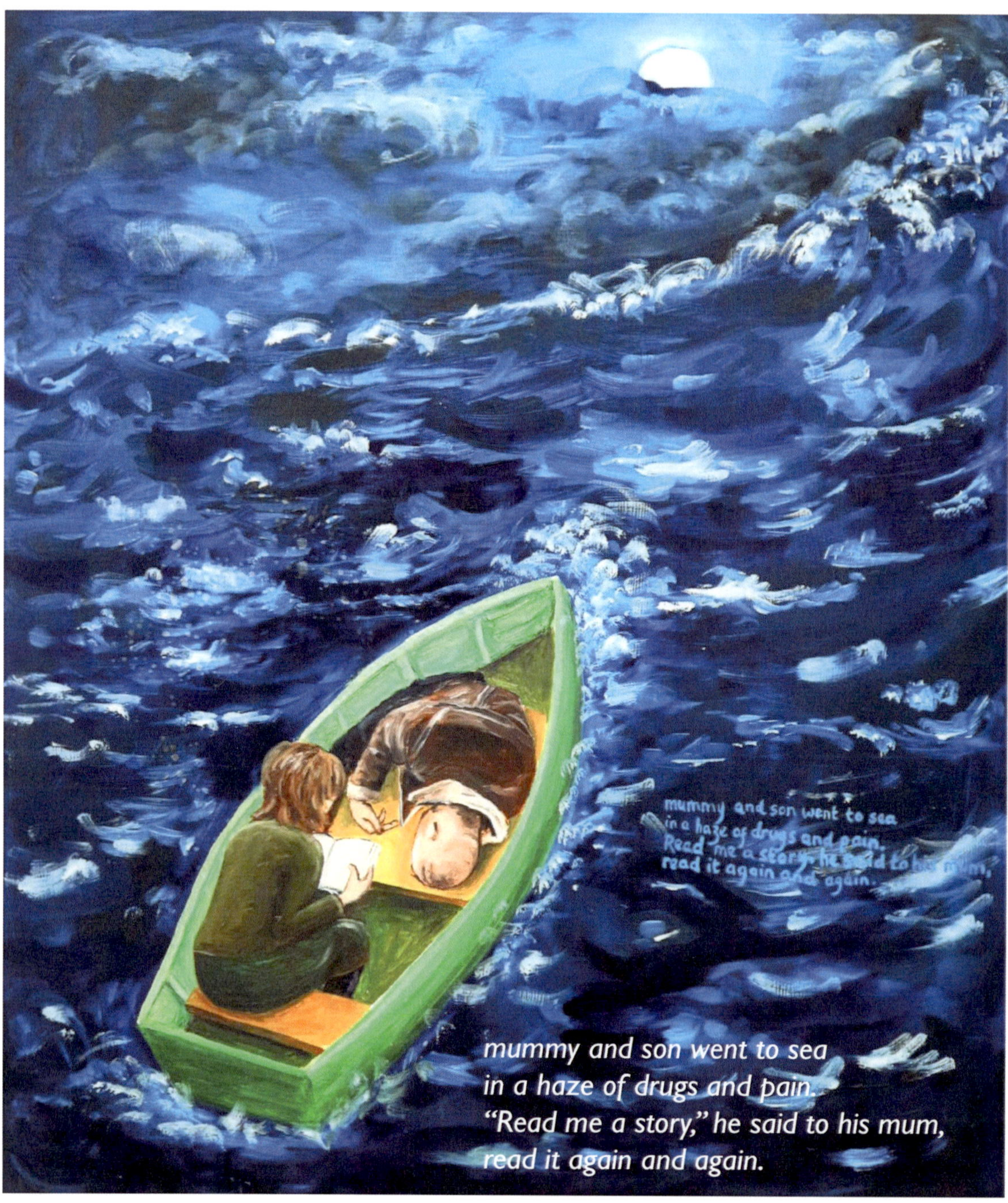

After a terrible night of drugs and drink, Costya saw me in his room. He'd been unconscious. "Read me a story," he said and as there was only one book on sociology in the room, I read him that. Later, someone said it sounded like the Owl and Pussy Cat going to sea, amidst a storm, and the pea green boat an oasis of calm. So I painted that.

And yet, my lovely boy, I love you + I am waiting for you to find a chink in your armour so that we can be friends, + so that I can show you off for the wonderful, clever, funny + eccentric masterpiece that you are.

What I want to say to you today is that I miss your amazing voice. I miss your clever sense of humour + I miss you being such fun to be with. I don't want you to be living away like this.

Mae's words -

I spent my childhood terrified of my parents due to their addictions, mental illness, volatile relationship, and unpredictability. I was emotionally abused and witnessed domestic violence, drug overdoses, and poverty.

To survive I had to prioritize the needs of others constantly on guard for little red flags that my parents might abuse me. I grew up feeling fundamentally bad, deserving of only conditional love, unable to express my needs or emotions without deep panic and fear.

Life is full of surprises, we either survive them or change them for the better. I'm doing everything within my power to change this generational trauma, I'm doing this for myself, my children and my community. I am slowly healing and growing with my beautiful children.

I am gentle, respectful, kind, and valuable.

I'm proud, and I will no longer be silent, scared, or feel threatened for sharing my experience.

I am breaking the cycle and I'm taking you all with me.

Mae

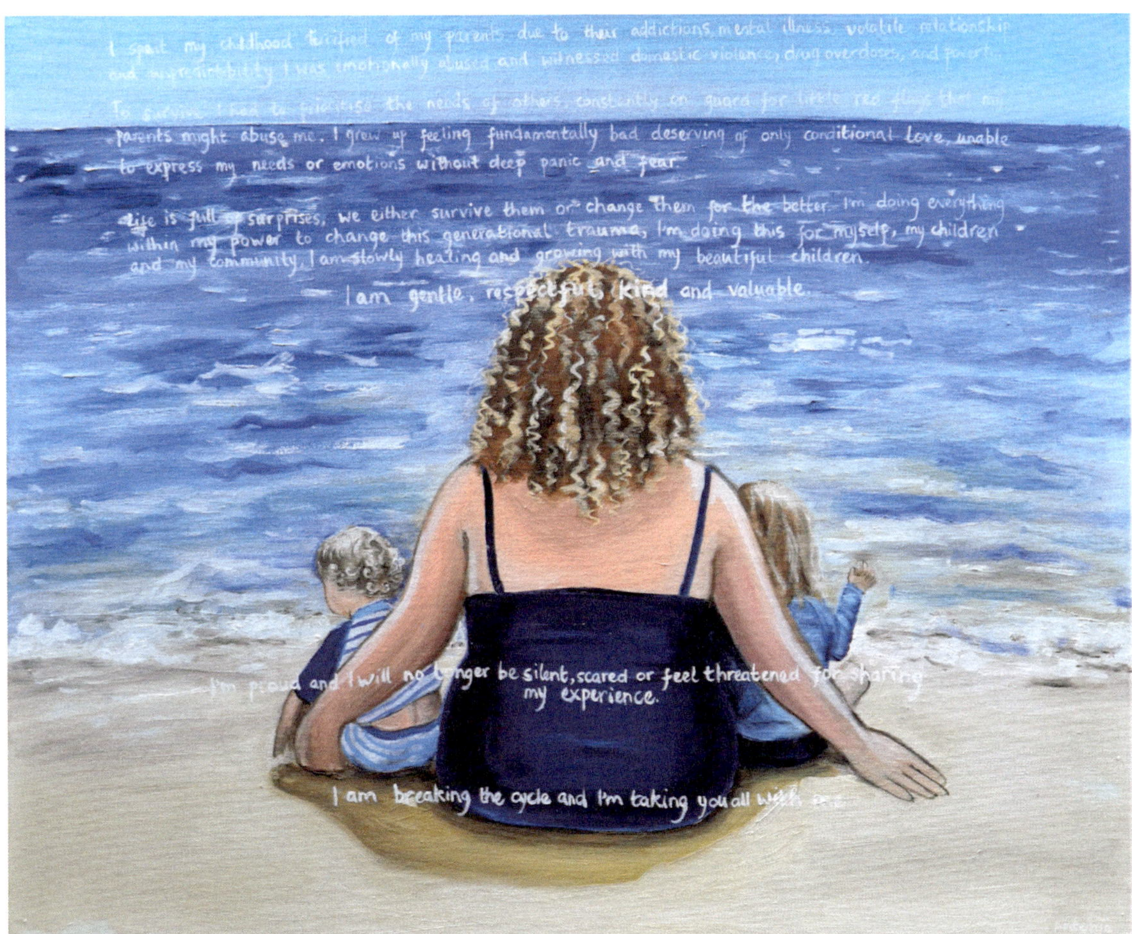

Not her real name, Mae has to remain anonymous. She is learning who she is, now she is a young mother. The oldest of 5 children to addicted parents, Mae did not have a childhood. "I'm breaking the cycle," she says, "and I'm taking you all with me."

Gill's words -

So chatty, friendly, open, and outgoing.

She was so elegant once. So beautiful. How much damage is done to our minds when not robust? When traumatized? When in the hands of a psychopath?

It all happens for a reason. When we find out - IF we find out -

A week before she died, she was still worried about stigma of mental health help. She wouldn't see a psychiatrist.

I miss her.

Complicates grief, police, coroner, post mortem.

Life ahead without her - I don't want to think about it.

I know she was an addict. I lost my SISTER, who was an addict. I lost HER.

She never spoke about anything. Hid everything. I think she knew.

She had an addiction. It changed her over twenty years. Get to know that person with addiction. That's who they are.

But she was also traumatized. Upbringing. Mad upbringing - married a psychopath - so fragile, + then she drank.

Maybe the cause of her death, not alcoholism.

The drink changed her. But it becomes familiar. The awfulness of family life. She never made good choices.

Still hiding things when she died. I wish she'd had more wisdom. She wouldn't let him call 999. Then we wouldn't be in so much pain. She'd have died in hospital. Then no autopsy, complication, police arrests -

but maybe it was still going to be complicated.

No will court cases, deaths, hoarding. But it would have been LESS complicated, less mess.

Gill

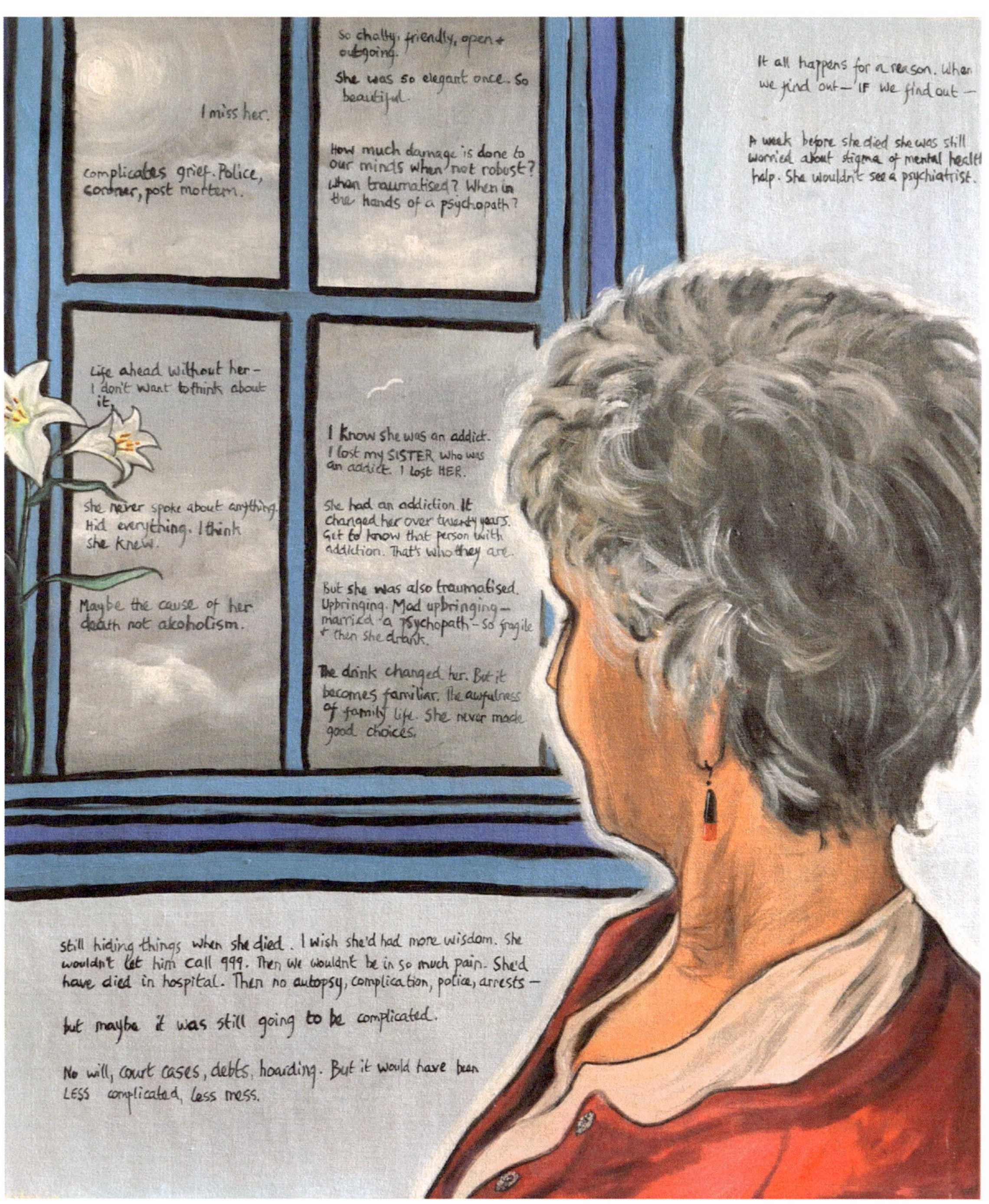

Gill loved her sister, Charlotte. In a troubled and chaotic family, Gill looked after Charlotte from when she was born. Gill was only 8. Charlotte was beautiful, creative and lost to alcohol. Her sudden death from alcohol was complicated and traumatic. "I lost my SISTER who was an addict," Gill said. "I lost HER."

David's words -

Addiction, no one wants to be an addict, majority of users don't become addicted, addiction is often driven by trauma.

Why take drugs? Have you ever been to the Gorbals? Why wouldn't you take something that took you to heaven from the harsh reality of life?

Drugs policy makes everyone worse. Led by USA, seeing addiction as a moral failing, not a mental health problem.

Almost all drugs policies are based on politics, not health.

America forced UK banning drugs (heroin) on prescription in 1940s, making drug taking 'morally repugnant'.

Nixon created the war on drugs deliberately to distract people from the failing war in Vietnam. It was successful, and deflected attention and problems onto black people and ethnic minorities.

War on drugs has always been a scam.

Failure of the Conservative government de-investing in addiction services, removing them from medical to social policies. Most appalling in my lifetime.

Emerging evidence of psychedelics to help addicts.

Decriminalization is the best way to stop drug use. Drug testing centres to minimise opioid deaths from Fentanyl, safe injecting rooms.

Drug laws and policies allow us to dehumanize addicts, and allow us to punish them. Sadistic.

Banning of therapeutic drugs is the worst censorship of research in the history of the world over the last 50 years. Drugs policies, laws, all because it gets politicians votes. As sensible as banning insulin for diabetics.

My sacking is the Government Drugs Advisor, a Rosa Parks moment created a live debate suddenly.

We are all vulnerable.

David Nutt

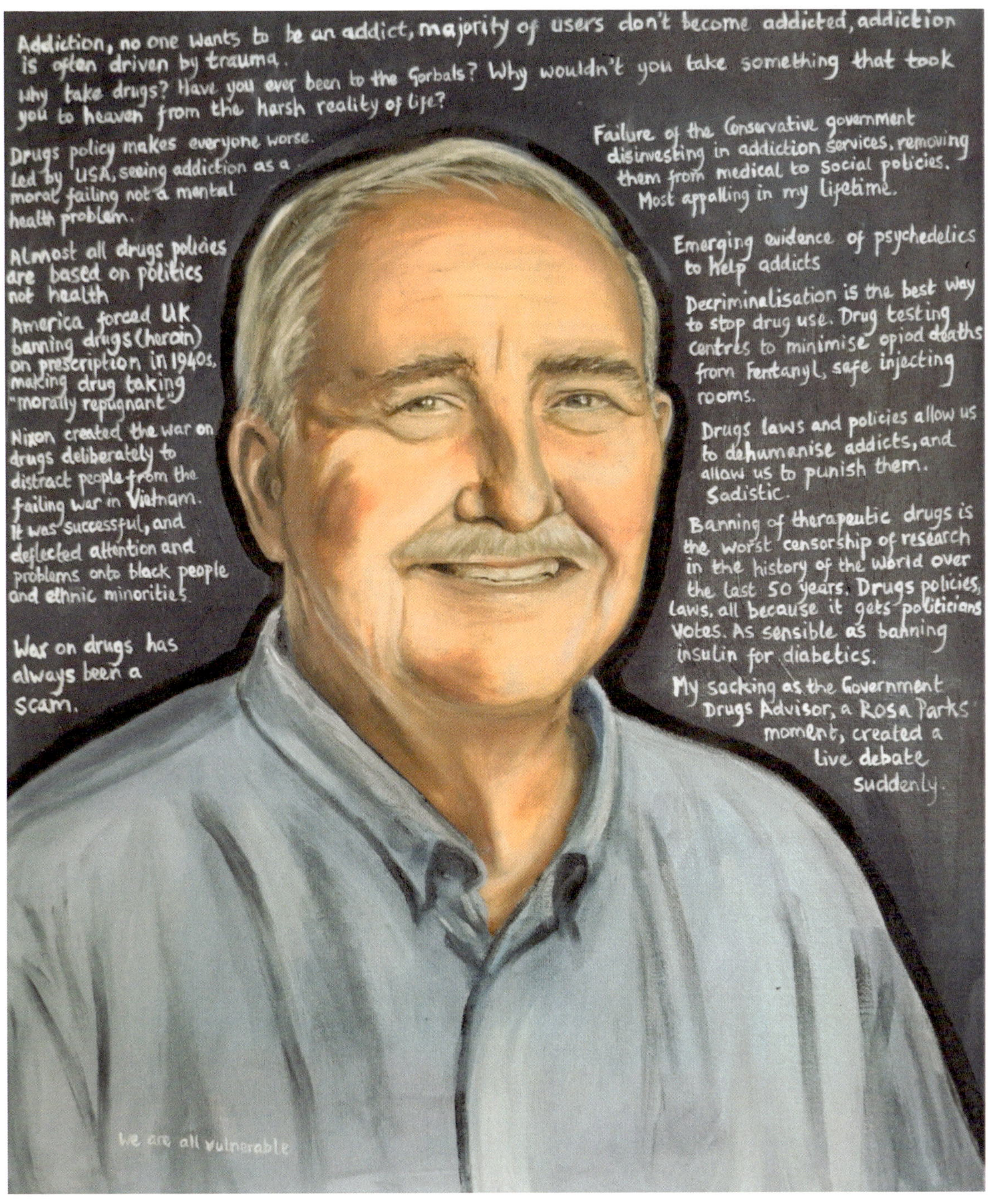

I asked Professor David Nutt to take part in this exhibition because of his tireless courageous and compassionate research into helping mental health and addiction. Speaking truth to power, accepting no funding whatever, he created Drug Science Organisation with his team for totally independent research.

Jodie's words -

I don't know who I am. I feel like it's been taken away from me. No safe place to find myself. My life chance to grow and mature my mind too consumed as a child.

Mum to my mum. Make sure she's at home. One night she didn't come. I called her 200 times. Missed calls. I am 13. She's out.

No parental support. Household to run and to go to school.

We were so close. Slept in the same bed till age 10.

Scared. I'll go into her room and she's dead. Image always in my mind.

Loss of my mum before she dies.

Anytime she's her old self? Split seconds. She doesn't have the time for me. I say half of what I want to say and she has to go. Got to go now.

I smoke dope to get numb to it. Weed opinion.

When I went to therapy, it was consumed by mum.

Grieving a person I haven't lost yet. Going downhill.

Makes me feel low. Mum abandoned me. Gave up on me.

Comes in to be nice to get something off you.

Now, I don't want to give her money and things. Manipulative. Persistent.

I want to leave. I used to want my mum to be sober.

Perfect world I want mum to click back to how she was.

Used to have an amazing relationship with my mum. We had a good life, love and care, attention conversation. But not anymore.

Mum - "Leave me alone fuck off, cunt. Fuck off." Me - "Am I a piece of shit? If you weren't doing crack all night, you'd be able to take the cat to the vet."

Grieving stages - Accepting she's doing it - Not let them manipulate you - Accepting you can't fix them. Like me saying, I'll give you food. I'll lay there with you while you're sick. I'll stroke your hair - Never enough. I'll never be enough. Trying to understand my mum. She had alcoholic parents. Abusive partners. Kids early. Dreams ripped from her.

56

Jodie

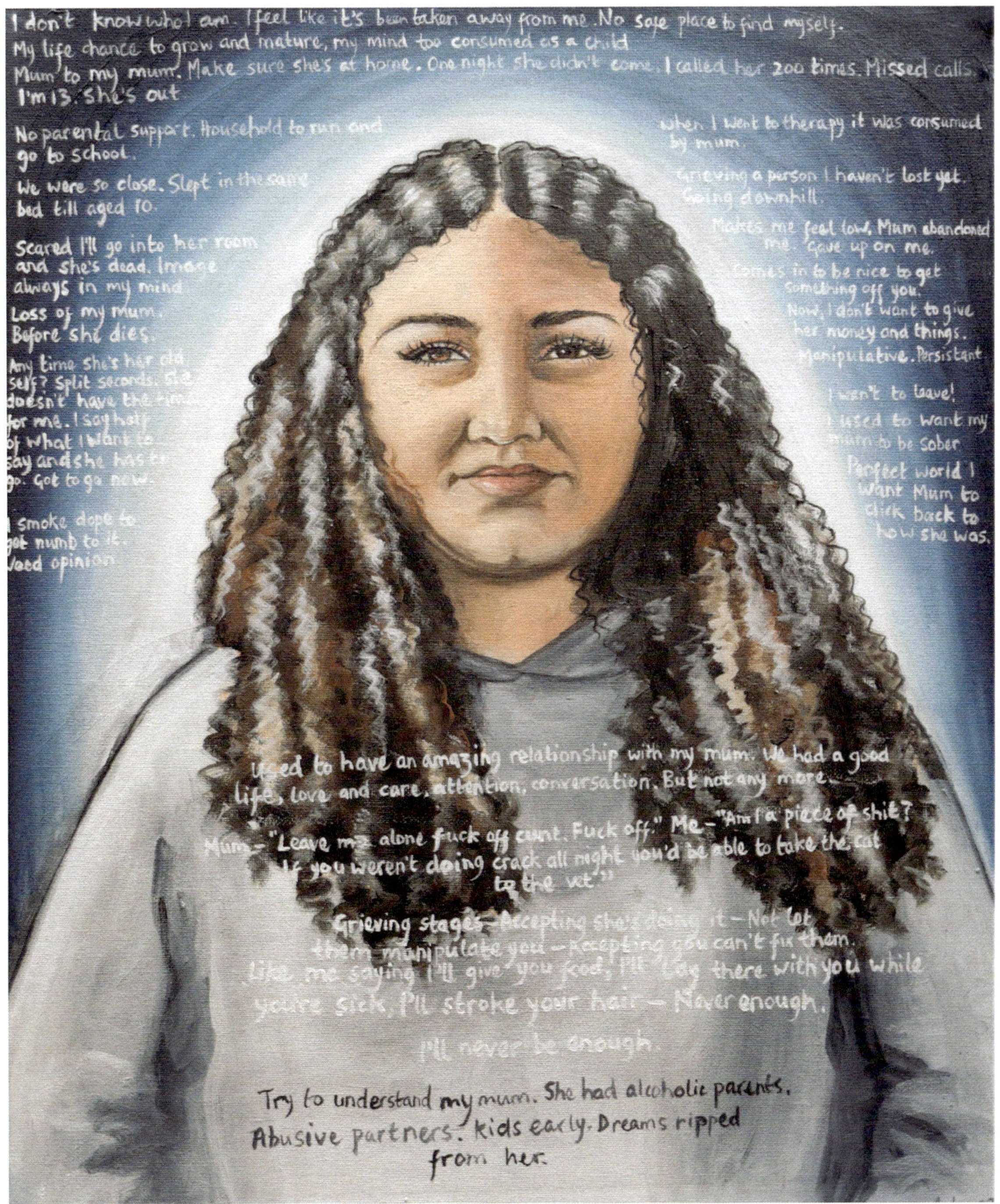

I met Jodie and Kevin at the first showing of Addicts and Those Who Love Them. I was taken with Jodie's story, and Kevin's, and asked them to take part. Jodie's mother is an addict and life has not been easy.

Kevin's words -

My experience with addiction, similar to Jodie, much less personal. Hidden. Discreet. My dad, taking drugs as far back as I remember.
My mum didn't know in 15 years marriage he was taking drugs, hidden behind alcohol. Told me as a kid, oh, drugs don't affect me. I can take them.
I believed him. He wasn't an addict. He hid it, spending all his wages on coke and drink.

Friends told me why your dad got so many rolled up coke wrappers. I thought it was lottery tickets. He'd go to a dealer "for a friend" in a pub and spend 15 minutes in bathroom. I didn't understand. Excuses from my dad, couldn't ever give us money. Hiding and sneaky with it.

He works only to get drugs.

Very hidden. I hadn't a clue.

How do I feel about him?

Because it was so hidden. I don't have bad feelings to him.

His life is disgusting to me.

It's so fake. It's so wrong.

I started to piece things together at 15. I can't put it into words.

Disappointed. He lied all my life.

We never had argumentative relationship. But other people said he was nasty and narcissistic.

Sword, fighting with plastic swords. When I was a small child, I poked his eye and he tried to break my arm.

I didn't notice straws, rolled up things in his house. So many people took drugs. Now I can see who takes drugs past the lies. I couldn't see past the lies.

The pub is where the dealers are, not just the pints.

WHO ARE YOU? My whole life I thought my Dad was one person, and now I don't know him.

Kevin

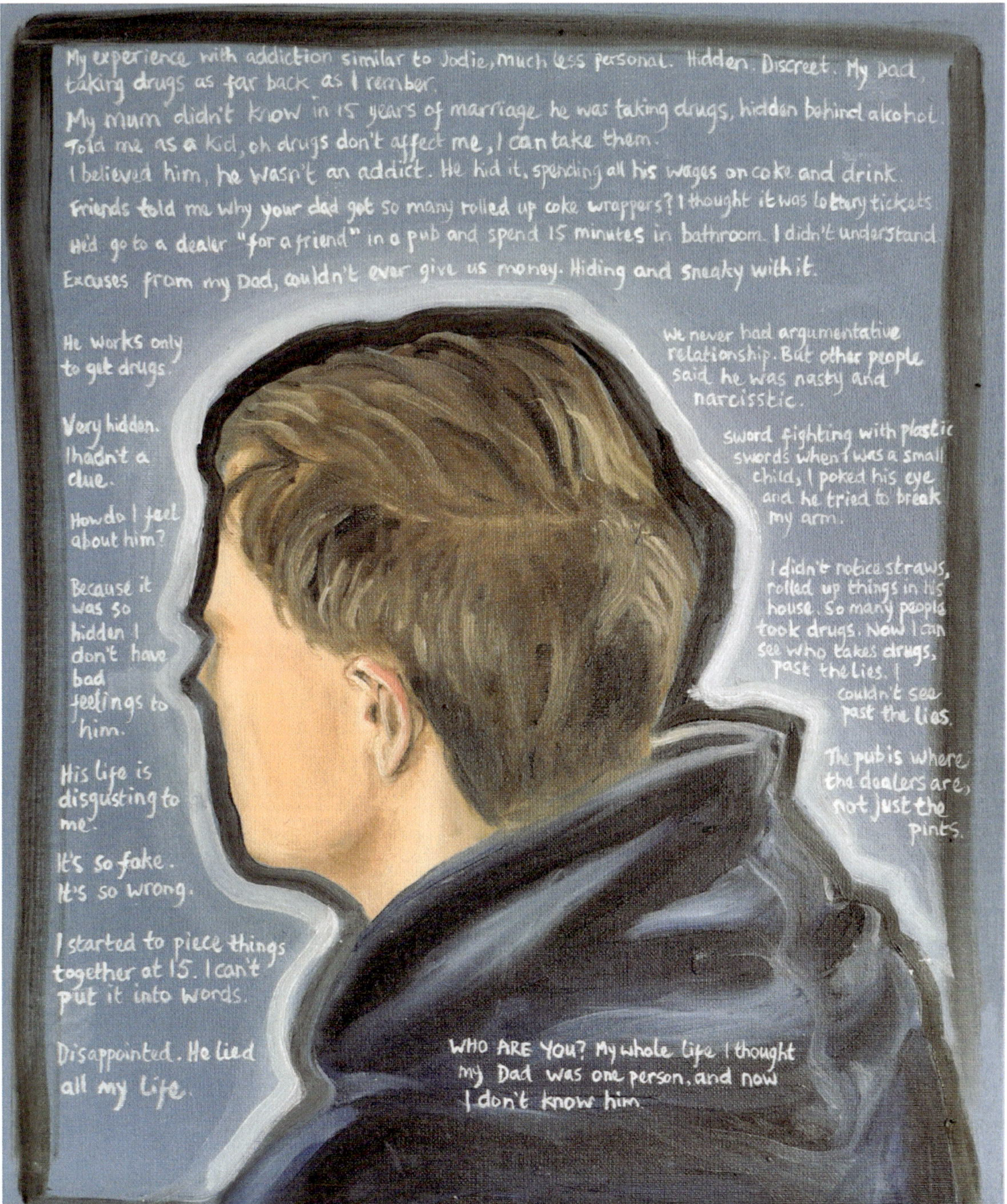

Kevin doesn't want to be identified. Partner to Jodie, together since they were 13, Kevin's dad is an addict. Kevin and Jodie support each other and both want to find somewhere to live and start again.

My Love,

*I did see you, but not as expected, and not on my terms, which often happens with us.
I am very sad and want to offer you a hot bath, cook you a meal, wash your clothes
and make sure you sleep soundly before going back to your life. That isn't possible
though. If it was, we would be coming and going without my stress, panic and worry
about what we were going to put up with, to change the plans and arrangements we
had agreed to, for you being back in the house.*

*I went to the cafe with your Christmas present. I didn't expect you to come and
thought if you did and I wasn't there, it would look bad. So I sat on my own and had
a pot of tea. Facebook said later that you were Christmas shopping in London with a
hangover that day; you must have ignored the text to show me what you thought of it.
I had sent you a message to ask if you would meet me before Christmas, at 11am on
Christmas Eve, at the cafe. I missed you, and wanted to see you before Christmas.*

*That night at 11pm, you texted to say you were stuck, unable to get a taxi or train
or bus, from the station and if I really wanted to do something I could collect you.
If I didn't you would have to sleep rough by the sea there. And your phone is out of
battery. It couldn't have been more inconvenient. Your sister, after mammoth amounts
of night duty and utterly exhausted, was asleep at last with her husband in my room.
Her car was parked in the drive blocking mine. My car had hardly any petrol. How
do I get the keys to move her car, how do I get petrol at 11pm on Christmas Eve, and
why is it so late and why have you allowed this to happen? So I do wake her husband,
get the keys, move the car, and go off slowly to find petrol, which I do manage, and
then go to collect you at nearly midnight. Waiting at the station, you smelt of drink,
looked dirty and unhealthy, and told me you had nowhere to go. It was obvious you
wanted to come home with me.*

*I took you to Chichester becasuse I didn't want you in my house. It was awful to say
no, but it turns out you went back to where you were staying anyway, and it wasn't
quite that you had nowhere to go, it was just that it was as usual, chaotic. At no point
did you thank me or acknowledge that I had come out to help you.*

*So, on Boxing Day, after your Christmas spent with the people you call your real
family, I received a text from you wanting advice and help. After meeting you in a cafe
here, I hear how everything kicked off badly on Christmas night, where your friends
all had a punch up, with drink and drugs, and now you are stranded here, dirty, cold,
hungover, afraid and unable to go anywhere.*

I was so distressed to say no to all your messages pleading to come and sit in our house and be warm. I am so sorry that you couldn't come home, it would be the worst thing ever. You would have abused it, and me, and everything in it. It would have been chaos and you would not have gone. You would have taken over, and without you ever having understood anything at all about how your behaviour has ruined everything. More control and more taking me for granted.

But it made me see that you are nice and respectful when you need something. When you see that the people you say you prefer and are your real family, when they are out of control, threatening, using you and making you afraid to go back to them, then my nice warm house seems wonderful. And because I have always been a pushover for you, you think it won't take much for you to make me say yes. I am weak and stupid to you, it is easy to get what you want from me and manipulate me, all the time taking no responsibility for anything you have done, do and say.

I wish I could have taken you home though, and given you a bath, some food, somewhere to rest and recover. I know you are recovering from alcohol, I know you are stuck in a cycle of despair and abuse. I know you are suffering terribly. You are my darling child. It is the worst thing I have ever had to do, to not help and not come to you when you feel so dreadful. It is because it never works. You never do feel any better. You take all you can and feed it into this gaping black hole of need and unresolved pain, and you don't even notice what has been offered to you. It is more important that you keep yourself the way you are, in pain, addicted, stuck, a victim, because then you don't ever have to look at yourself, and at your choices, and take the risk to face them all. It is more painful to look at yourself than it is to remain at risk of total destruction in the life you are living at the moment.

I will end here. I keep checking on Facebook to see if you are OK. I have been of no help to you ever, I was never strong when I needed to be, never truthful when I should have been, and not consistent with my ways of dealing with you. I don't blame you for being so angry with me. But, I do wish you were in my life, living nearby, where we can have a wonderful time seeing each other and being friends.

I love you,

Mum xx

Antonia Rolls

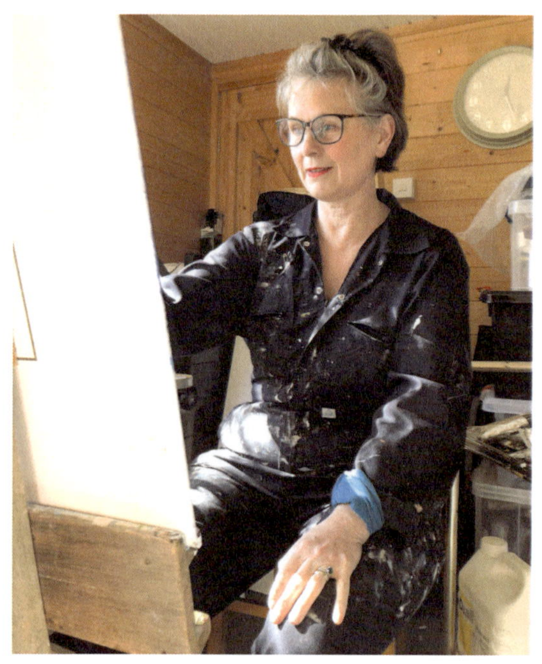

Antonia Rolls is an artist, listener, writer and speaker. She uses her painting and writing to explore difficult subjects with compassion and truth.

Her exhibitions cover the end of life, addiction and suicide, and addiction deaths. She has lost two sons this way, and shows how to look for the light.

www.antoniarolls.co.uk
YouTube: @antoniarolls

THE INTREPID SAGA

Being the oldest of the Aeon 14 series, the three books of The Intrepid Saga have seen their fair share of covers. Four different cover artists have been involved in creating these.

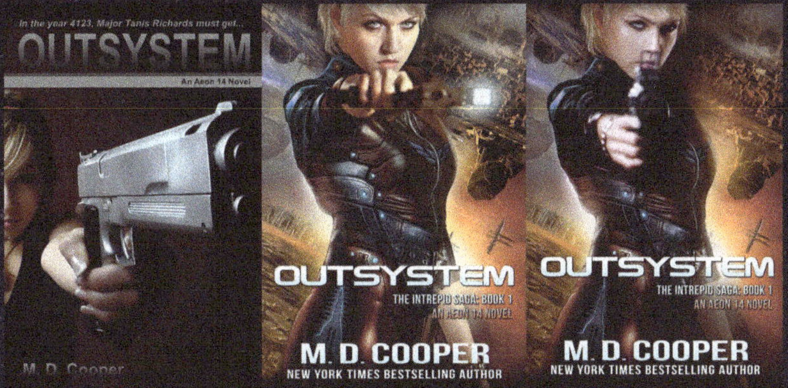

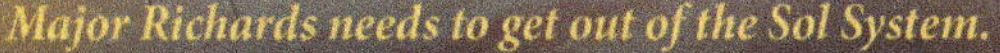

Demoted by the military and hung out to dry, the media labels her the Butcher of Toro. Despite her soiled record, Tanis is still one of the best military counter-insurgency officers in the Terran Space Force.

And they need her to find the terrorists responsible for trying to destroy the GSS Intrepid, a massive interstellar colony ship, in the final phases of construction at the Mars Outer Shipyards.

It'll be her ticket out of the Sol system, but Tanis discovers she is up against more than mercenaries and assassins. Major corporations and governments have a vested interest in ensuring the Intrepid never leaves Sol, pitting Tanis against factions inside her own military.

With few friends left, Tanis will need to fight for her life to get outsystem.

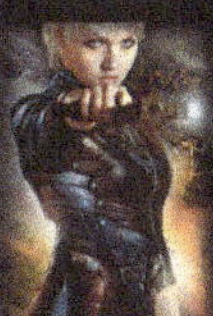
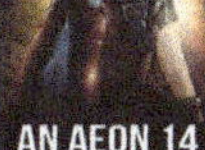

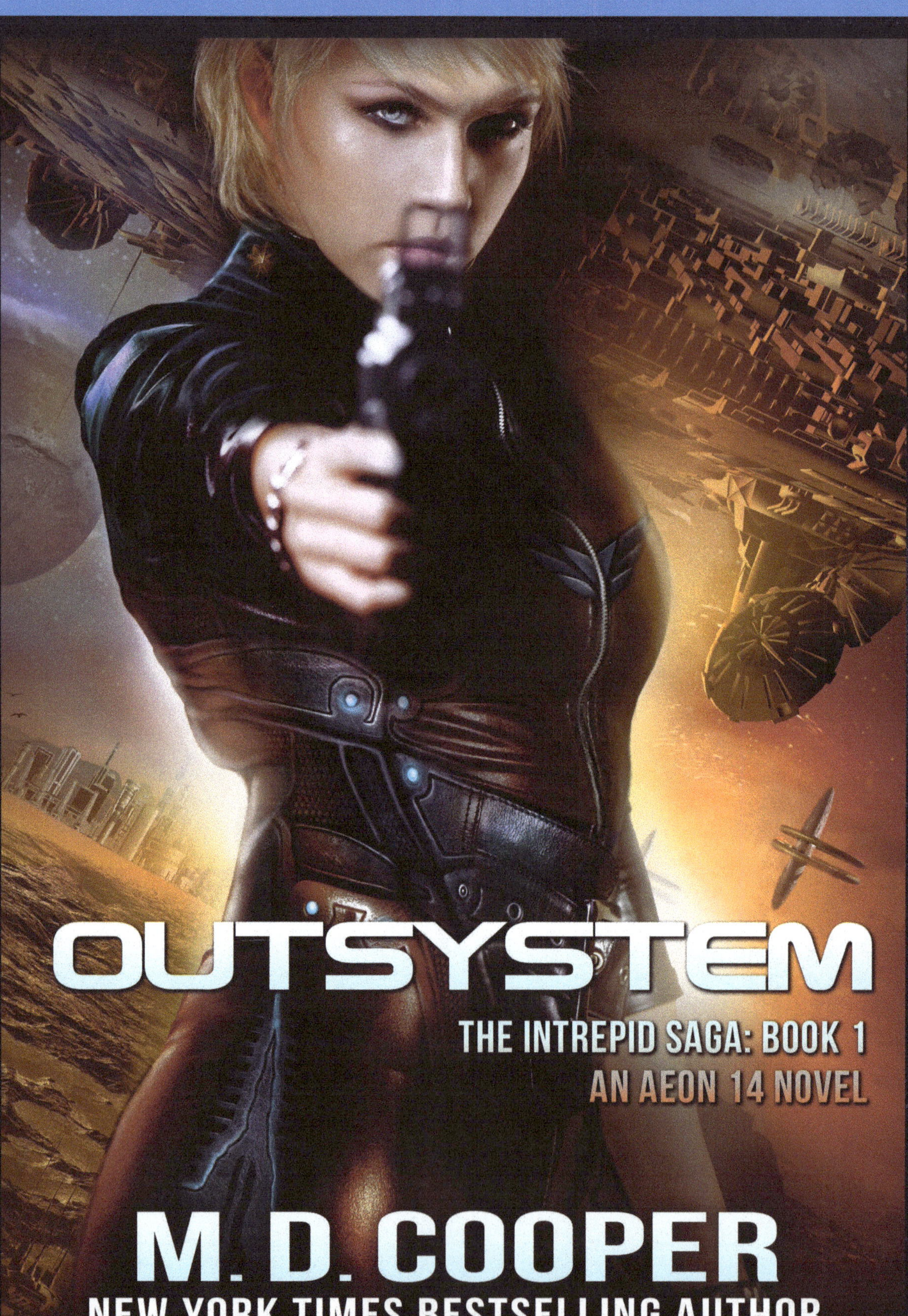

Left: third edition Outsystem cover.

Right: fourth edition Outsystem cover.

Many readers took issue with Tanis's "gangsta" pose on the second edition Outsystem cover.

In the summer of 2016, the ebook was updated to have this cover.

There was never a print edition with this cover.

Up until February 2018, all of the covers in Aeon 14 (with the exception of the Perseus Gate books) used stock model images. Unfortunately, there are only so many poses available with stock images, and the images were beginning to show up on other books.

The cover on the right was the first to feature the new Tanis model and custom armor made for the photoshoot.

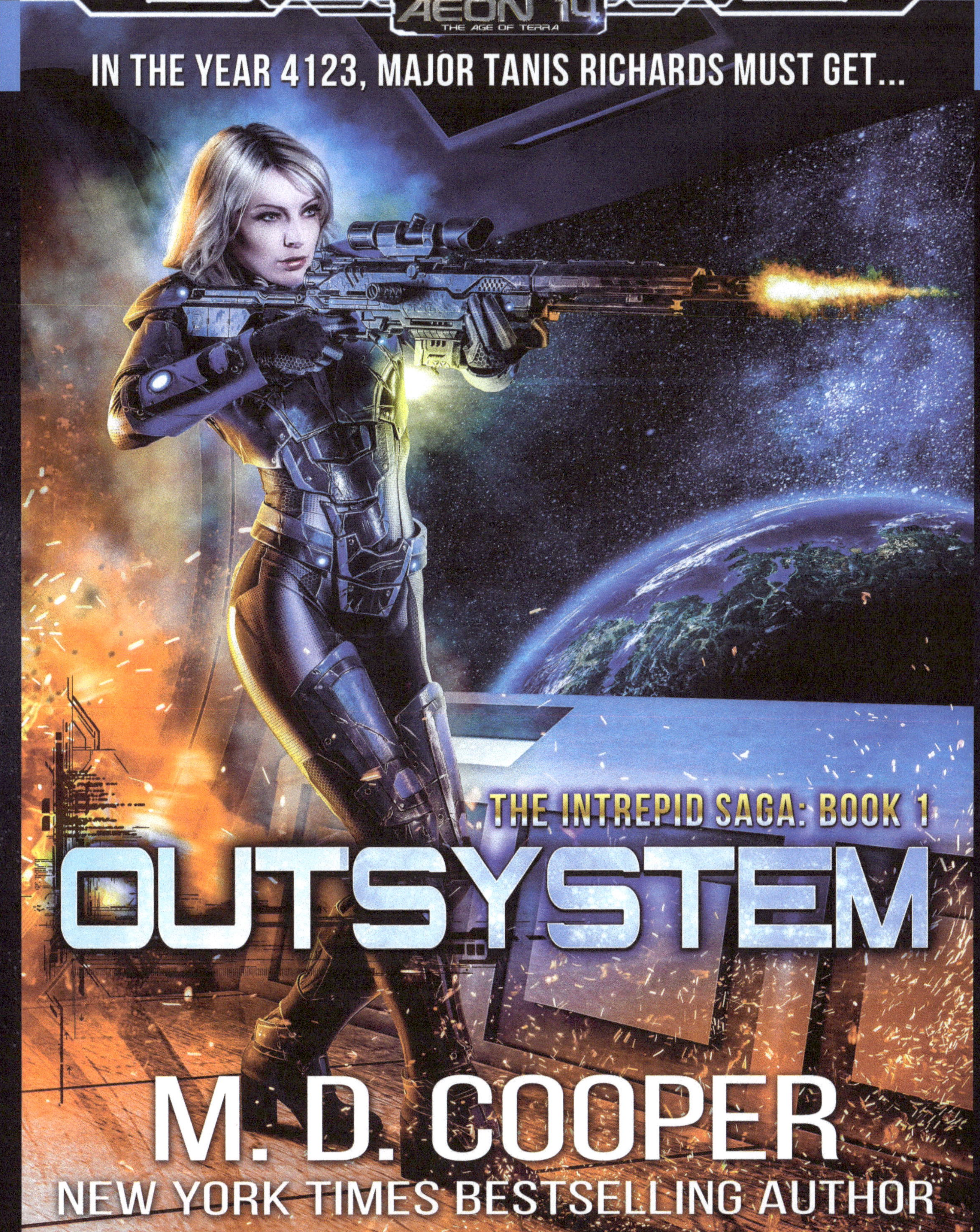

AEON 14
THE AGE OF TERRA
IN THE YEAR 4123, MAJOR TANIS RICHARDS MUST GET...
THE INTREPID SAGA: BOOK 1
OUTSYSTEM
M. D. COOPER
NEW YORK TIMES BESTSELLING AUTHOR

OUTSYSTEM

THE INTREPID SAGA: BOOK 1

In 4123, the greatest colony ship ever built is leaving the Sol System, and Major Tanis Richards has secured a berth.

Demoted by the military and hung out to dry, the media calls her the Butcher of Toro. However, despite her soiled record, Tanis is still one of the best military counterinsurgency officers in the Terran Space Force.

The backers of the colony mission need her to stop the terrorists trying to destroy the GSS *Intrepid*, during the final phases of its construction at the Mars Outer Shipyards.

Getting the job done will be her ticket out of the Sol System, but Tanis discovers she is up against more than mercenaries and assassins. Major corporations and governments have a vested interest in ensuring the *Intrepid* never leaves Sol, ultimately pitting Tanis against factions inside her own military.

With few friends left, Tanis will need to fight for her life to get outsystem.

AEON14.COM

1
THE INTREPID SAGA

OUTSYSTEM

M. D. COOPER

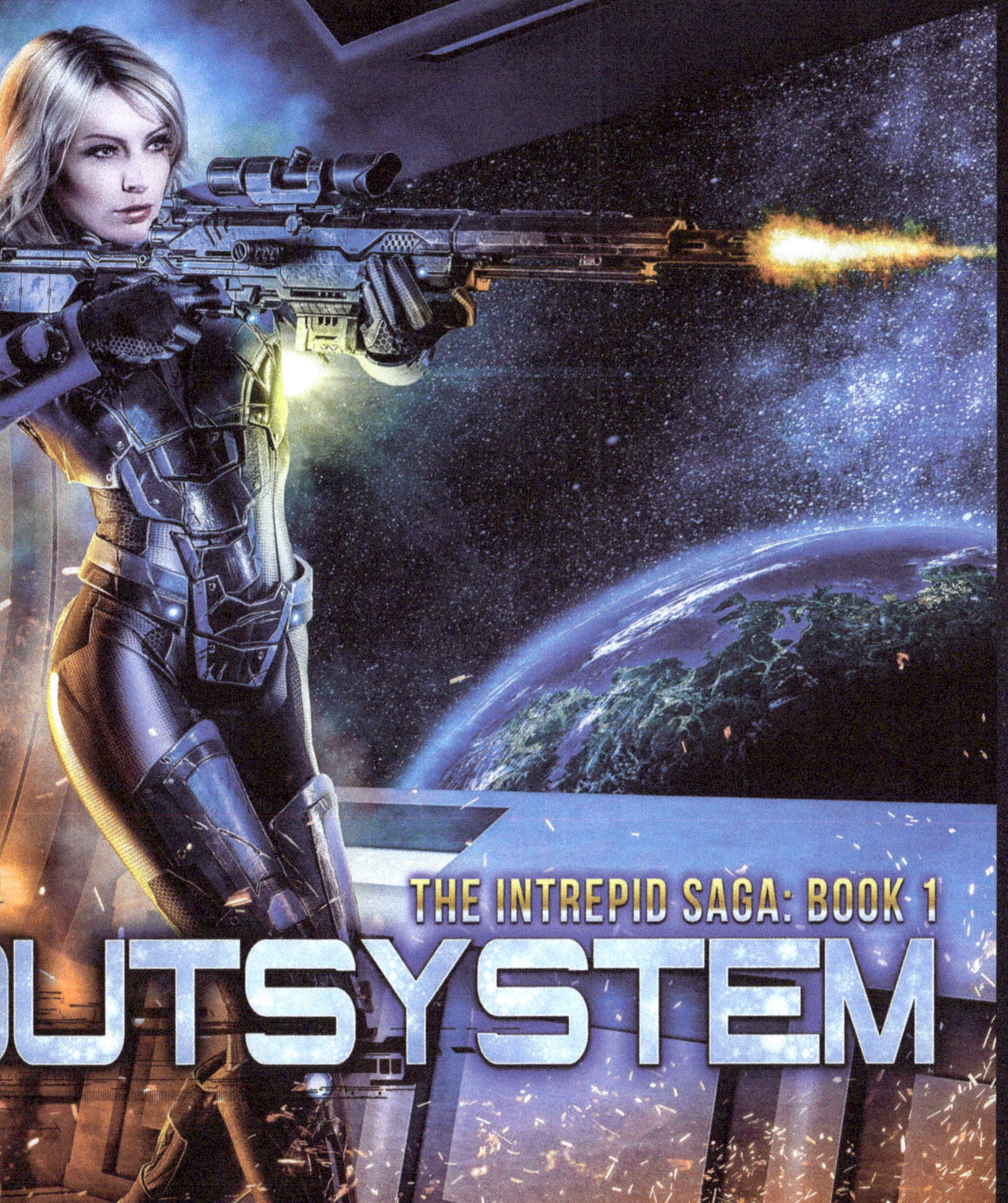

Once the re-covering of the books began, all Aeon 14 books took on a similar spine and back cover treatment.

This is what the "full wrap" with typography looks like, which won't be displayed for all books in this edition.

This cover also features the Aeon 14 header logo that now appears on all Aeon 14 books.

The fourth edition is the only Outsystem cover where Tanis isn't "shooting at the reader". Poses where a gun is pointed at the reader are often rejected for ads. This cover pose was selected to avoid that issue.

The model who portrayed Tanis did a fantastic job, and the armor that was custom made fit perfectly and really upleveled the art.

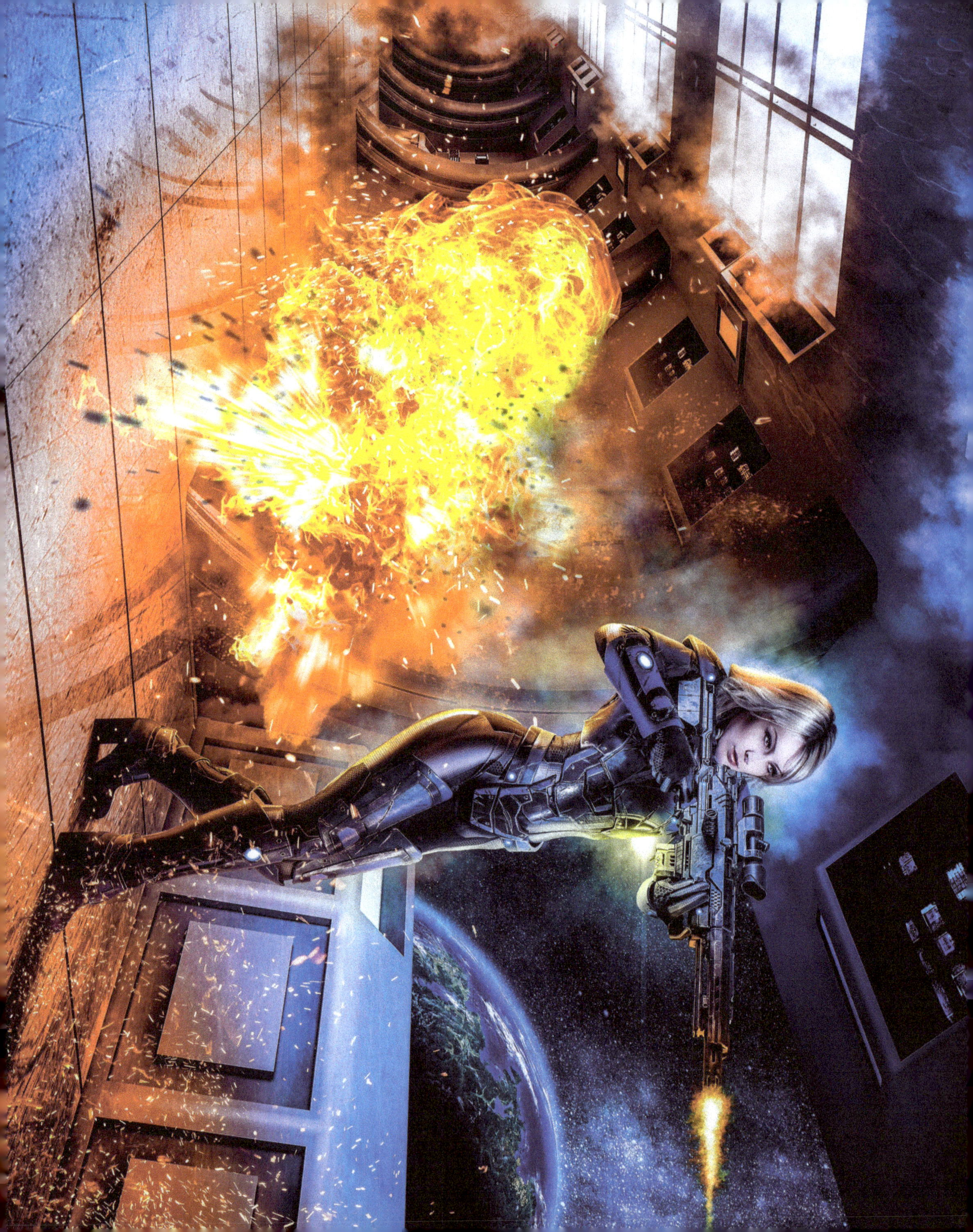

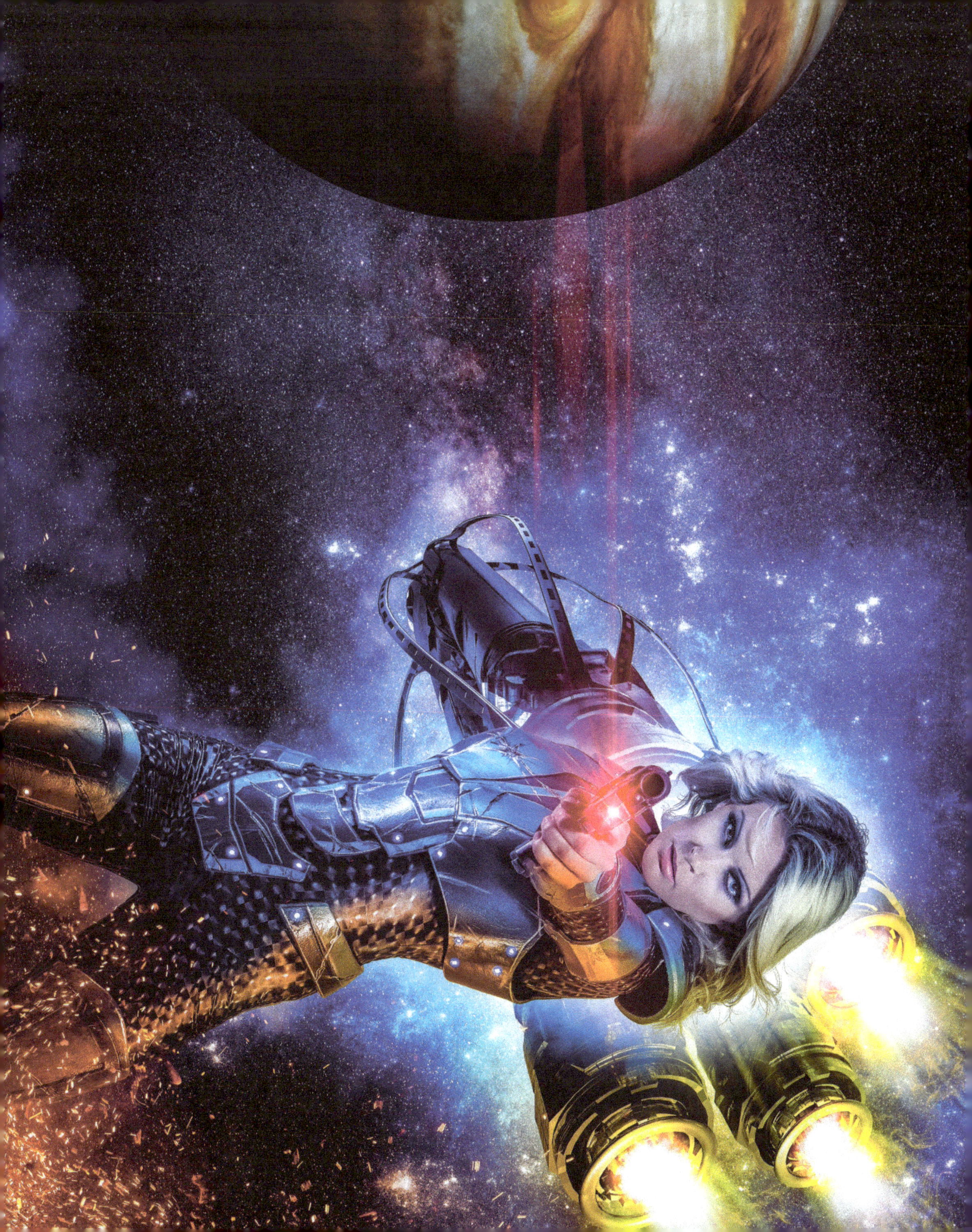

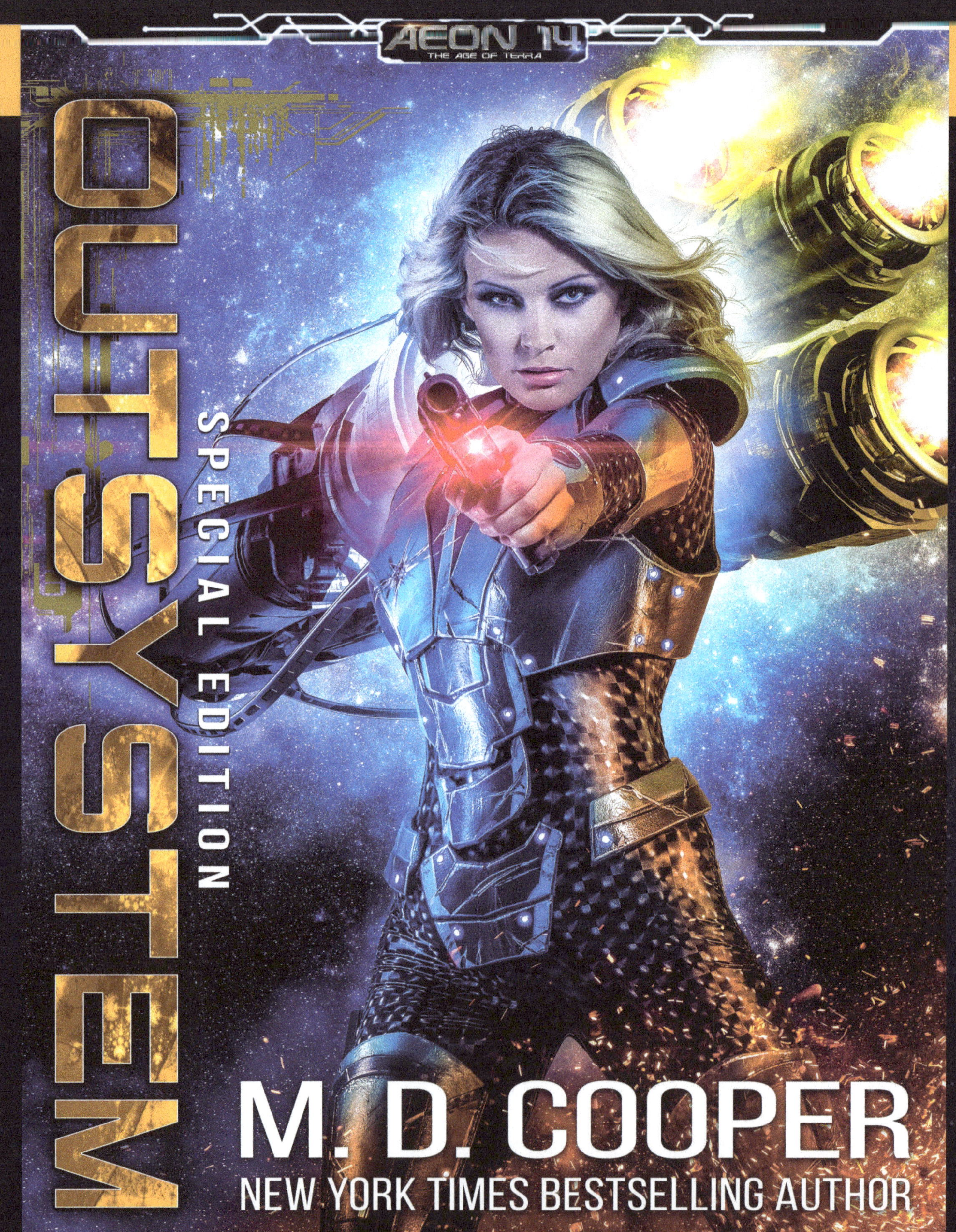

AEON 14
THE AGE OF TERRA
OUTSYSTEM
SPECIAL EDITION
M. D. COOPER
NEW YORK TIMES BESTSELLING AUTHOR

In mid 2018, a soundtrack to Outsystem was released. Fans had the opportunity to purchase a "Deluxe" edition of the soundtrack which came with a special edition of Outsystem.

This version is longer (contains some parts from Destiny Rising) and is not available to purchase anywhere other than with the Deluxe Editon of the album.

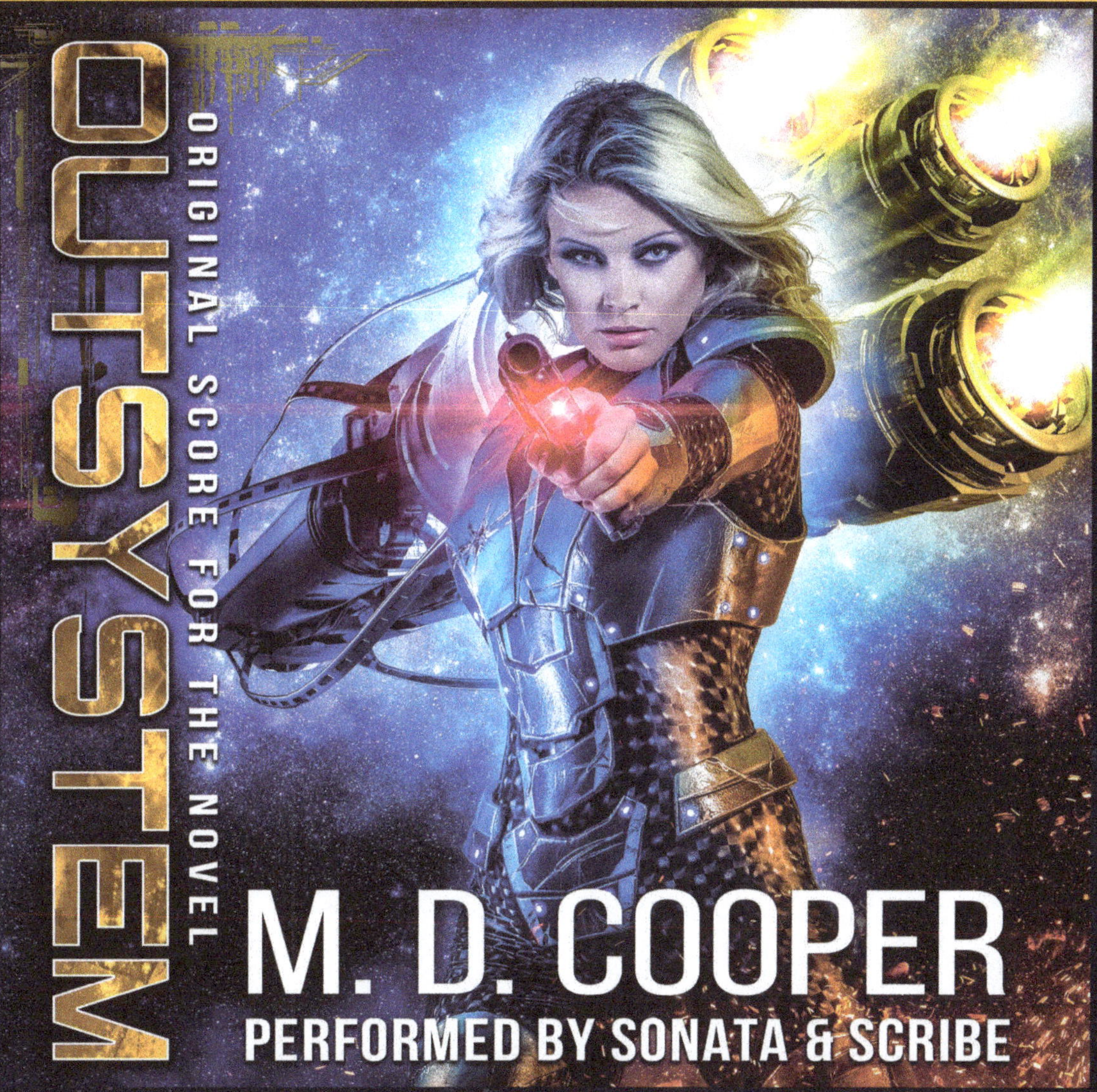

OUTSYSTEM

ORIGINAL SCORE FOR THE NOVEL

M. D. COOPER
PERFORMED BY SONATA & SCRIBE

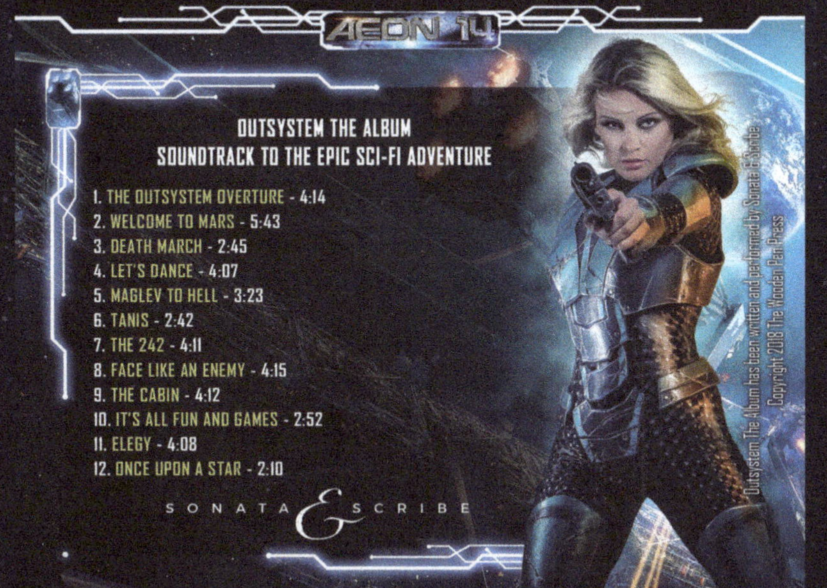

Opposite: the full front cover of the Outsystem Special Edition.

Above: the digital cover for the album, which is available through major retailers.

Left: the back of a post card listeners can order from and have signed.

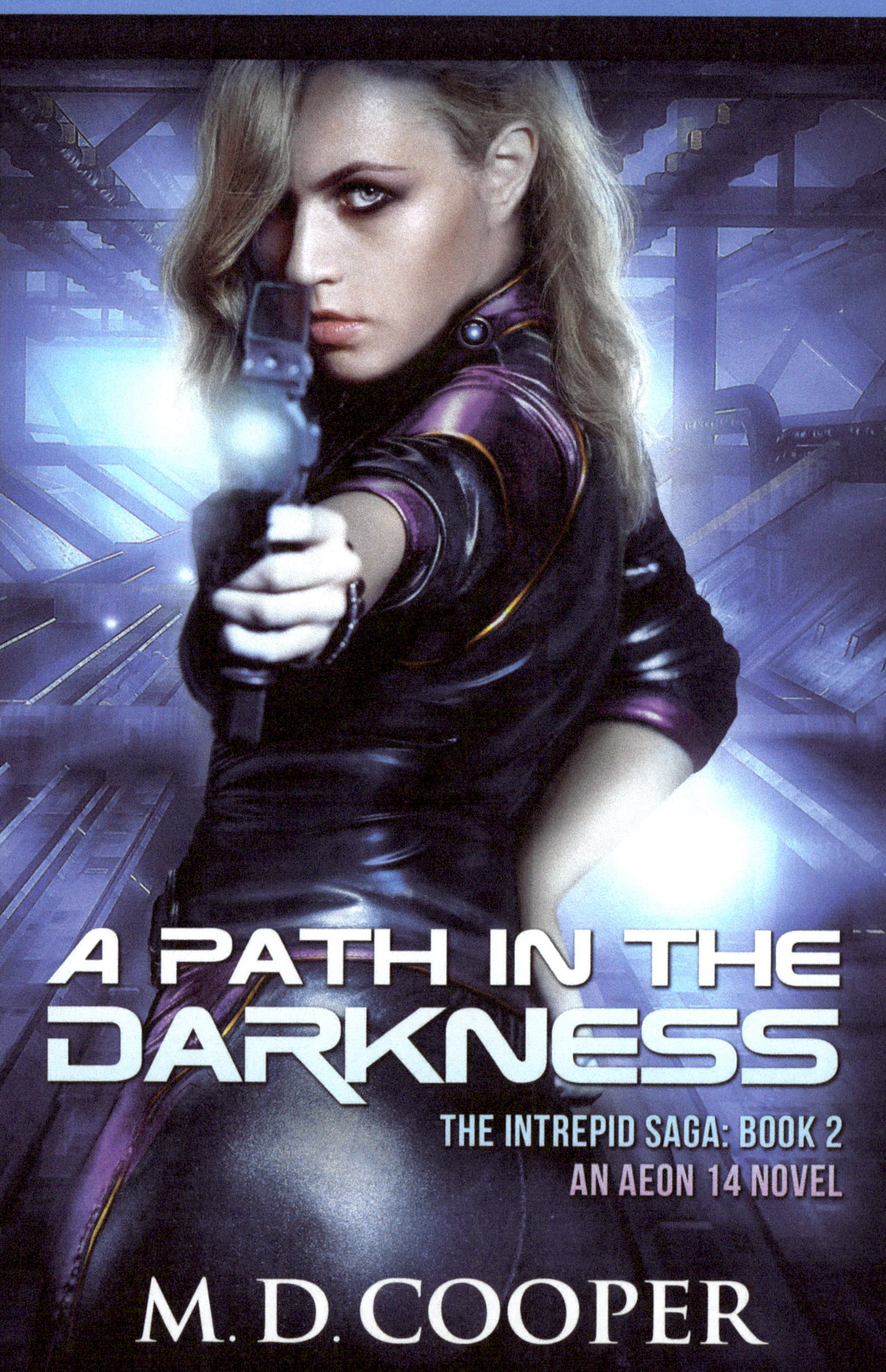

A PATH IN THE DARKNESS

M. D. Cooper

For a brief time the self-made cover pictured above was used on aeon14.com.

However, the book was only ever published with the cover right and opposite.

It's worth noting that the cover on the right is the first of the iconic rear-end shots to show up on Aeon 14 covers. In my defense, the cover artist was female and was the one to select this pose.

The version of the cover opposite is the first to show Tanis in the stealth suit she took from the assassin in Outsystem. Though it is destroyed in this book, Earnest recreates the technology for her at a later date.

For the photoshoot, we found a holographic suit that embodies what the effect could look like when the suit's stealth systems are enabled.

AEON 14
THE AGE OF TERRA

WITH HER SHIP LOST, TANIS RICHARDS MUST FIND...

THE INTREPID SAGA: BOOK 2

A PATH IN THE DARKNESS

M. D. COOPER

NEW YORK TIMES BESTSELLING AUTHOR

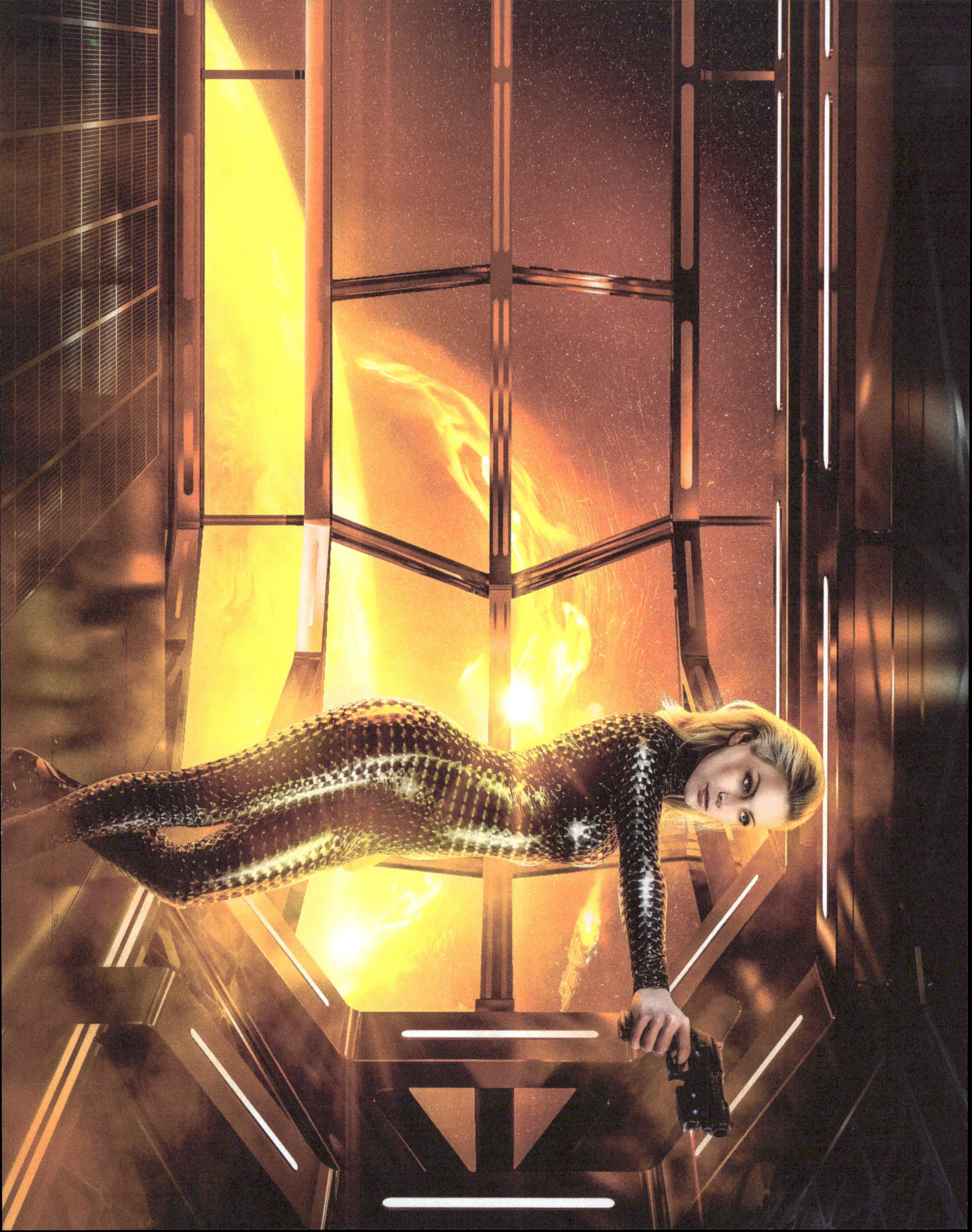

When the time came to release Building Victoria, I knew that the *Intrepid* needed to make an appearance.

Because the ship is so iconic, I couldn't use some existing stock imagery, and I had to find a an artist who could desgin a 3D model of the ship and render it.

As luck would have it, Tom Edwards is both a great cover artist and a fantastic 3D modeller.

He designed this initial version of the *Intrepid*, as well as the cover.

I've always liked this pose and expression for Tanis. She looks like someone is going to have a very bad day.

It is also the first time we see her lightwand on a cover.

On the following page, we see the updated version of this cover, featuring both Tanis and Jessica.

Right: the original cover for Building Victoria.

Left: full art for A Path in the Darkness. Note that Lt. Collins's ship is visible fleeing the impending collision with Estrella de la Muerte.

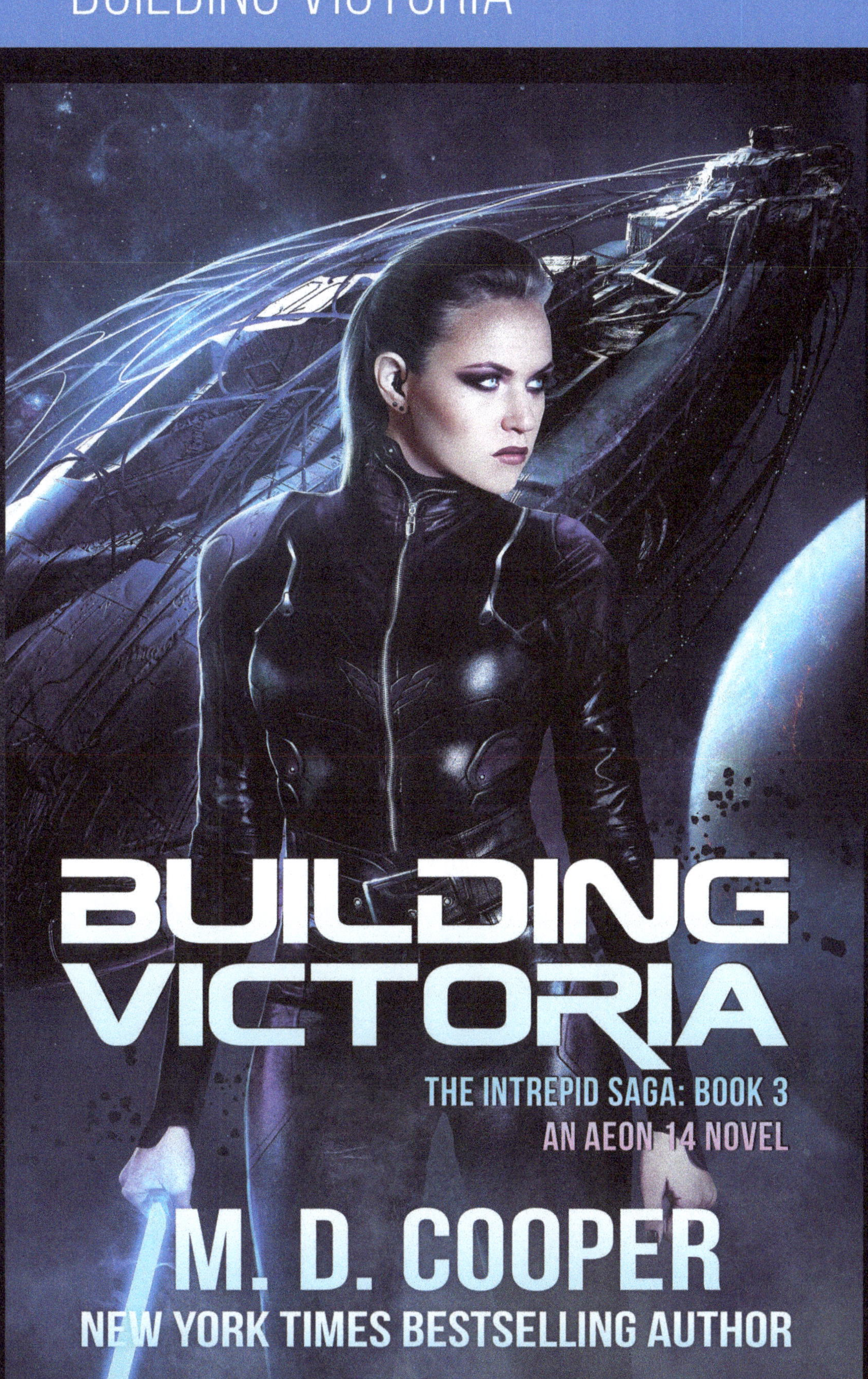

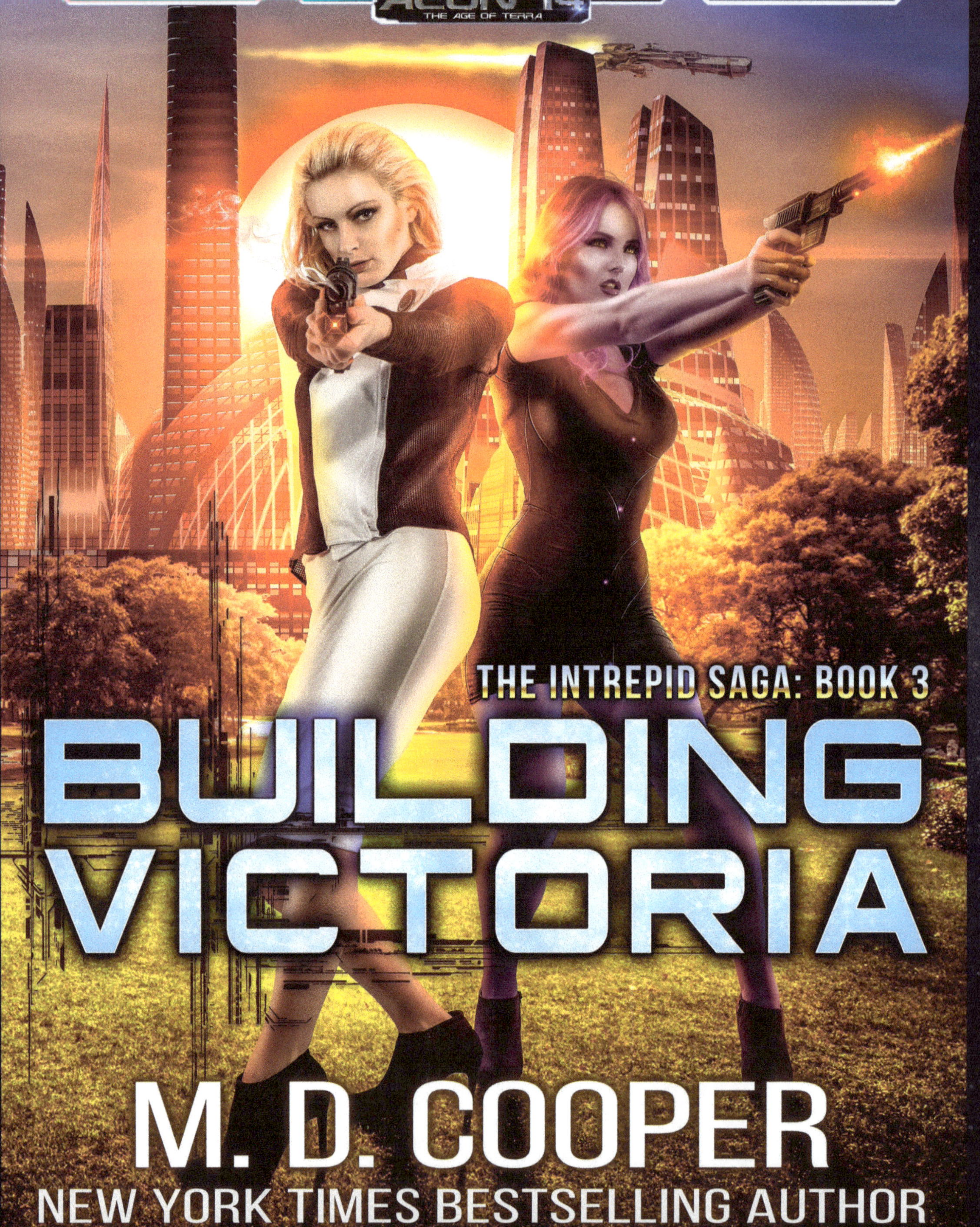

AEON 14
THE AGE OF TERRA
THE INTREPID SAGA: BOOK 3
BUILDING VICTORIA
M. D. COOPER
NEW YORK TIMES BESTSELLING AUTHOR

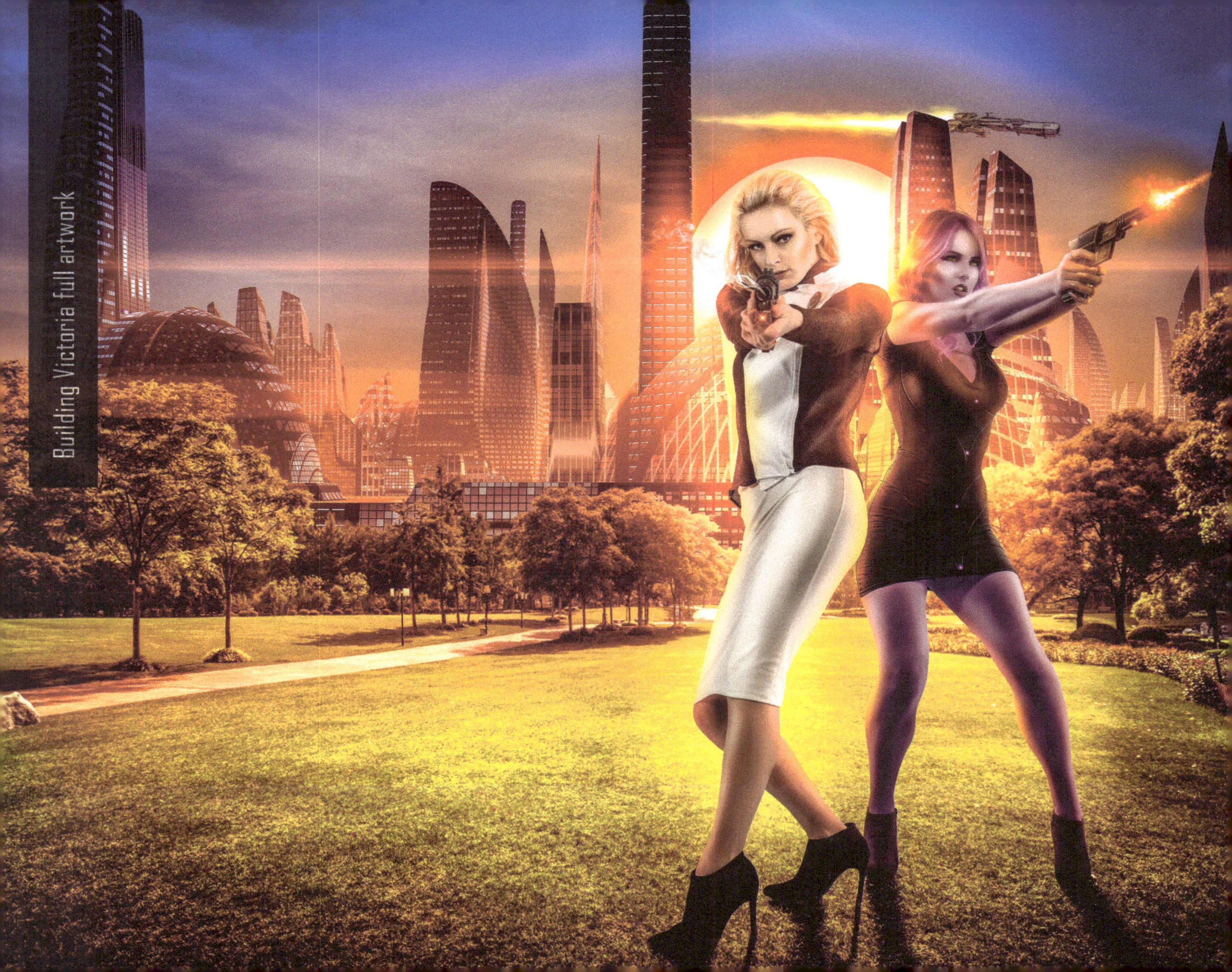
Building Victoria full artwork

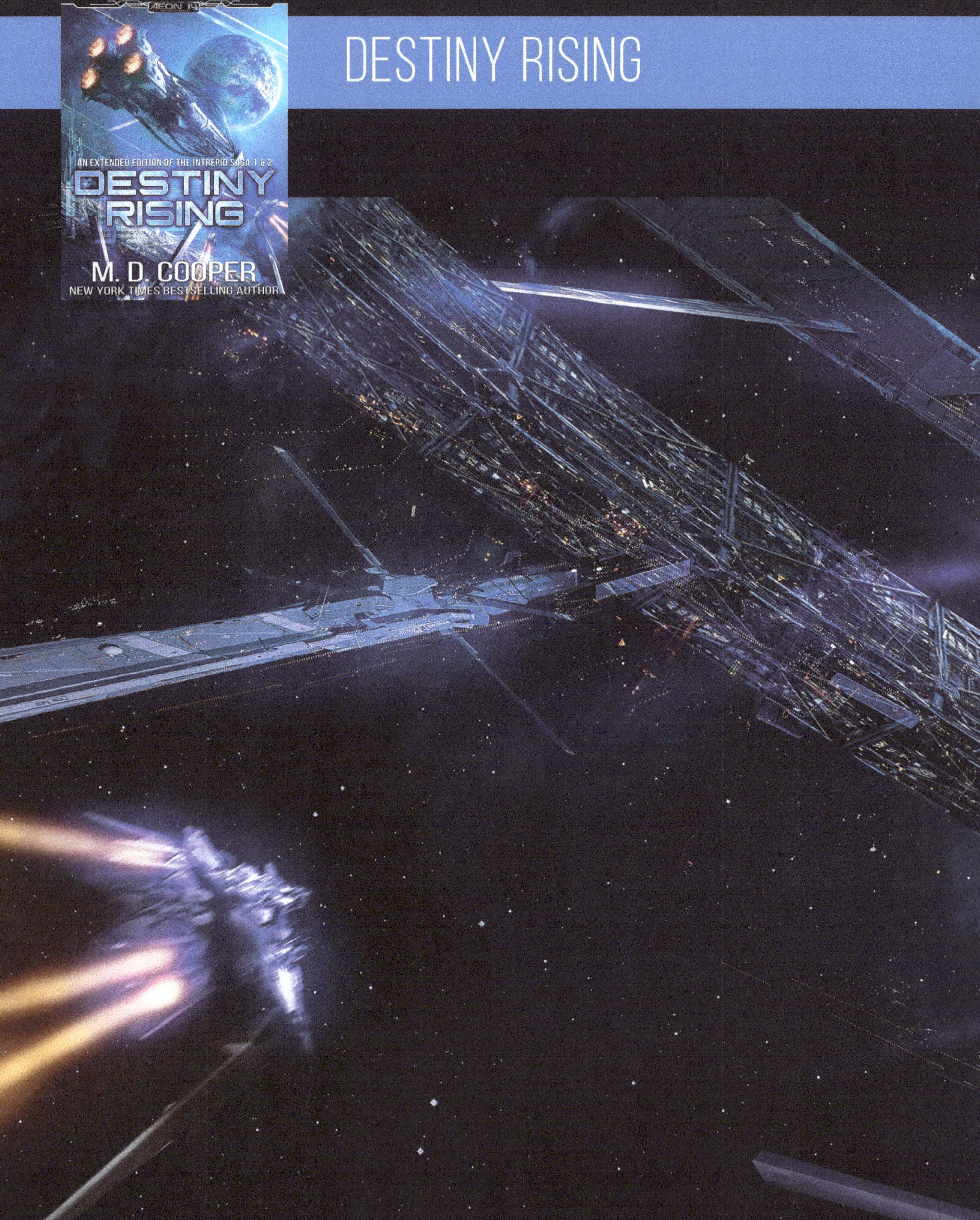
AN EXTENDED EDITION OF THE INTREPID SAGA 1 & 2
DESTINY
RISING
M. D. COOPER
NEW YORK TIMES BESTSELLING AUTHOR

Destiny Rising is an extended edition of *Outsystem* and *A Path in the Darkness*. It contains deleted scenes and a serial story told from Joe's point of view. I wanted this cover to be something special, and reached out to Adam Burn, an artist whose work I had admired on deviantart.com for some time.

Below, we have one of the most iconic images of the series thus far. In the distance is a terraformed Mars surrounded by the Mars I Ring, and the MCEE further out. Hanging off the MCEE are spur stations. And of course, the *Intrepid*.

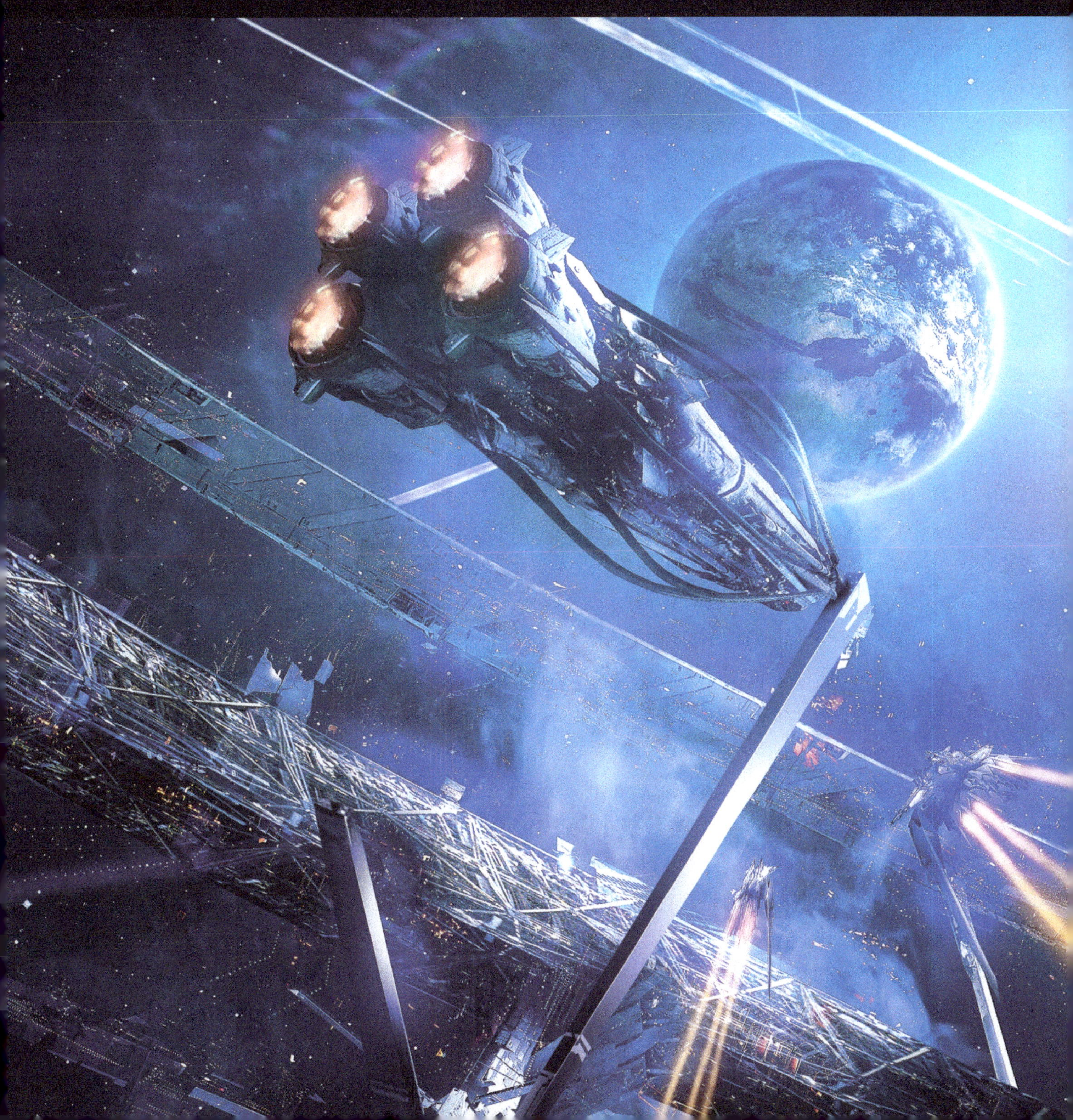

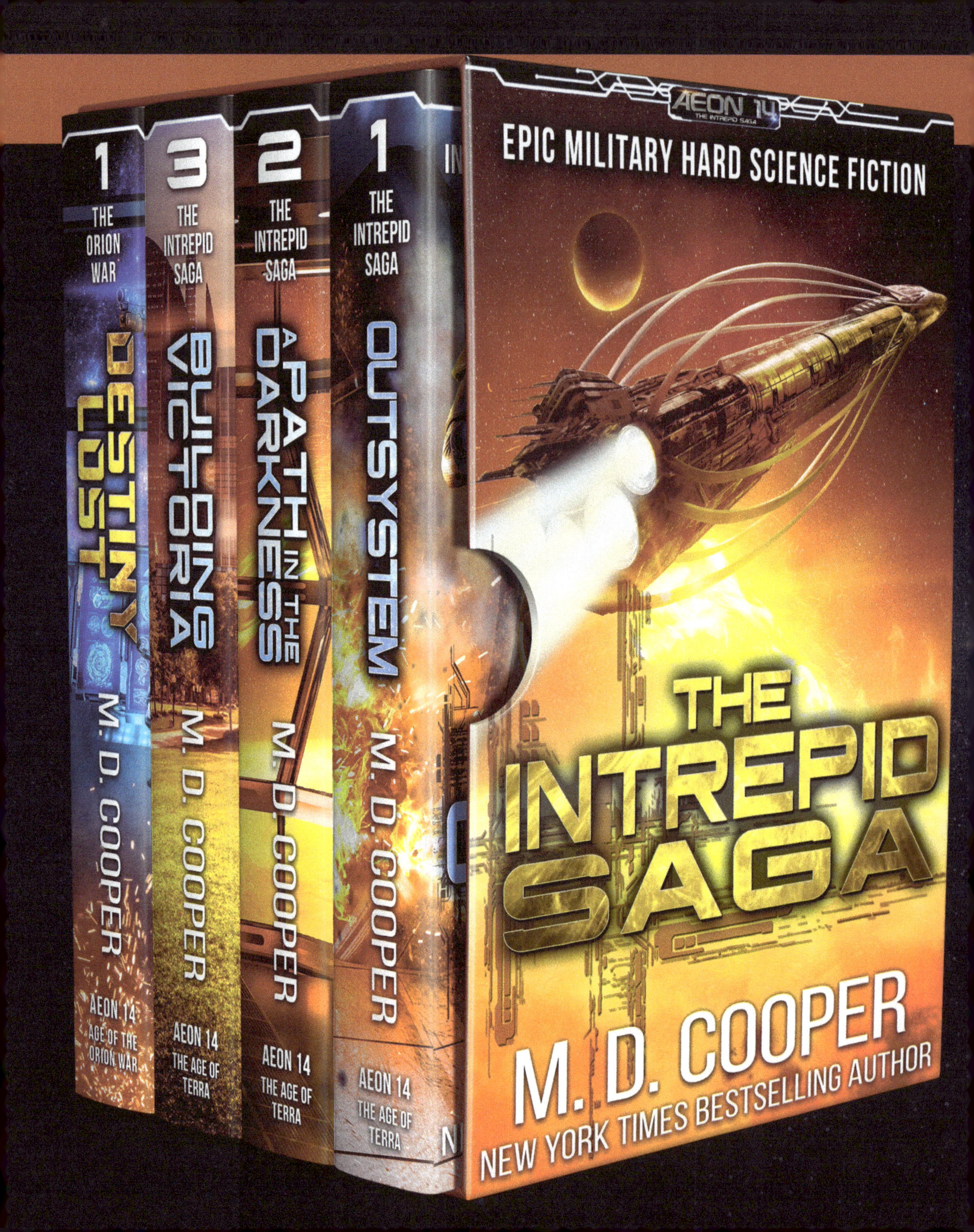

1
THE ORION WAR
DESTINY LOST
M. D. COOPER
AEON 14
AGE OF THE ORION WAR

3
THE INTREPID SAGA
BUILDING VICTORIA
M. D. COOPER
AEON 14
THE AGE OF TERRA

2
THE INTREPID SAGA
A PATH IN THE DARKNESS
M. D. COOPER
AEON 14
THE AGE OF TERRA

1
THE INTREPID SAGA
OUTSYSTEM
M. D. COOPER
AEON 14
THE AGE OF TERRA

AEON 14
THE INTREPID SAGA
EPIC MILITARY HARD SCIENCE FICTION
THE INTREPID SAGA
M. D. COOPER
NEW YORK TIMES BESTSELLING AUTHOR

The first edition of the omnibus edition of The Intrepid Saga was released in the fall of 2016. It came with the promise that whomever purchased it would get an updated version containing (what was at the time) the 4th book in the series: Destiny Lost

Eventually Destiny Lost was made to be the fist book in the Orion War series, but it is still included in "The Complete Intrepid Saga" because I feel as though it is both the culmation of the first series, and the beginning of the second.

Left: the first cover of the omnibus (note the reuse of the *Intrepid* previously seen on Building Victoria).

Upper right: the updated cover with Destiny Lost added.

Below: The current print cover of The Intrepid Saga, using art originaly intended for New Canaan.

Opposite: the ebook omnibus cover of The Intrepid Saga.

This cover also uses the same version of the *Intrepid* seen to the right, but with the background from A Path in the Darkness.

THE THREE BOOKS OF THE INTREPID SAGA IN ONE OMNIBUS VOLUME

INCLUDING BOOK ONE OF THE ORION WAR: DESTINY LOST

Right after she finishes her BLT, disgraced Major Tanis Richards is off to save the day one more time.

Tanis is looking forward to a long journey in stasis before arriving at the newly terraformed world of New Eden. New Life. New Start. Getting berth on the Intrepid is her ticket out of the Sol system.

But nothing proves easy for Major Tanis Richards. Nothing is at it seems. What should be a simple journey is fraught with danger and adventure. A myriad array of forces seek to stop the Intrepid...no matter the cost, or lives lost. From competing corporations, to stellar eco-terrorists, it no one wants the Intrepid to arrive at New Eden.

Through their journey, the crew of the Intrepid will face rival planets, civil war, and the most wanted serial killer known to the galaxy. Pivoting their role from colonists to saviors.

Perhaps it's because the Intrepid carries the most valuable secret known to humanity.

Or maybe it's just Tanis's luck.

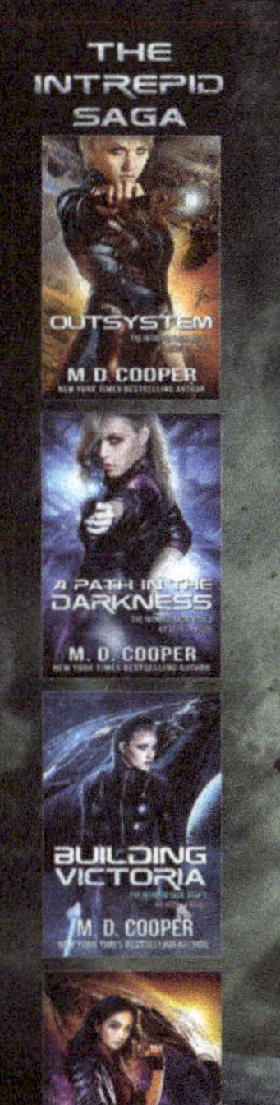

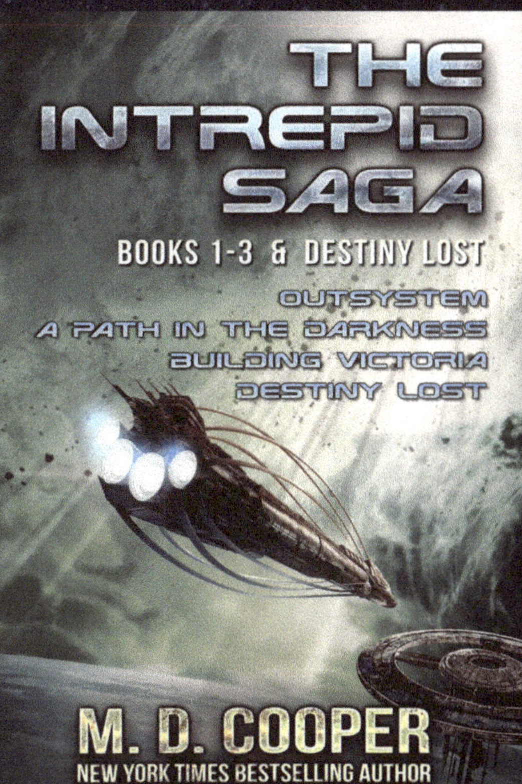

While it was the third Aeon 14 photoshoot, the Tanis and Sera shoot was a watershed event for Aeon 14 (Jessica and Reece had prior shoots). The shoot yielded over 2000 images. Now getting custom art made for the series' two main characters was easy, and would begin to happen far more often. A subsequent shoot was had with the model for Tanis, and a new model for Jessica. As of this writing, one more shoot is planned for Sera and Cara.

Select images from all shoots are shown.

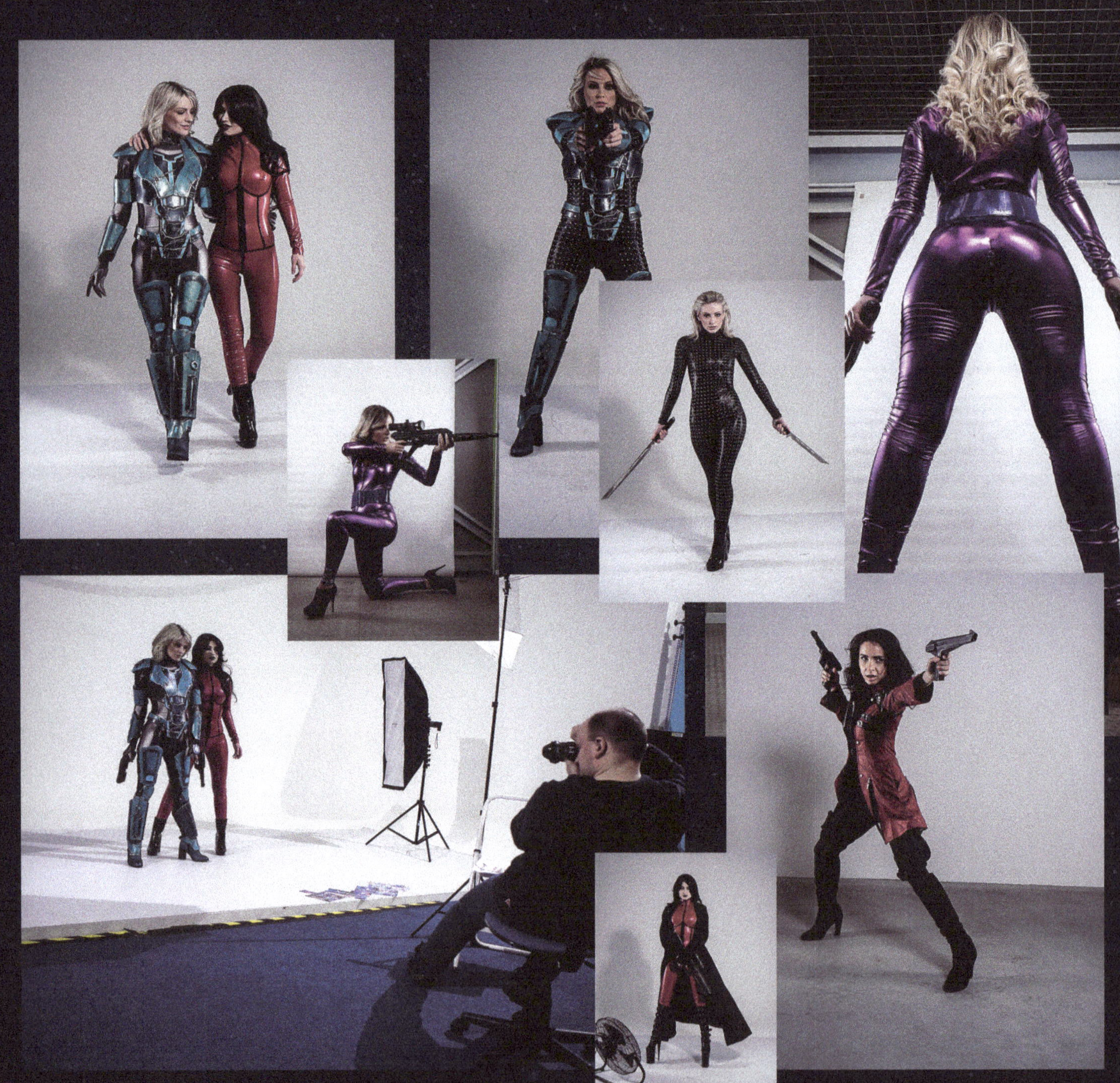

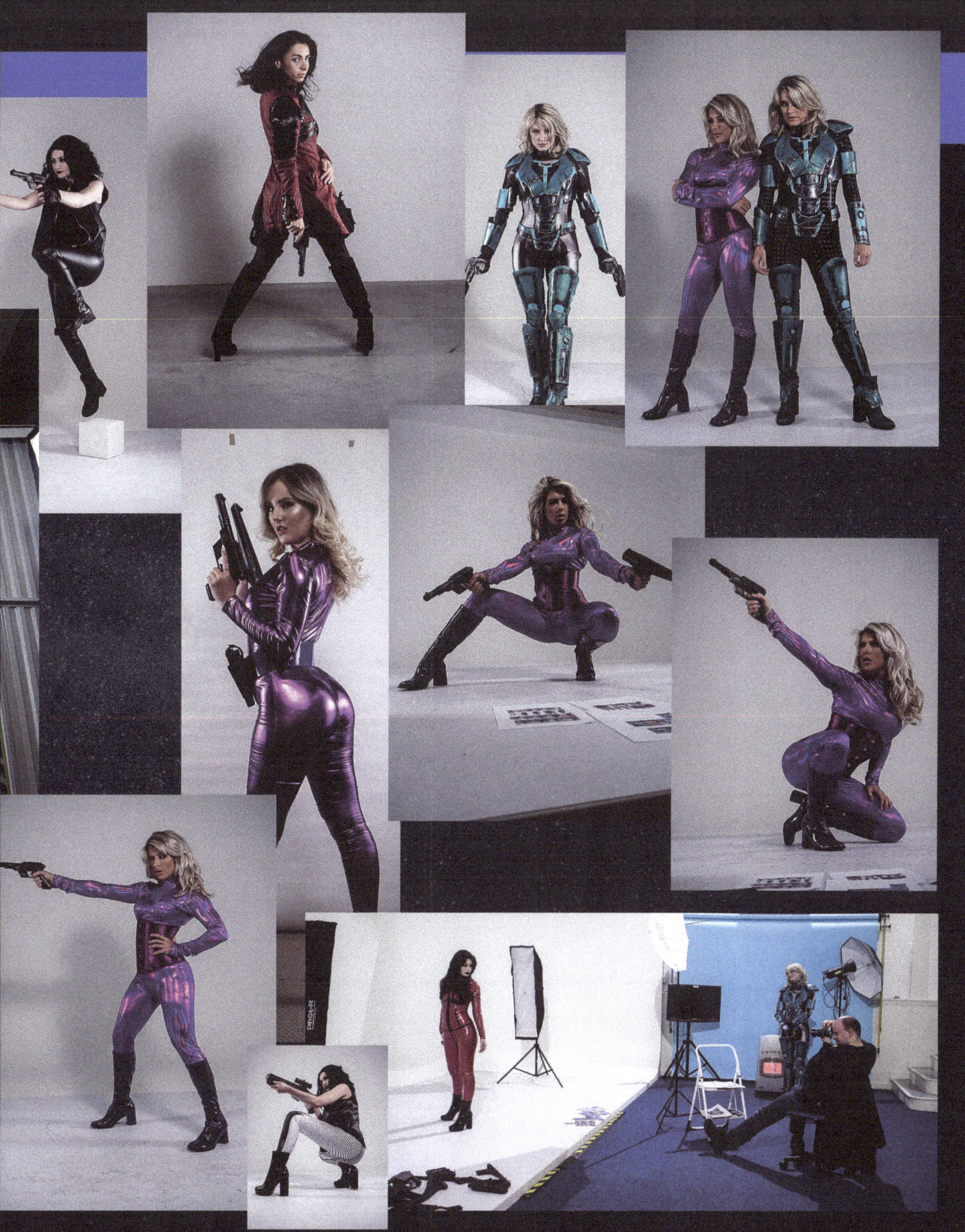

As mentioned on the prior page, Destiny Lost was once the 4th book in the Intrepid Saga, which is why these covers list it as such.

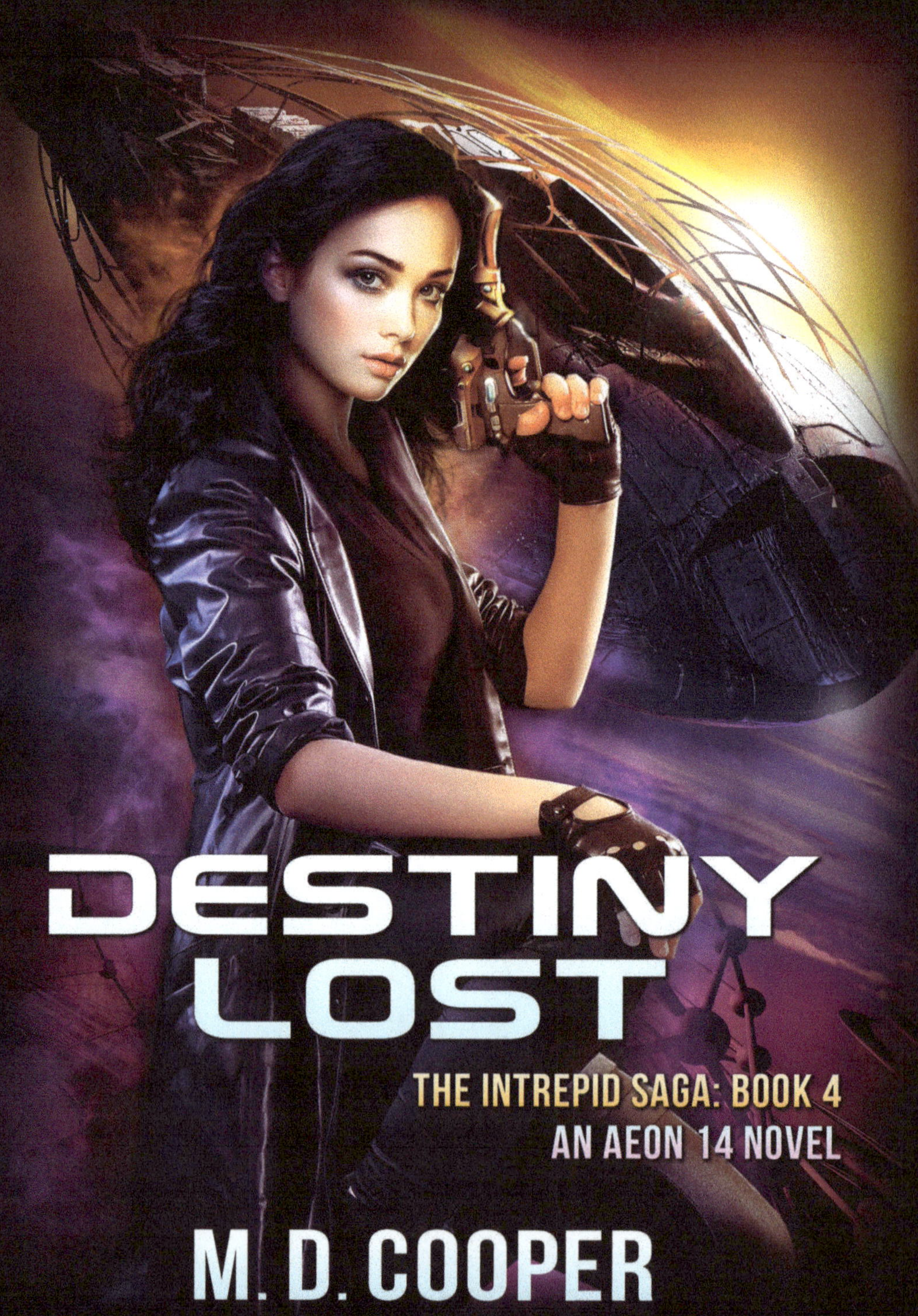

As mentioned on the prior page, Destiny Lost was once the 4th book in the Intrepid Saga.

To the left is a temporary cover I made for it to use on Aeon14.com until the release cover was made. Ravven, who made the original Outsystem and Path in the Darkness covers, was available for this work, and she produced the cover below. You'll note that we made good use of Tom Edwards' rendering of the ship.

While this depiction of Sera Tomlinson has always struck me as too young and sweet, this version of her has a special place in my heart.

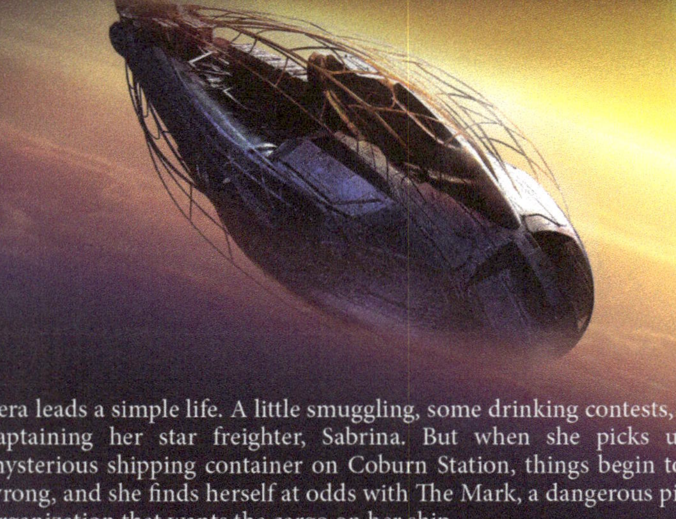

Sera leads a simple life. A little smuggling, some drinking contests, and captaining her star freighter, Sabrina. But when she picks up a mysterious shipping container on Coburn Station, things begin to go wrong, and she finds herself at odds with The Mark, a dangerous pirate organization that wants the cargo on her ship.

Inside the cargo she not only finds a woman, but a secret thought lost millennia ago. The woman is Tanis Richards, and she knows the location of the GSS Intrepid, the colony ship where she served as XO. The Intrepid comes from the golden age of human civilization, and is filled with advanced technology that The Mark will kill to get.

Sera knows how to help Tanis and the Intrepid. But to do that, she will need to reveal a secret that will pull her back into a life she left long ago. A life from which she was exiled in shame and disgrace.

Tanis doesn't trust Sera; and Sabrina's rag-tag crew is nothing like what she's used to, but she's going to have to rely on them to avoid capture and get back to the Intrepid. As Tanis and Sera battle pirates and interstellar governments—gunning not just for them, but for the Intrepid—they will forge a friendship that will forever shape the destiny of humanity.

DESTINY LOST

THE INTREPID SAGA: BOOK 4

M. D. COOPER

DESTINY LOST

THE INTREPID SAGA: BOOK 4

AN AEON 14 NOVEL

M. D. COOPER

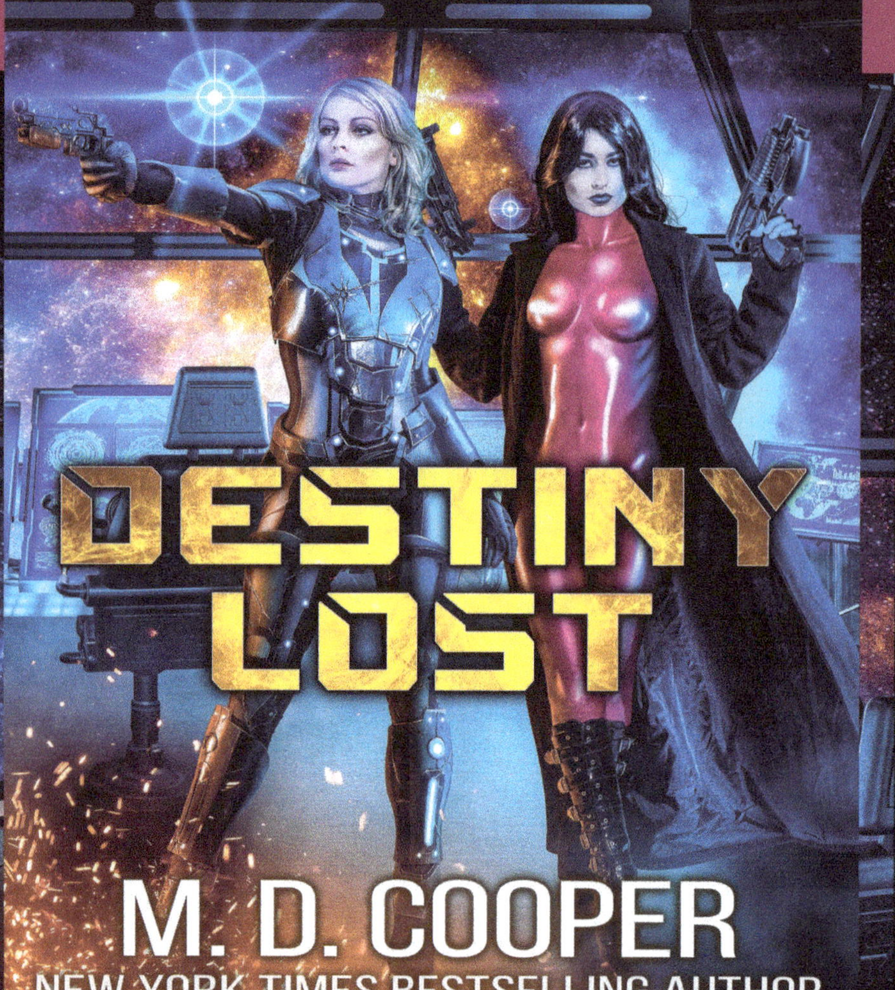

I had some trepidation about this cover.

For much of this book (and the series in general), Sera eschews clothing. Even at the begining of the book, she was not afraid to dress in a fashion that a 21st century reader would consider to be provocative, but when her skin is replaced with a hyper-sensitive bio-polymer, she throws clothing (barring boots and jackets) out the airlock.

The Perseus Gate covers featuring Jessica predate the updated Orion War covers (chronologically) by half a year. When doing those, I decided that being true to the characters as they were written was paramount, so I determined that Sera would appear on the covers as she does in the books.

Romanie, the model depicting Sera, is no stranger to provocative dress, and provided the latex catsuit she wore, as well as the tall buckled boots.

For this first cover, Andrew Dobell (the artist and photographer) altered the catsuit to make it appear as though it is Sera's skin. Not all subsequent covers show her like this because Sera often makes her skin appear to be a tight-fitting shipsuit.

Above: the second-edition Destiny Lost cover.

Right: the model in the outfit from the photoshoot.

Opposite (and under): the full art for Destiny Lost. This print is available on Society6.com

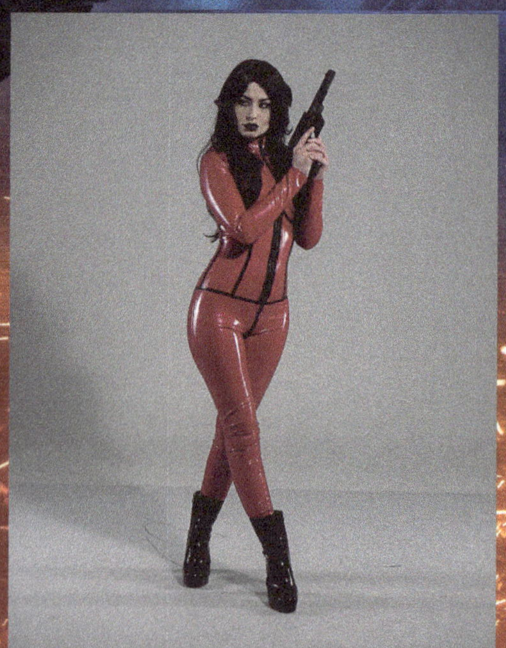

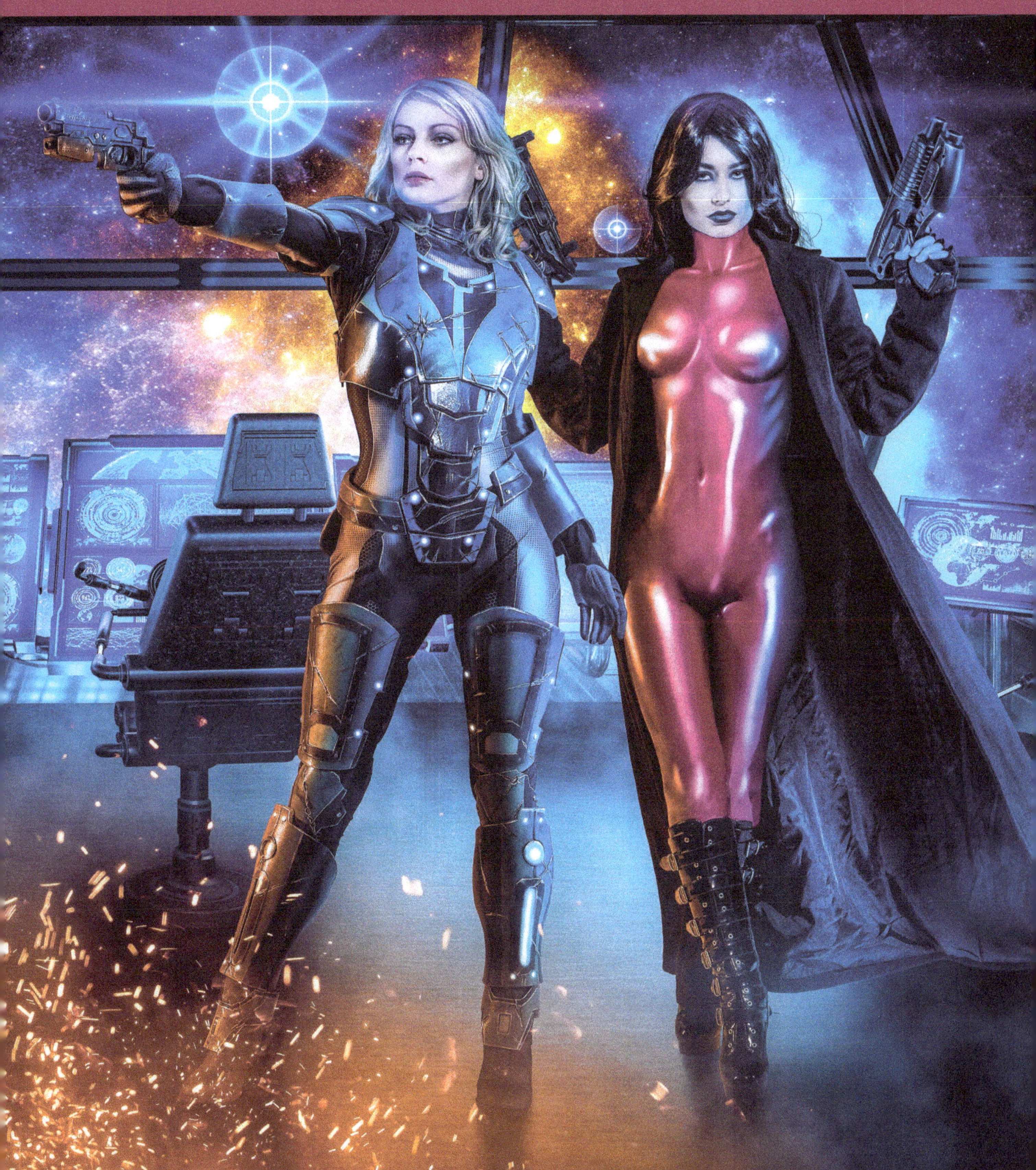

DESTINY LOST SECOND EDITION

99 DESIGNS & NEW CANAAN

When it came time to get the New Canaan cover made, my prior two artists (Ravven and Tom Edwards) were booked up for months. I'd not yet discovered Andrew Dobell, and so I decded to give 99 Designs a try. I ran a competition for the cover, and ended up buying the art from three of the artists, some of whose work you've already seen on prior pages.

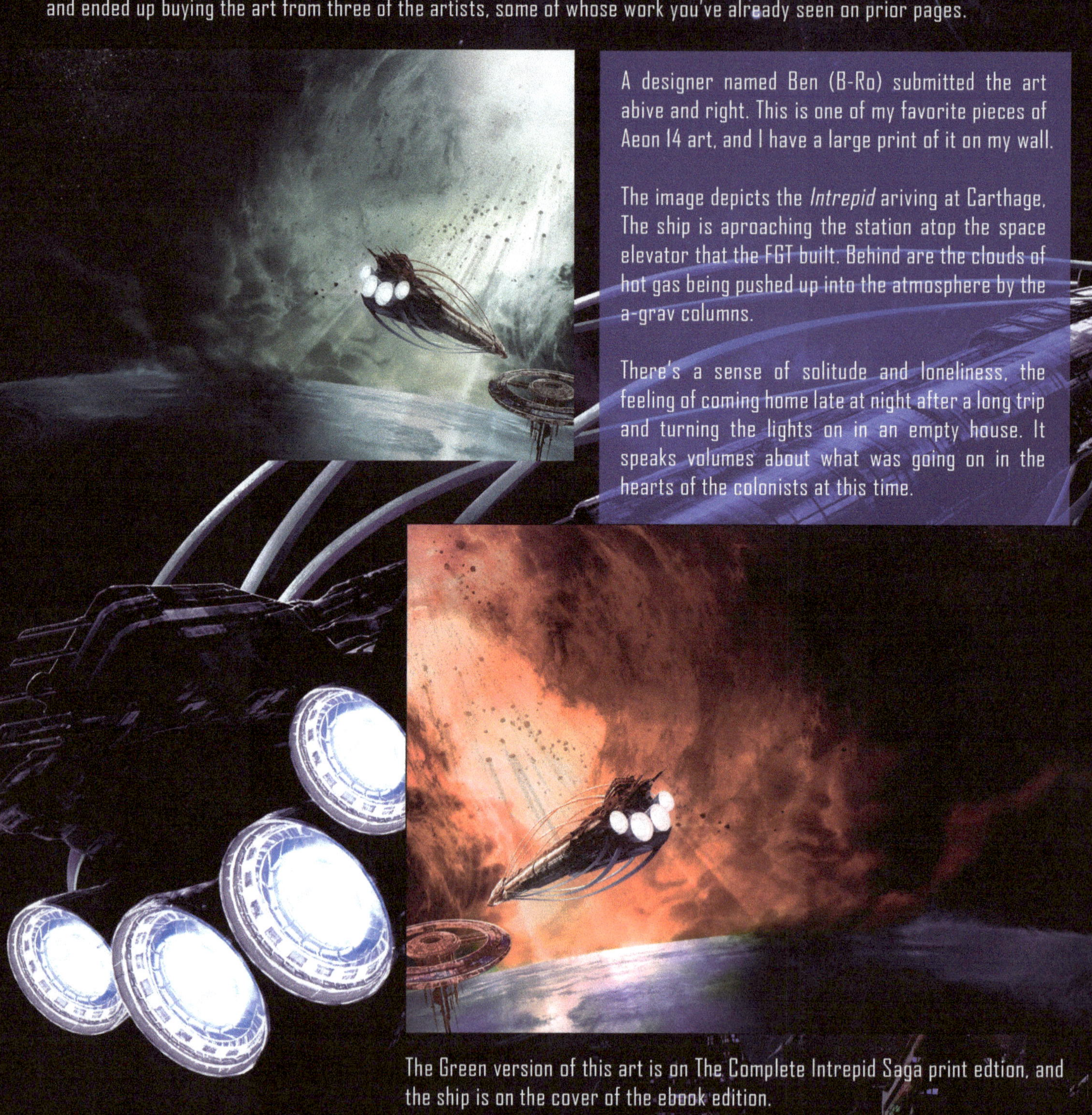

A designer named Ben (B-Ro) submitted the art abive and right. This is one of my favorite pieces of Aeon 14 art, and I have a large print of it on my wall.

The image depicts the *Intrepid* ariving at Carthage. The ship is aproaching the station atop the space elevator that the FGT built. Behind are the clouds of hot gas being pushed up into the atmosphere by the a-grav columns.

There's a sense of solitude and loneliness, the feeling of coming home late at night after a long trip and turning the lights on in an empty house. It speaks volumes about what was going on in the hearts of the colonists at this time.

The Green version of this art is on The Complete Intrepid Saga print edtion, and the ship is on the cover of the ebook edition.

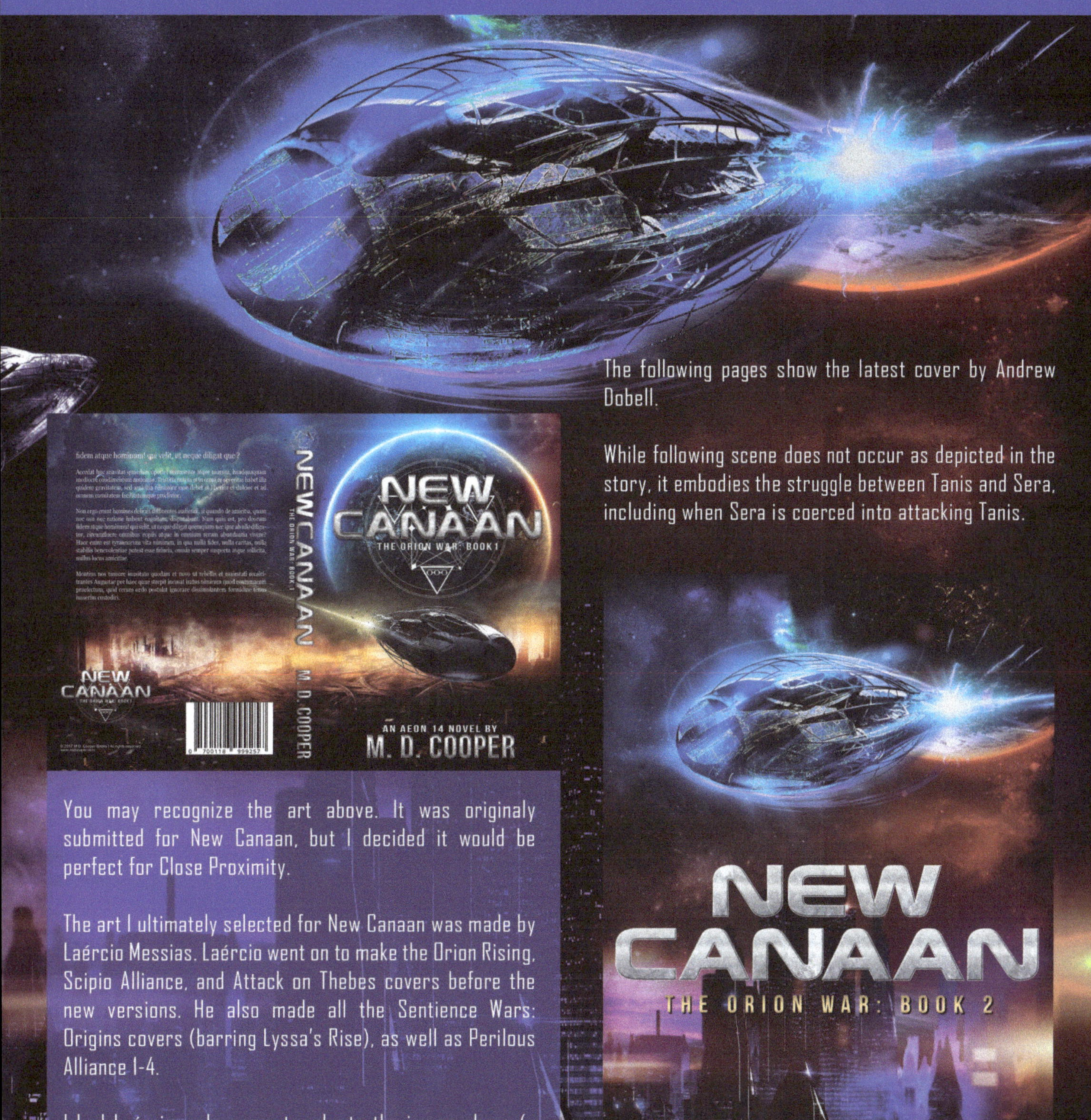

The following pages show the latest cover by Andrew Dobell.

While following scene does not occur as depicted in the story, it embodies the struggle between Tanis and Sera, including when Sera is coerced into attacking Tanis.

You may recognize the art above. It was originaly submitted for New Canaan, but I decided it would be perfect for Close Proximity.

The art I ultimately selected for New Canaan was made by Laércio Messias. Laércio went on to make the Orion Rising, Scipio Alliance, and Attack on Thebes covers before the new versions. He also made all the Sentience Wars: Origins covers (barring Lyssa's Rise), as well as Perilous Alliance 1-4.

I had Laércio make some tweaks to the image above (a new ship and different cityscape), and the format for the Perilous Alliance books was born.

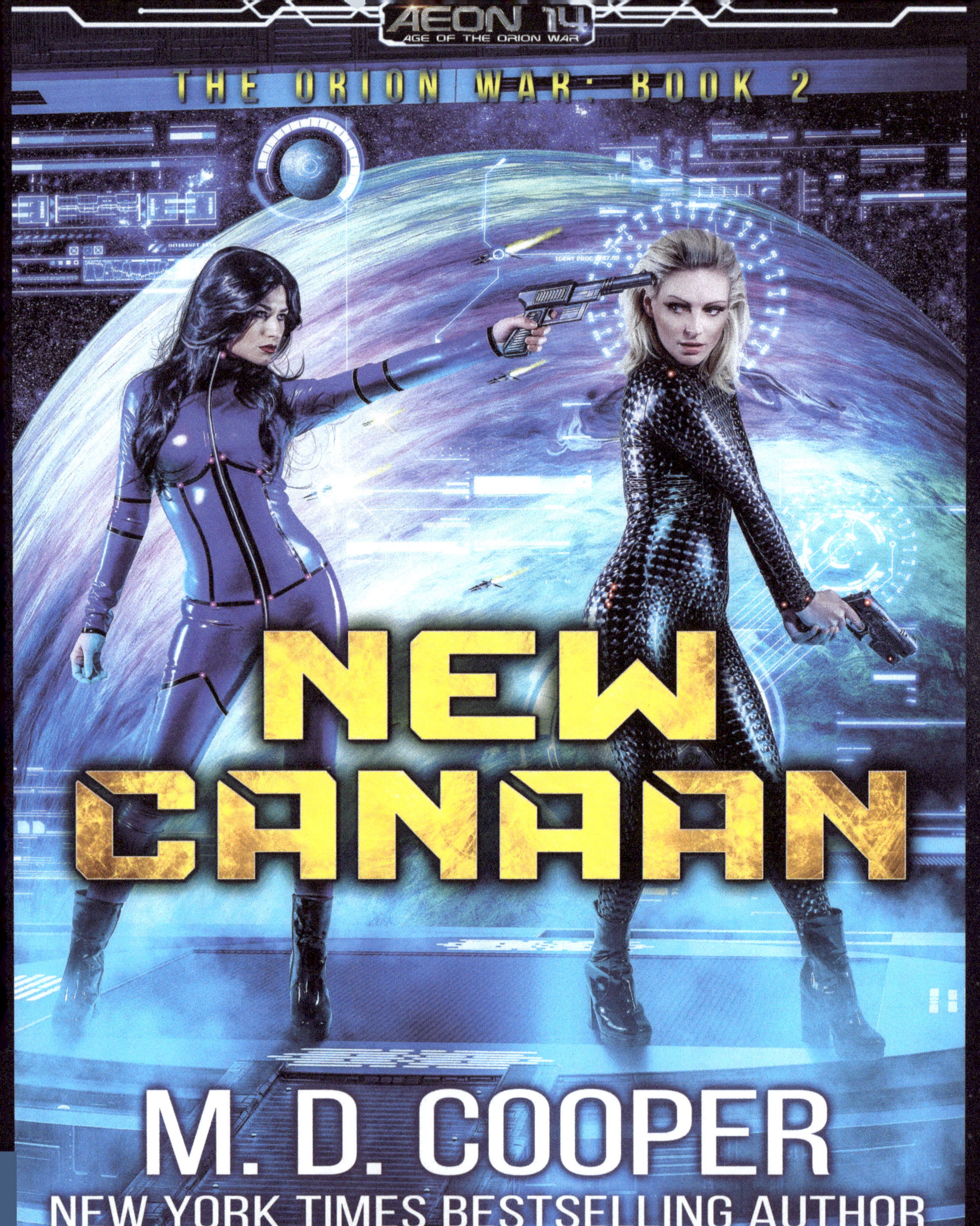

AEON 14
AGE OF THE ORION WAR
THE ORION WAR: BOOK 2
NEW CANAAN
M. D. COOPER
NEW YORK TIMES BESTSELLING AUTHOR

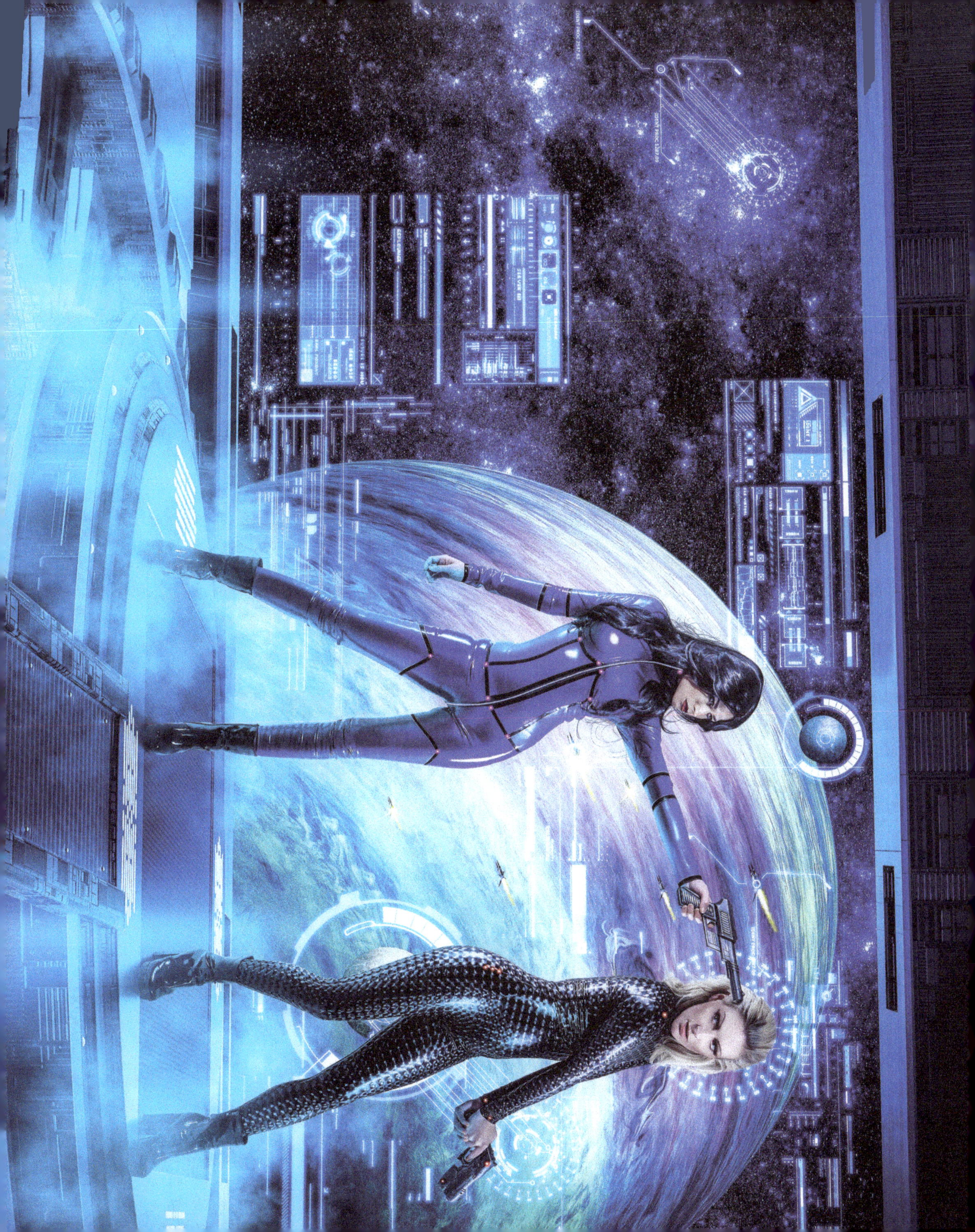

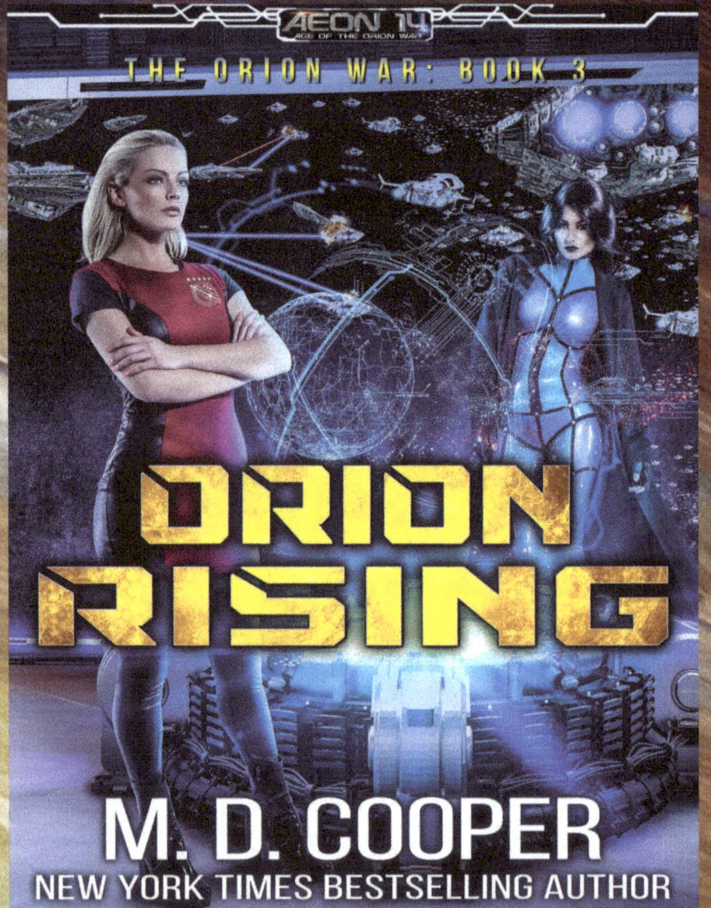

In the original version of Orion Rising by Laércio Messias, only Tanis was present. When Andrew Dobell recreated the cover we added Sera as she was certainly present for the battle.

Both, of course, depict the events of the battle from next to a holotank, which is where Tanis and Sera spent much of their time during this fight.

Left: the new cover featuring Tanis and Sera next to a holotank.

Below: Tanis on the bridge, also next to a holodisplay of the battle raging outside.

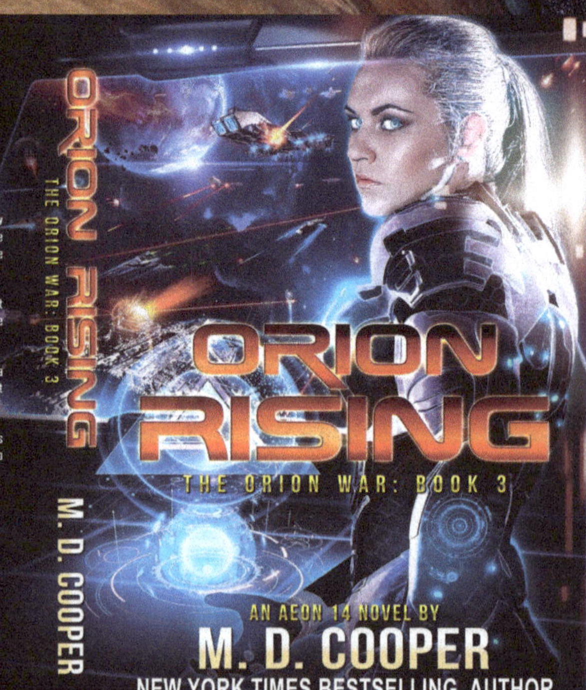

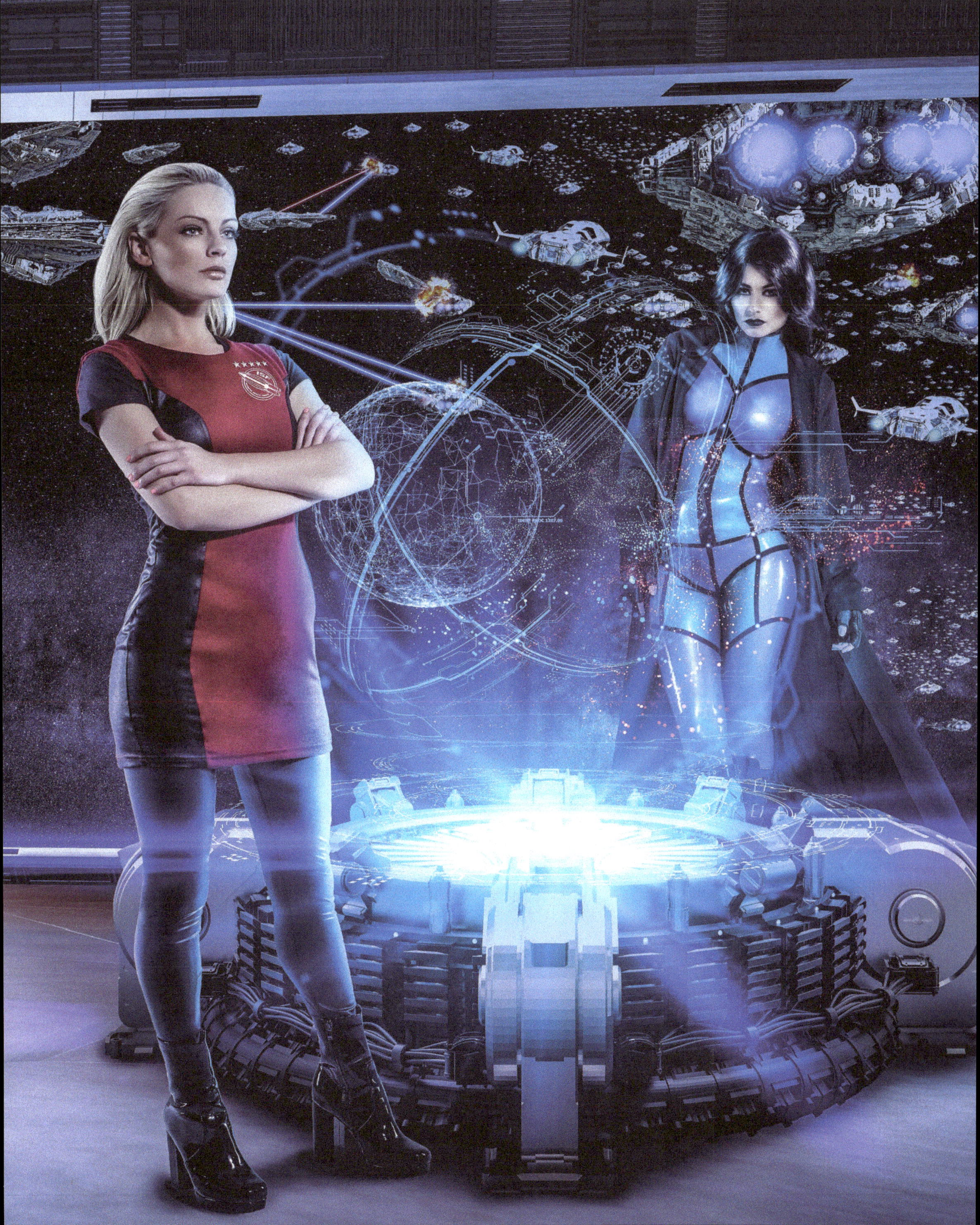

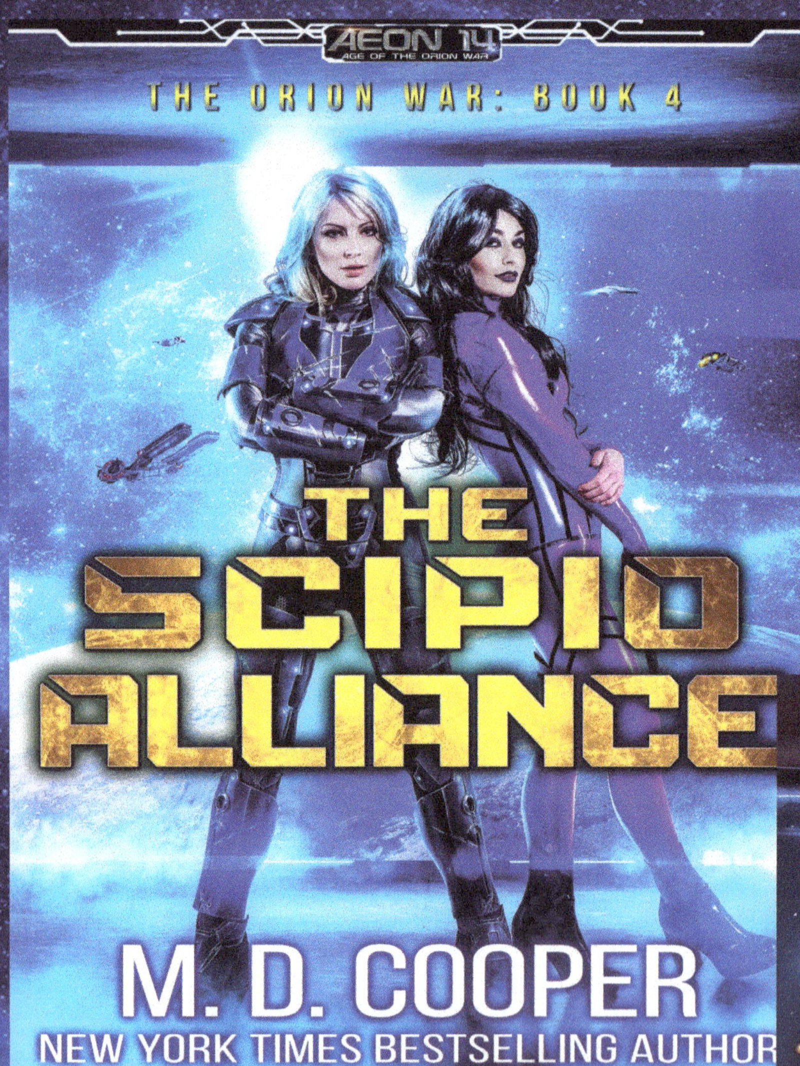

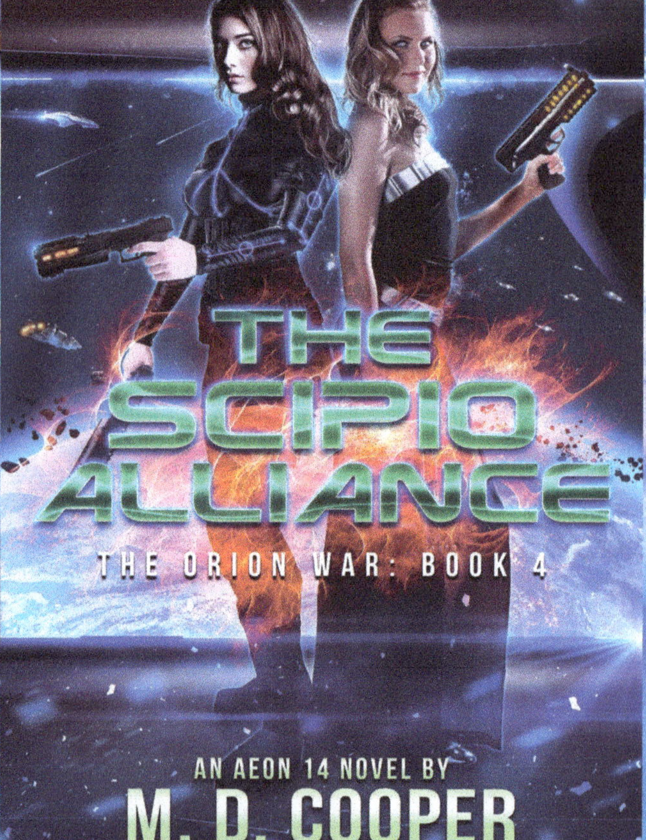

I unabashedly love thos cover. When I saw this image after the photoshoot, there was no doubt in my mind that it would grace the cover of this book.

The reason is that Tanis and Sera look happy.

That was something that I strove for with the original cover below (and achieved there as well).

This book is one of the few times we really see Tanis and Sera get to have a good time and relax. Everyone deserves that, right?

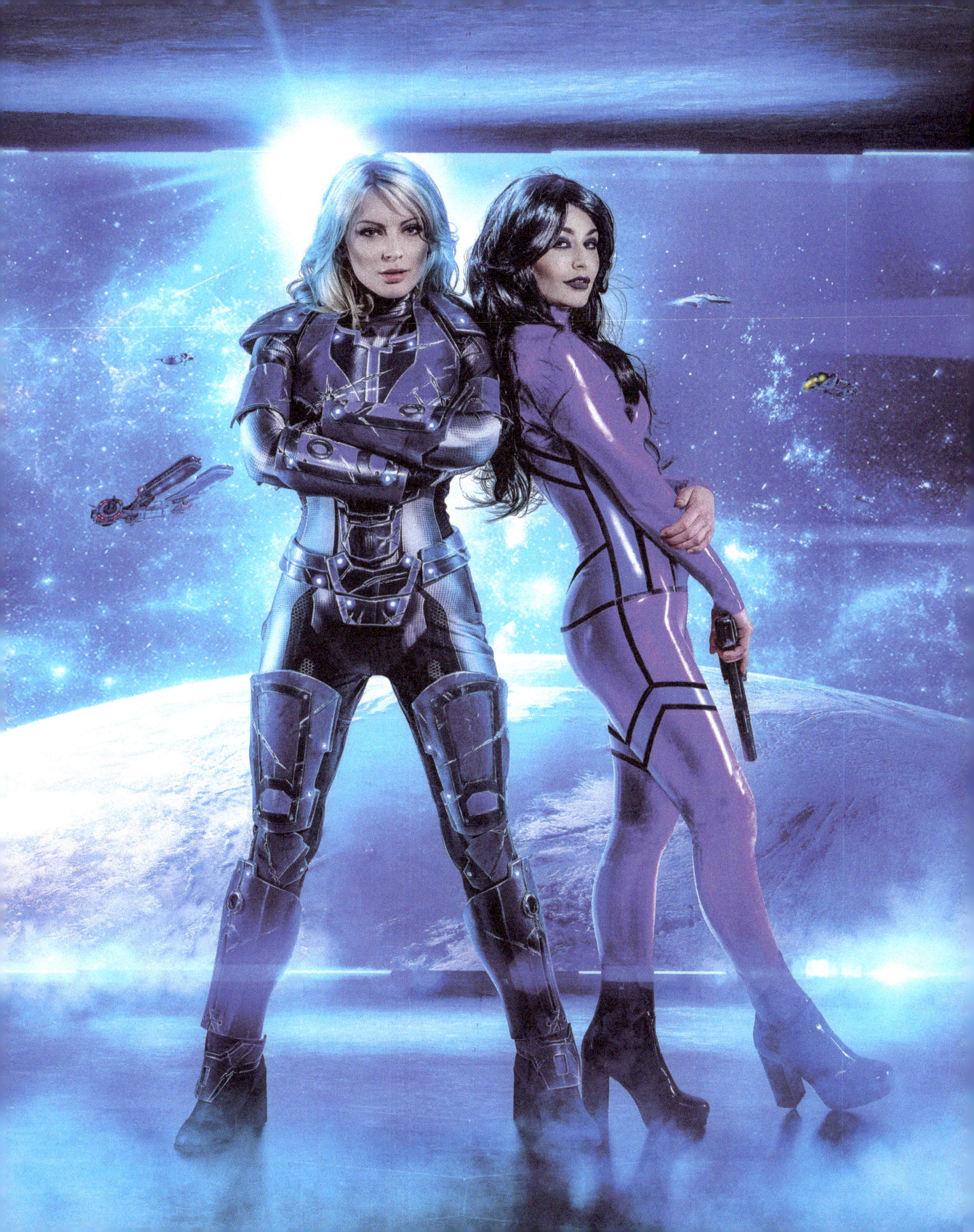

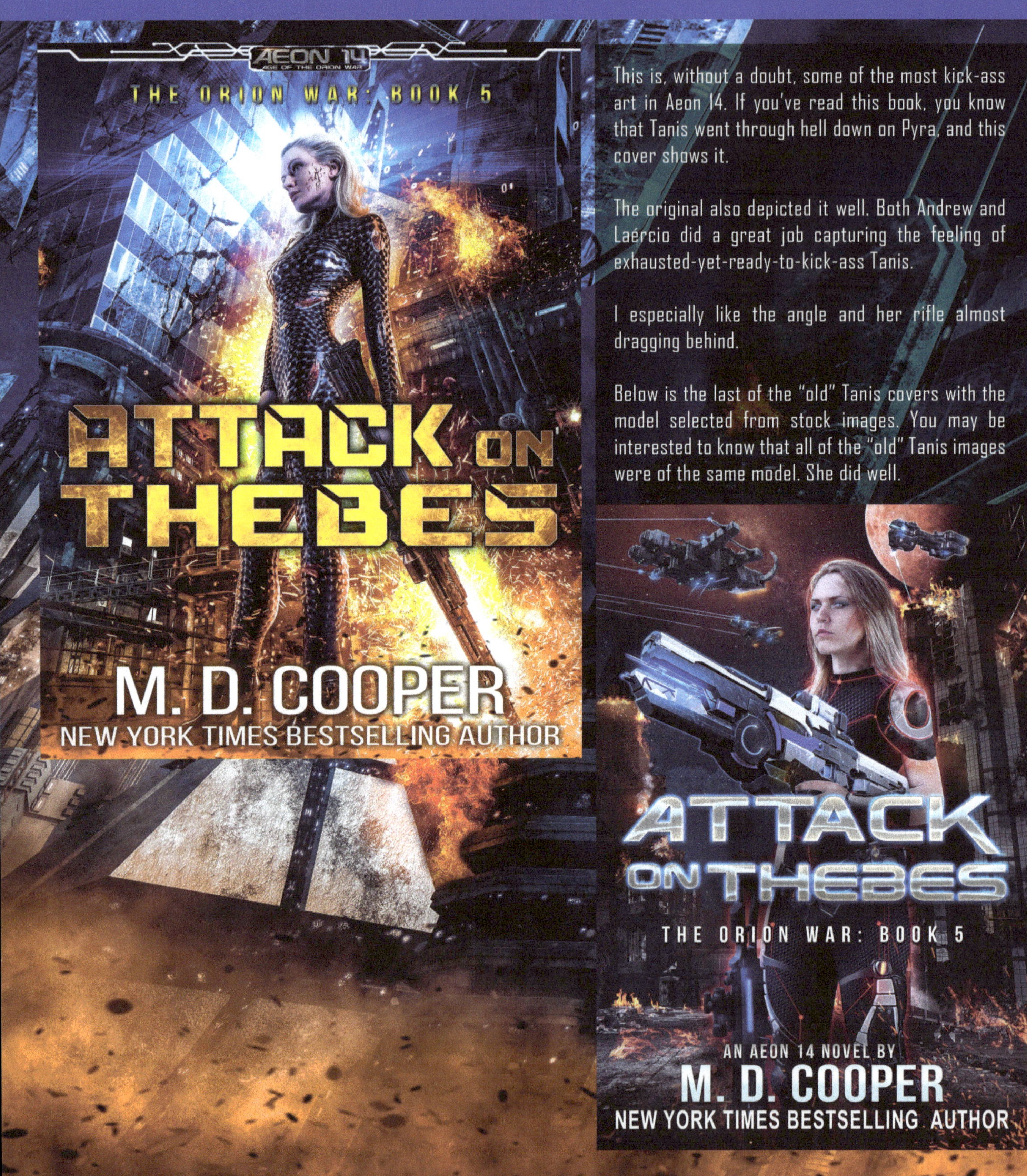

This is, without a doubt, some of the most kick-ass art in Aeon 14. If you've read this book, you know that Tanis went through hell down on Pyra, and this cover shows it.

The original also depicted it well. Both Andrew and Laércio did a great job capturing the feeling of exhausted-yet-ready-to-kick-ass Tanis.

I especially like the angle and her rifle almost dragging behind.

Below is the last of the "old" Tanis covers with the model selected from stock images. You may be interested to know that all of the "old" Tanis images were of the same model. She did well.

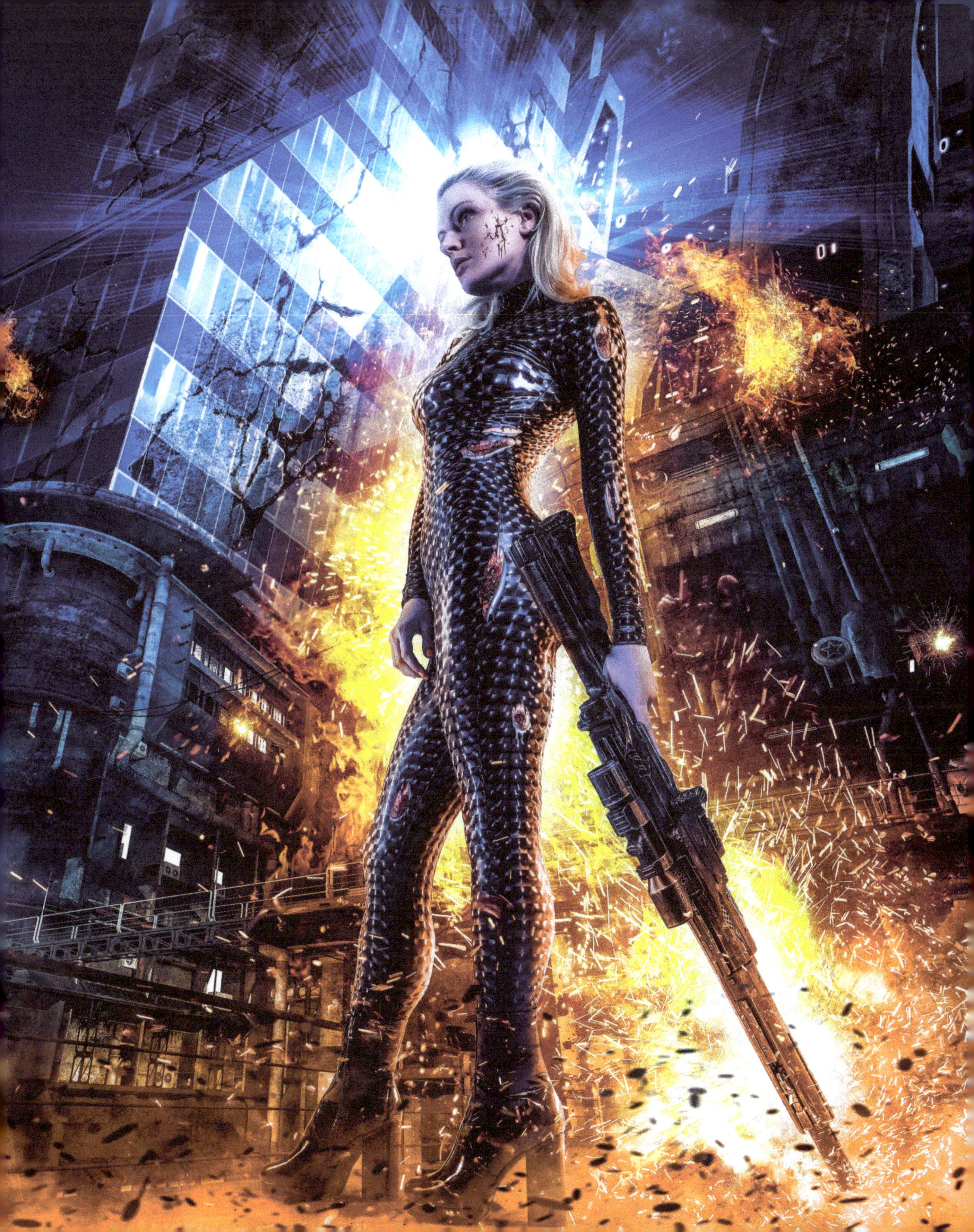

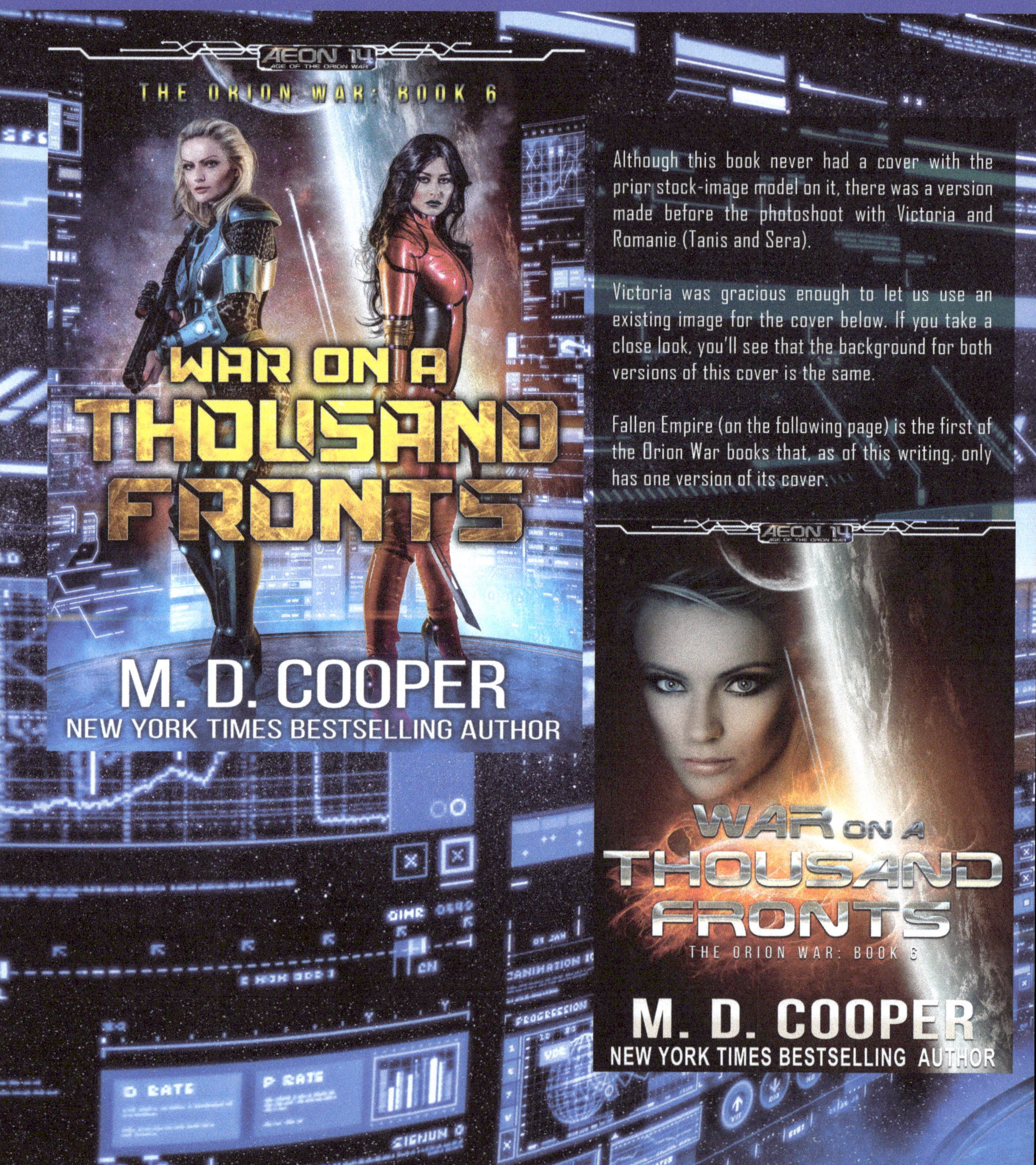

Although this book never had a cover with the prior stock-image model on it, there was a version made before the photoshoot with Victoria and Romanie (Tanis and Sera).

Victoria was gracious enough to let us use an existing image for the cover below. If you take a close look, you'll see that the background for both versions of this cover is the same.

Fallen Empire (on the following page) is the first of the Orion War books that, as of this writing, only has one version of its cover.

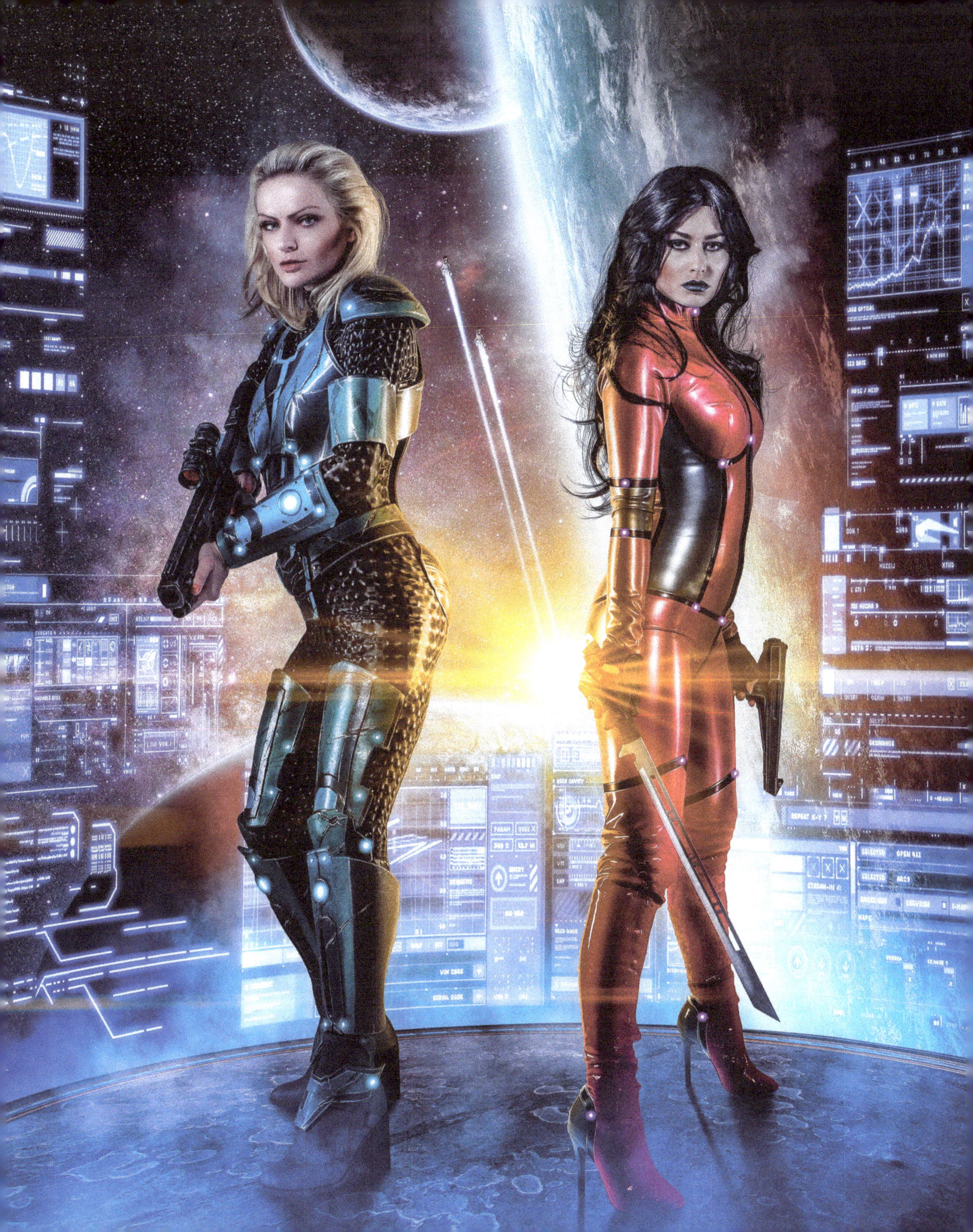

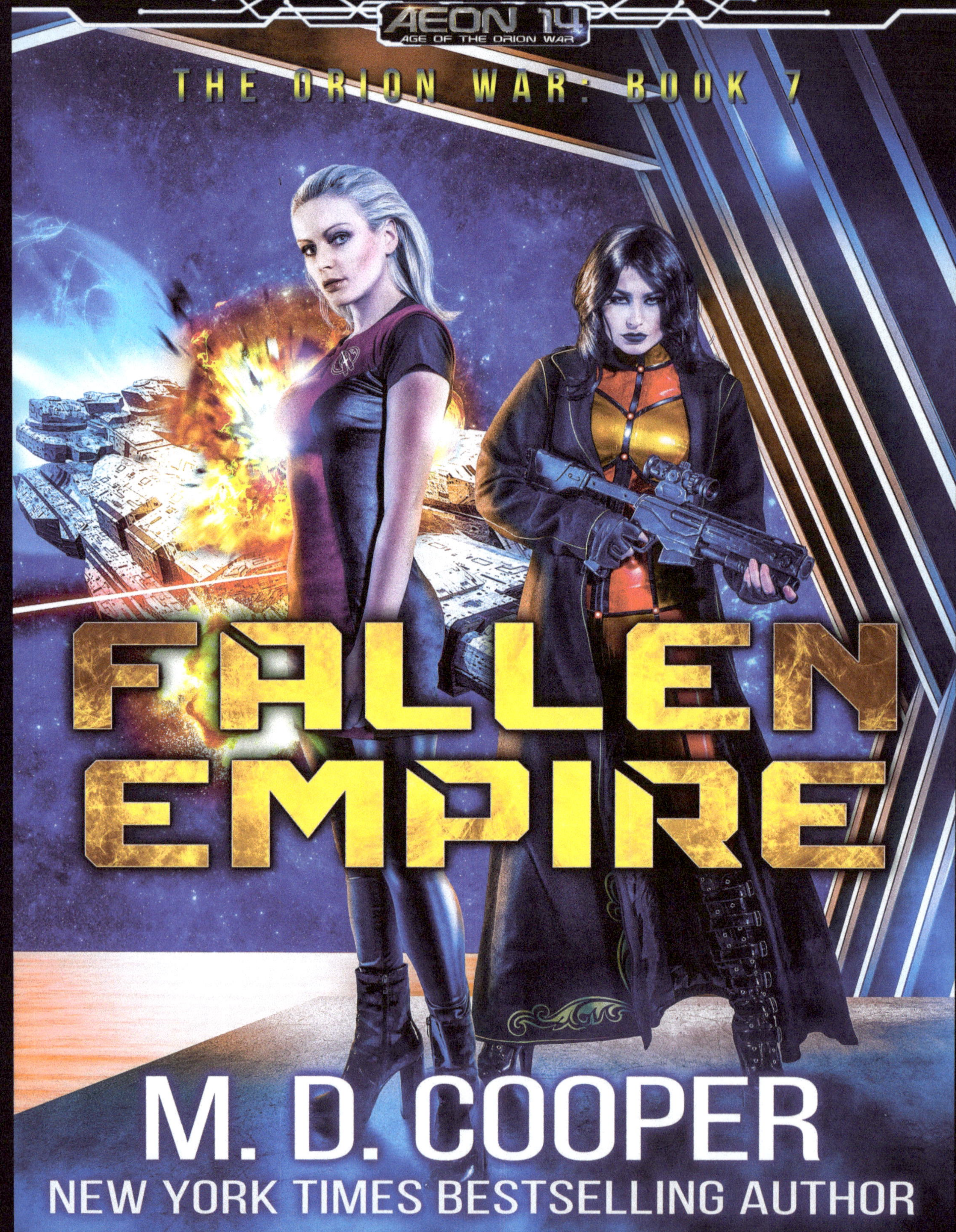

AEON 14
AGE OF THE ORION WAR
THE ORION WAR: BOOK 7
FALLEN EMPIRE
M. D. COOPER
NEW YORK TIMES BESTSELLING AUTHOR

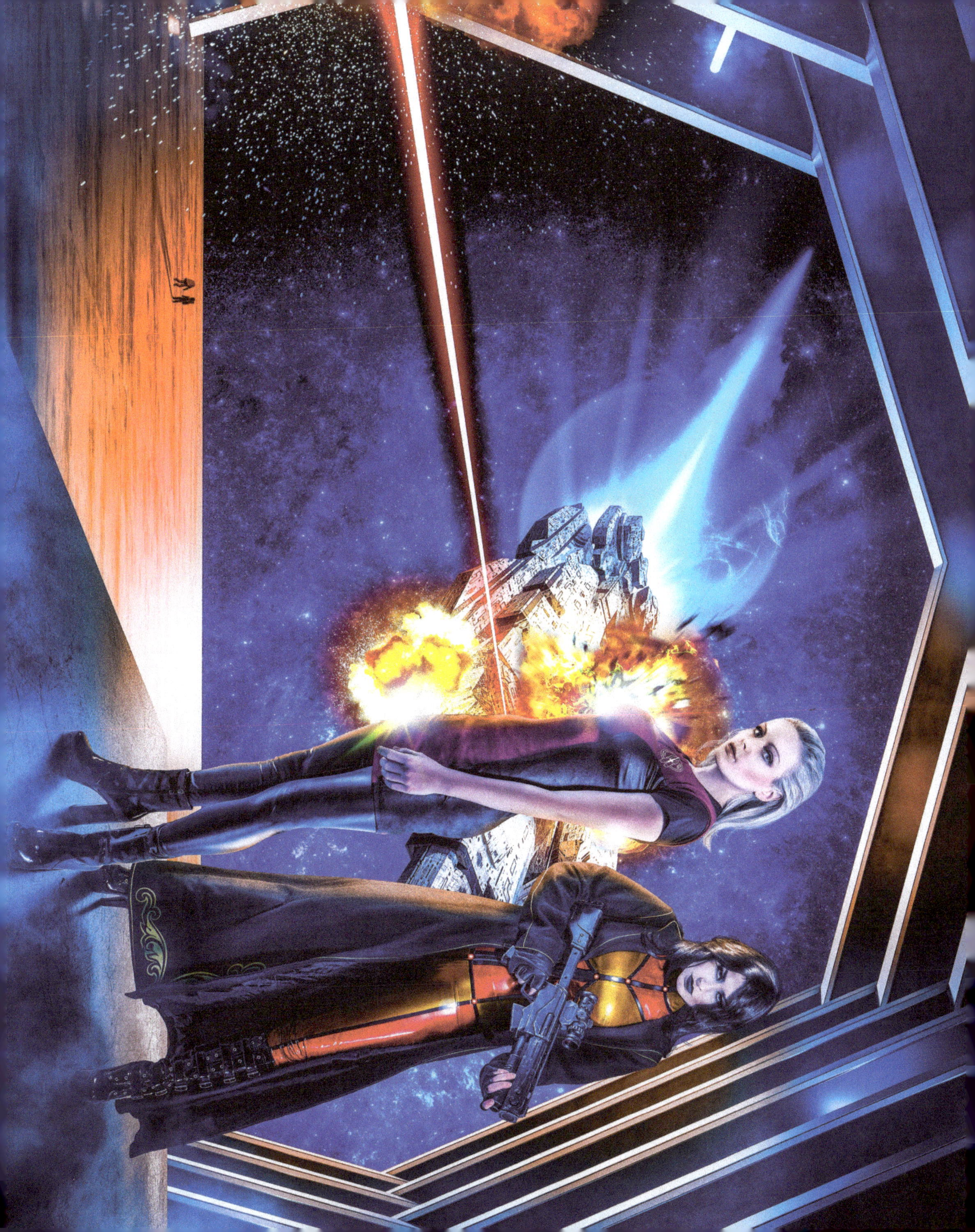

These three covers are all self-made. The covers right and below are for the editions available on Amazon.

To Fly Sabrina is a story only available to folks who sign up for the Aeon 14 newsletter.

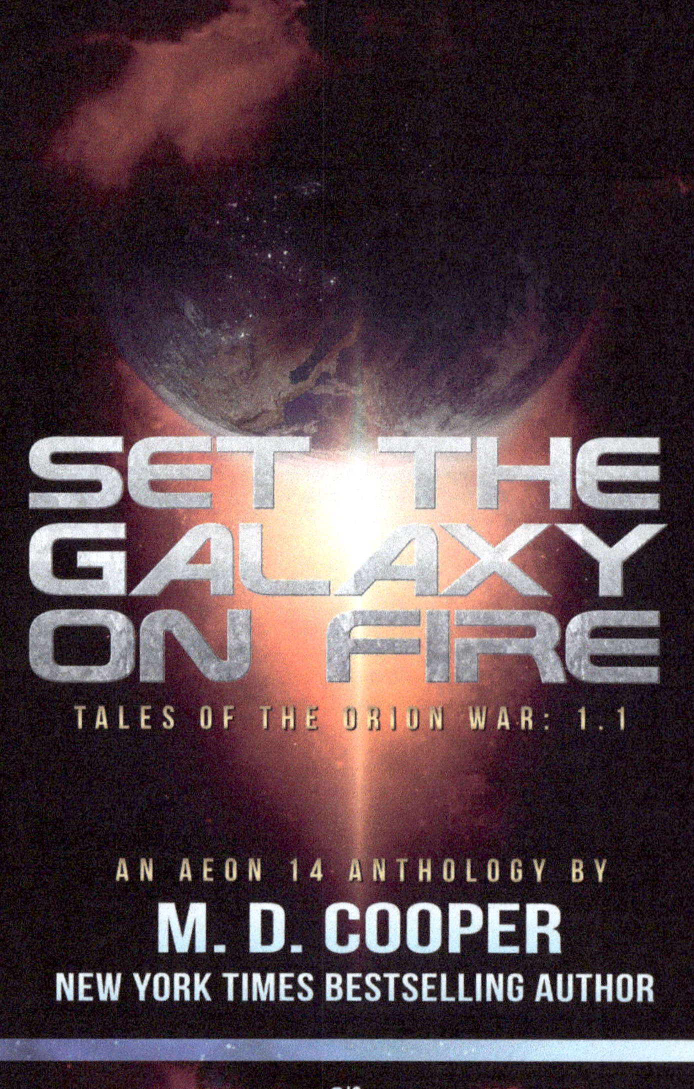

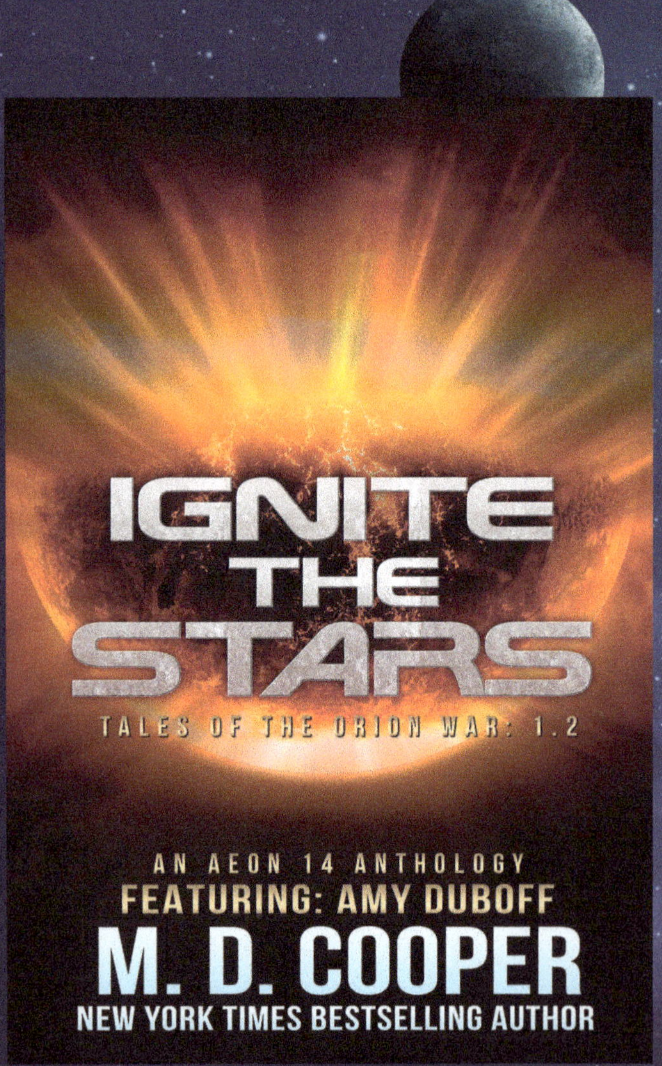

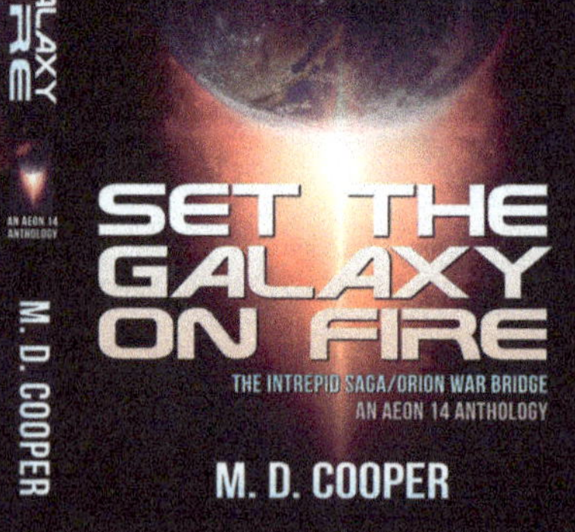

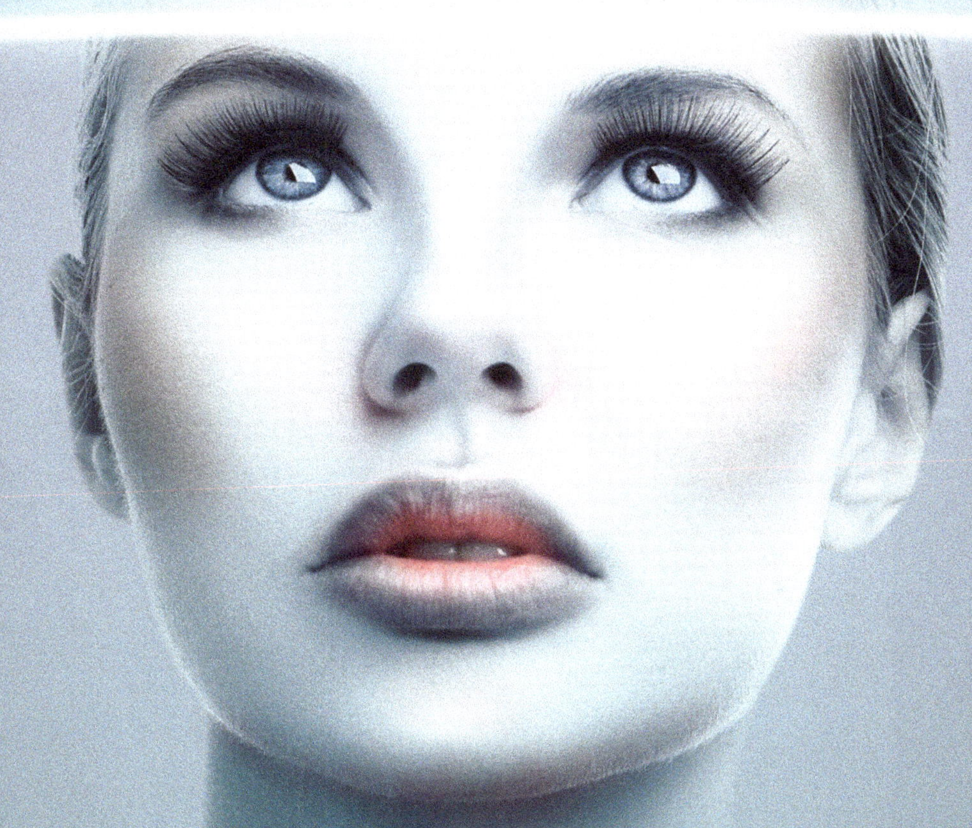

TO FLY SABRINA
ORION WAR PREQUELS
AN AEON 14 SHORT STORY
M. D. COOPER
NEW YORK TIMES BESTSELLING AUTHOR

The *Intrepid* is, without a doubt, a character in its own right. The first rendering of the great ship was done by Tom Edwards for the Building Victoria cover. Following that, the ship was depicted by Ben Ro (next page), Adam Burn (main image below), and a man who only goes by Kalishnaov (Fan fiction cover below and Carthage cover below).

Also included is concept art by Tom Edwards.

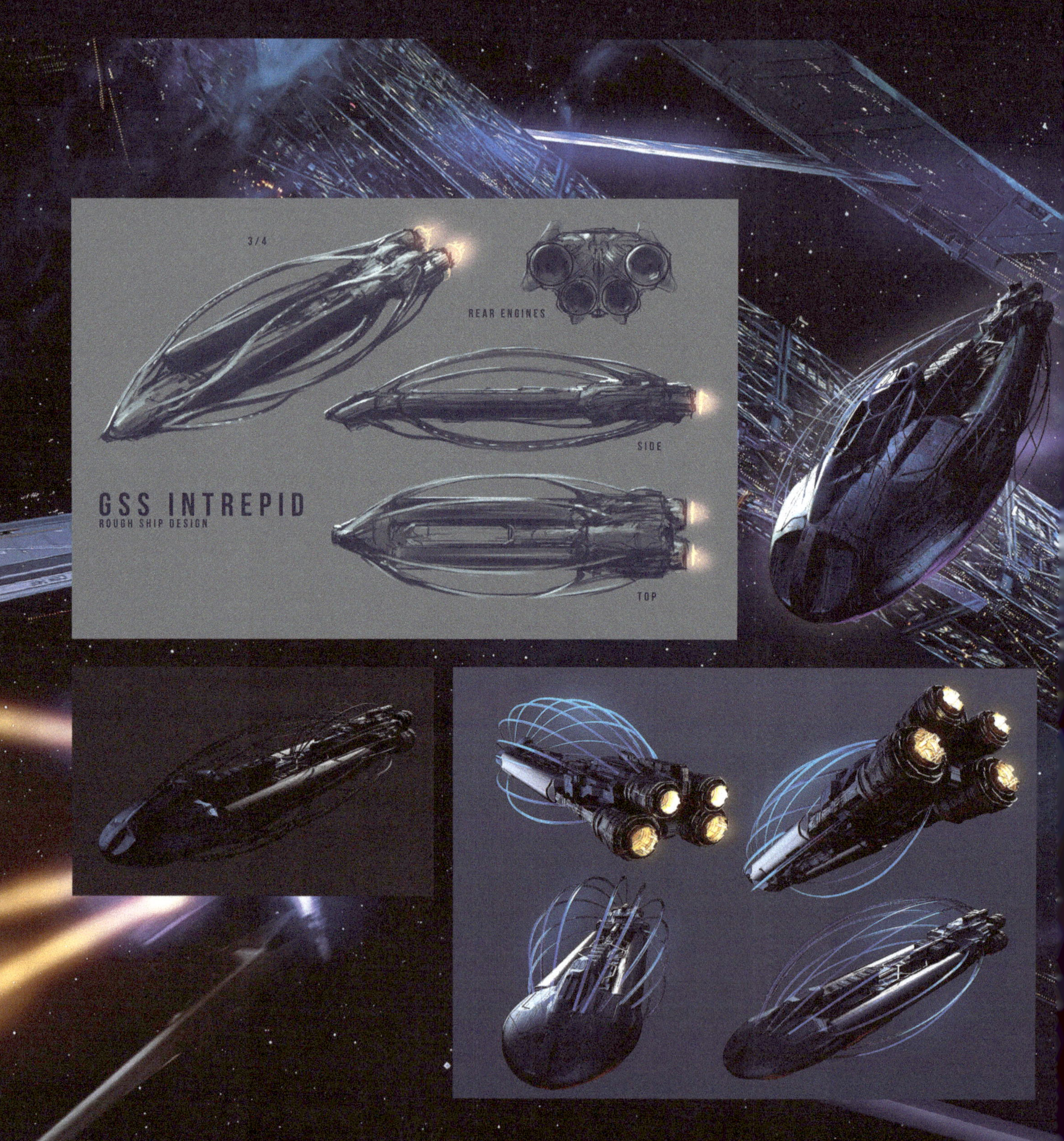

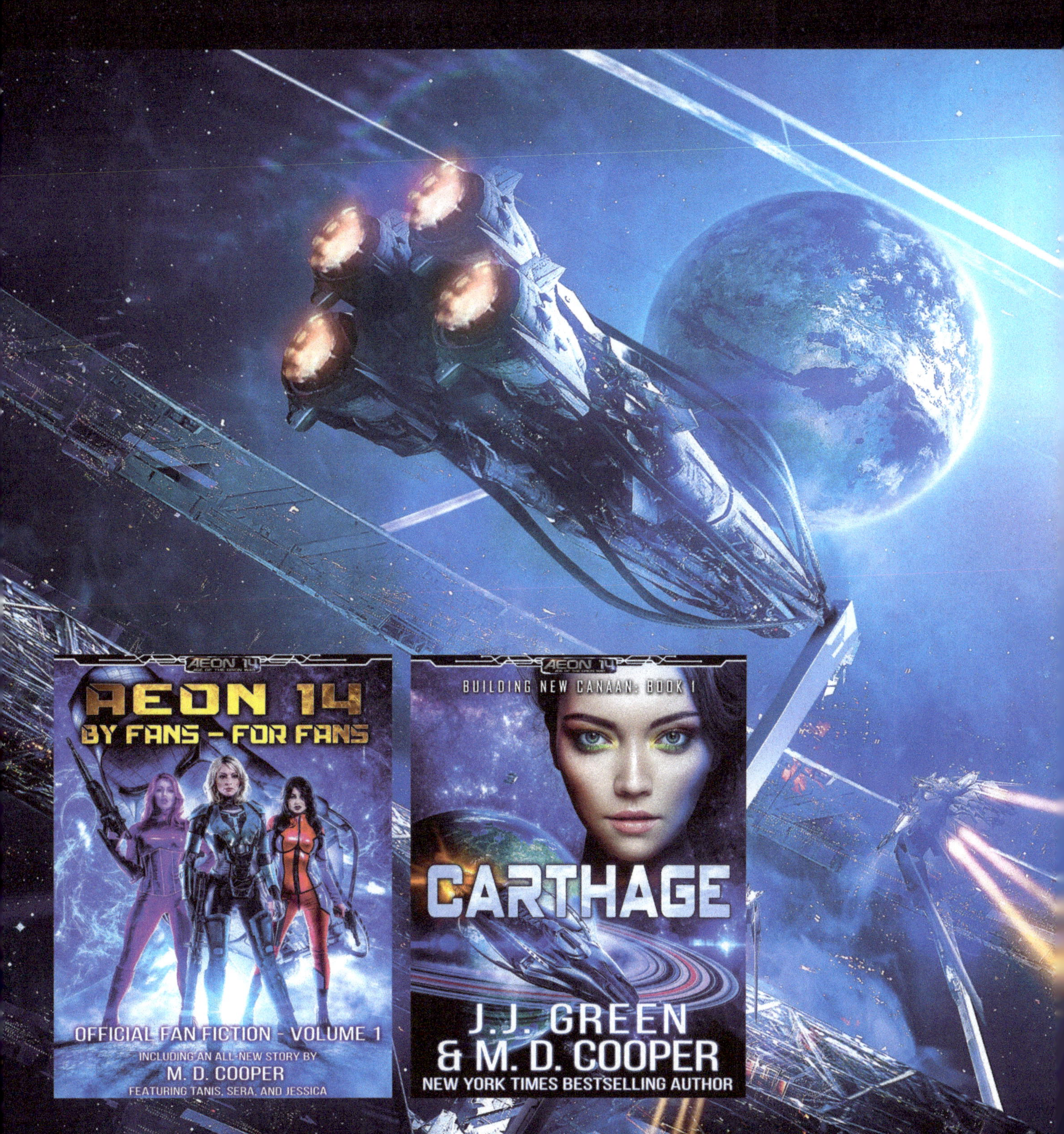
AEON 14
BY FANS - FOR FANS
OFFICIAL FAN FICTION - VOLUME 1
INCLUDING AN ALL-NEW STORY BY
M. D. COOPER
FEATURING TANIS, SERA, AND JESSICA
AEON 14
BUILDING NEW CANAAN: BOOK 1
CARTHAGE
J. J. GREEN
& M. D. COOPER
NEW YORK TIMES BESTSELLING AUTHOR

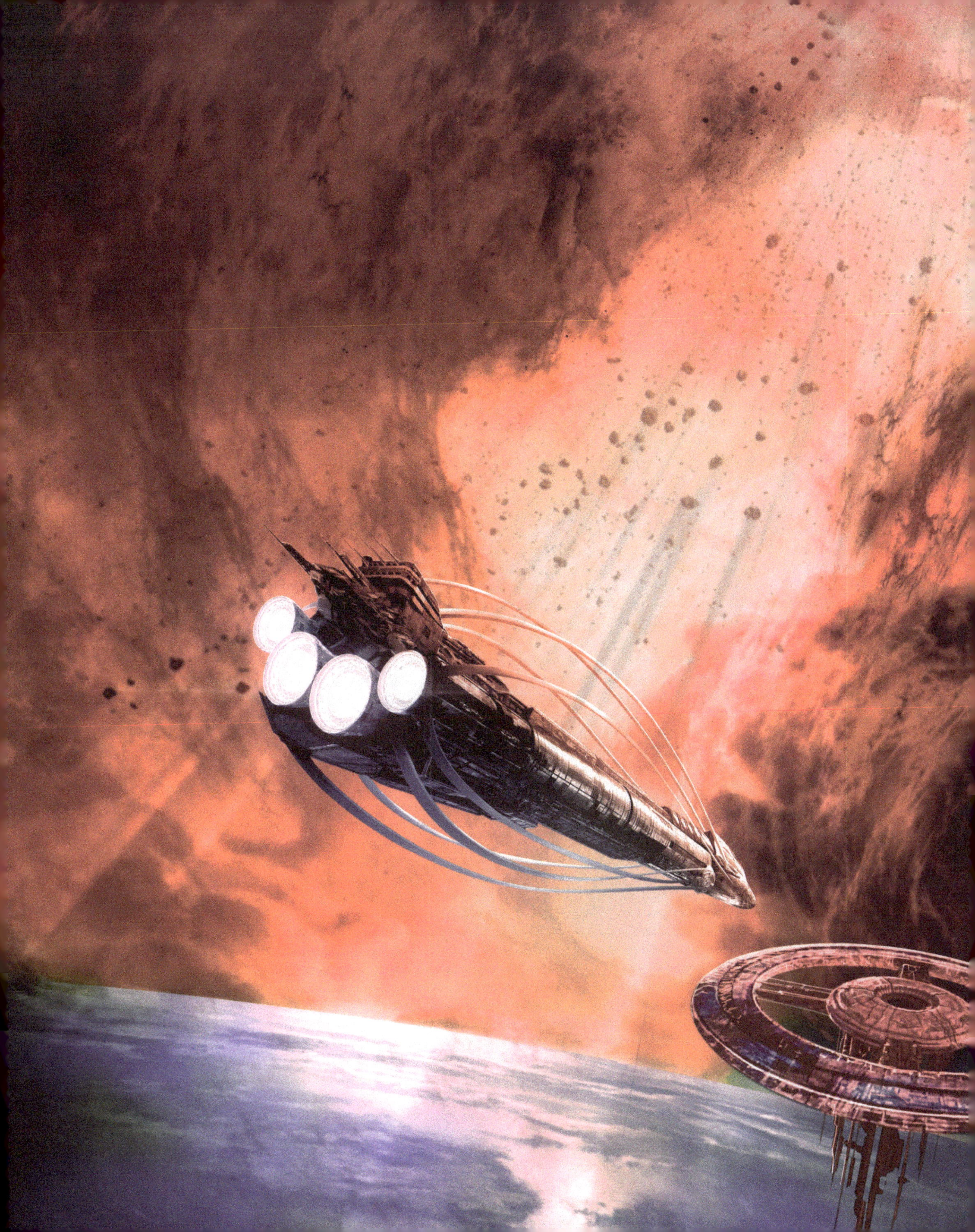

Close Proximity was the first co-authored book I ever wrote. As luck would have it, I wrote it with my wife, so the process was an enjoyable one.

Close Proximity was one of the first "ship only" covers (it came out shortly after New Canaan), and the theme of the covers has been consistent ever since. A ship in action, a looming planet of some sort, and the Perilous Alliance glyph. The one exception is the prequel cover below that has no ship. But there's a reason for that.

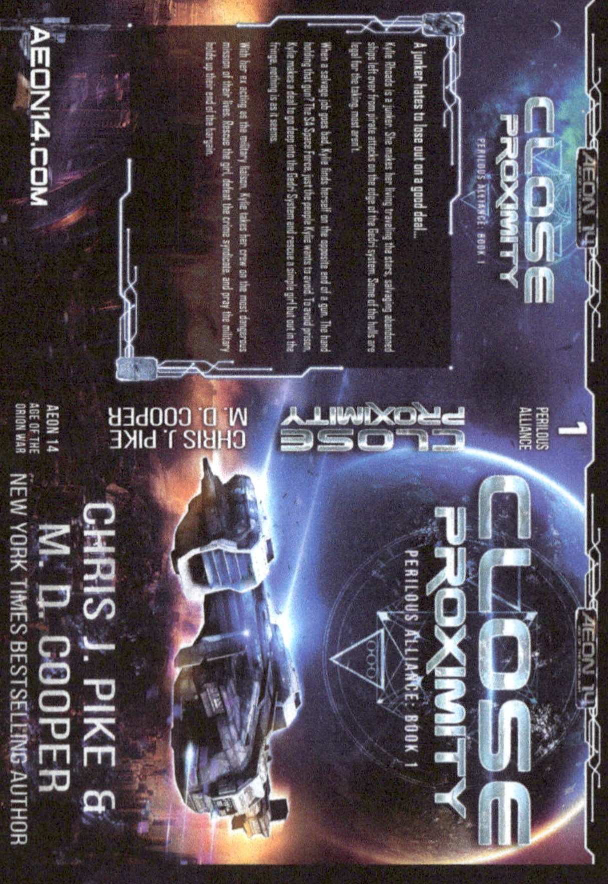

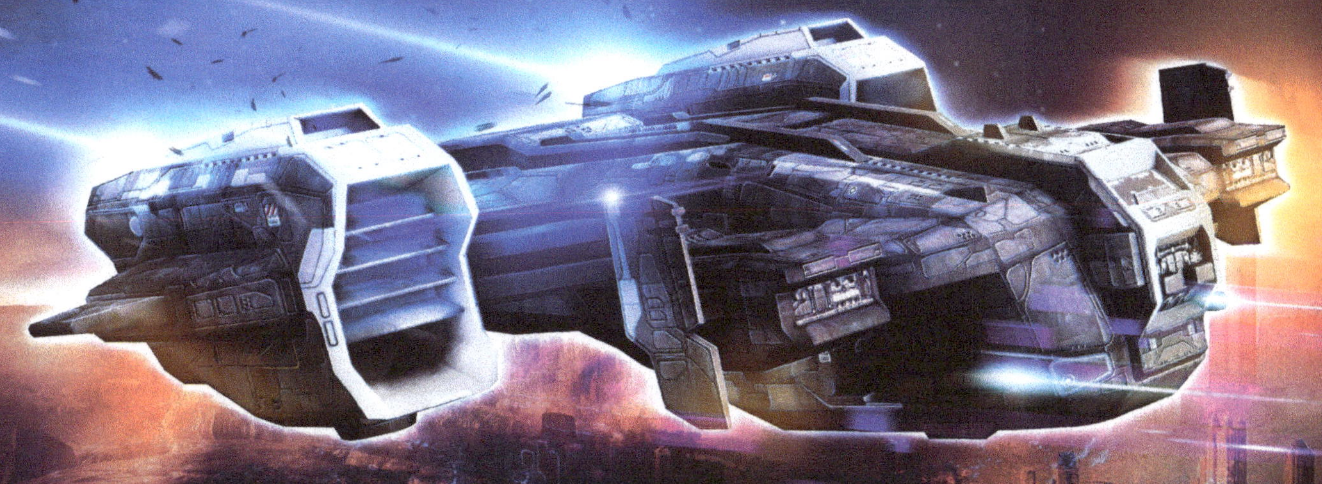

CLOSE PROXIMITY

PERILOUS ALLIANCE: BOOK 1

CHRIS J. PIKE &
M. D. COOPER

NEW YORK TIMES BESTSELLING AUTHOR

AEON 14
AGE OF THE ORION WAR
STRIKE VECTOR
PERILOUS ALLIANCE: BOOK 2
CHRIS J. PIKE &
M. D. COOPER
NEW YORK TIMES BESTSELLING AUTHOR

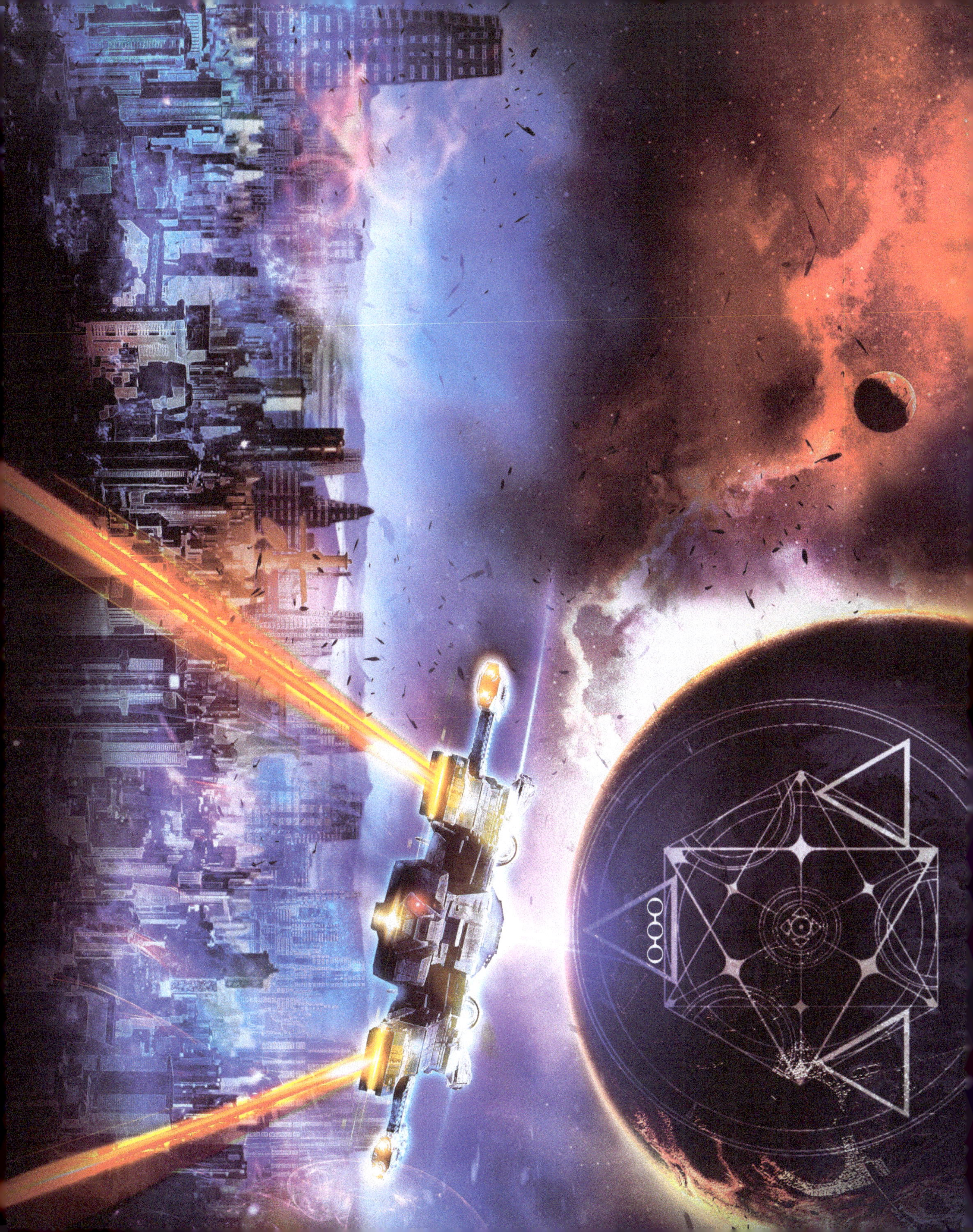

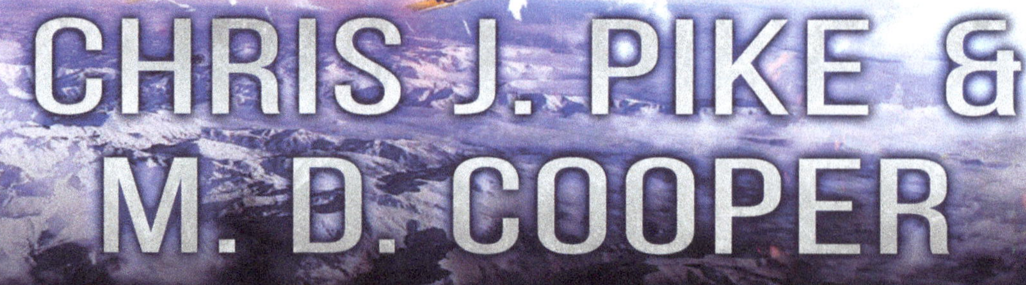

AEON 14
AGE OF THE ORION WAR
COLLISION COURSE
PERILOUS ALLIANCE: BOOK 3
CHRIS J. PIKE &
M. D. COOPER
NEW YORK TIMES BESTSELLING AUTHOR

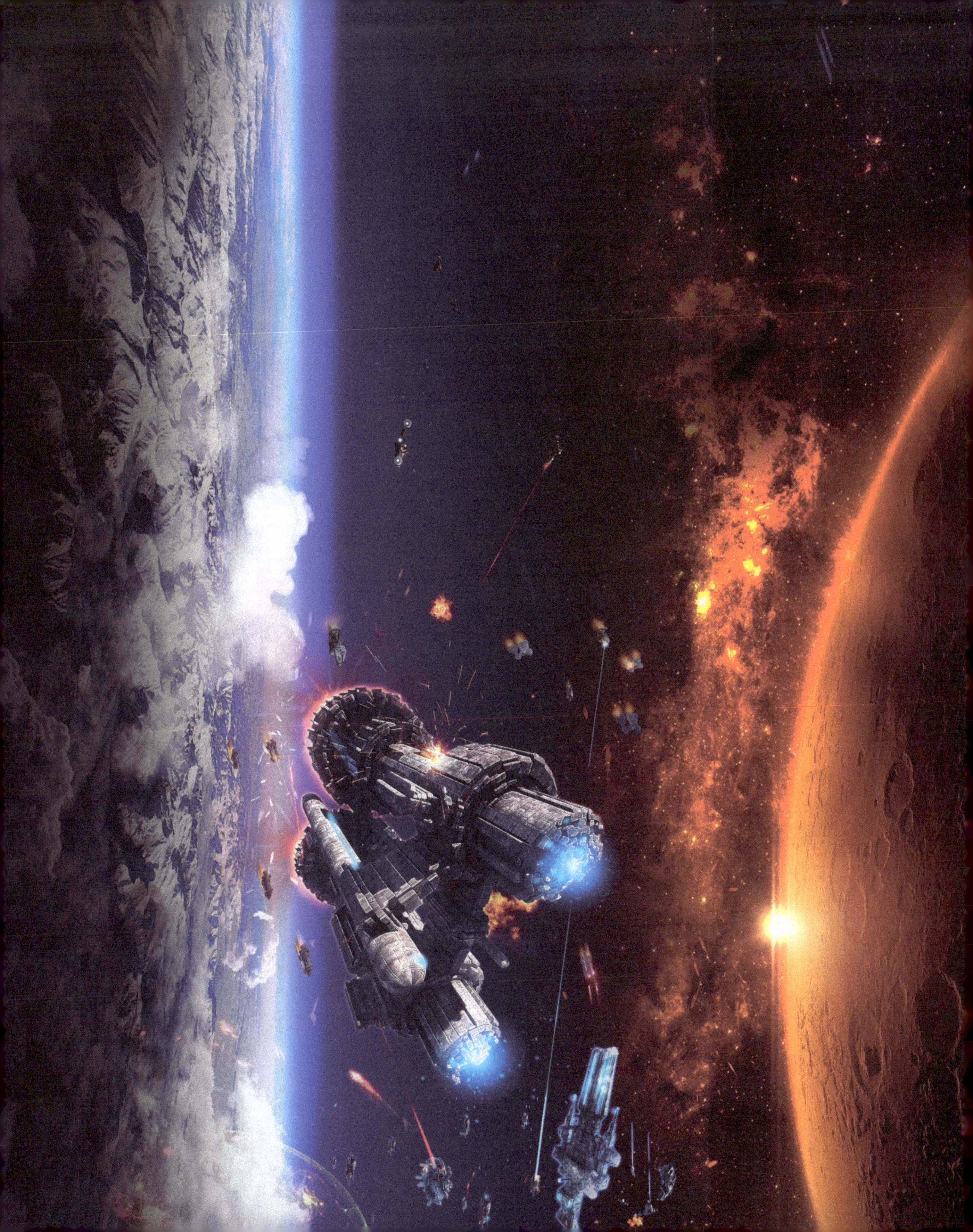

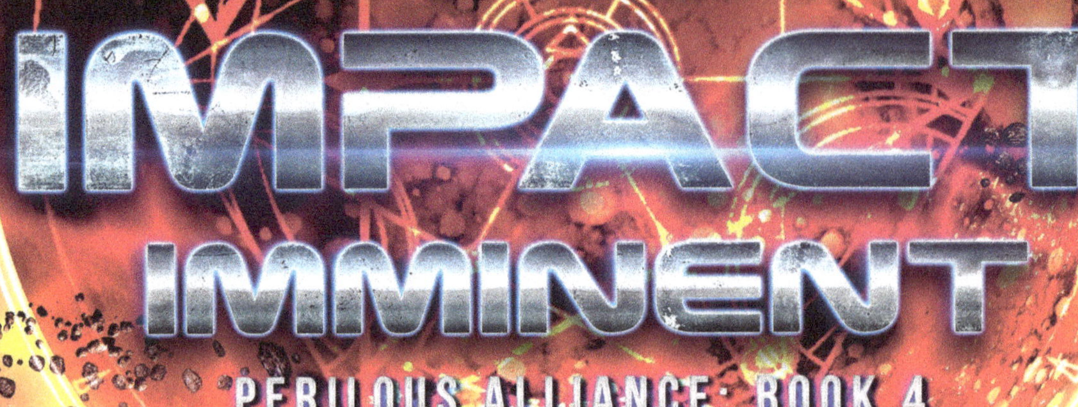

IMPACT IMMINENT

PERILOUS ALLIANCE: BOOK 4

CHRIS J. PIKE &
M. D. COOPER

NEW YORK TIMES BESTSELLING AUTHOR

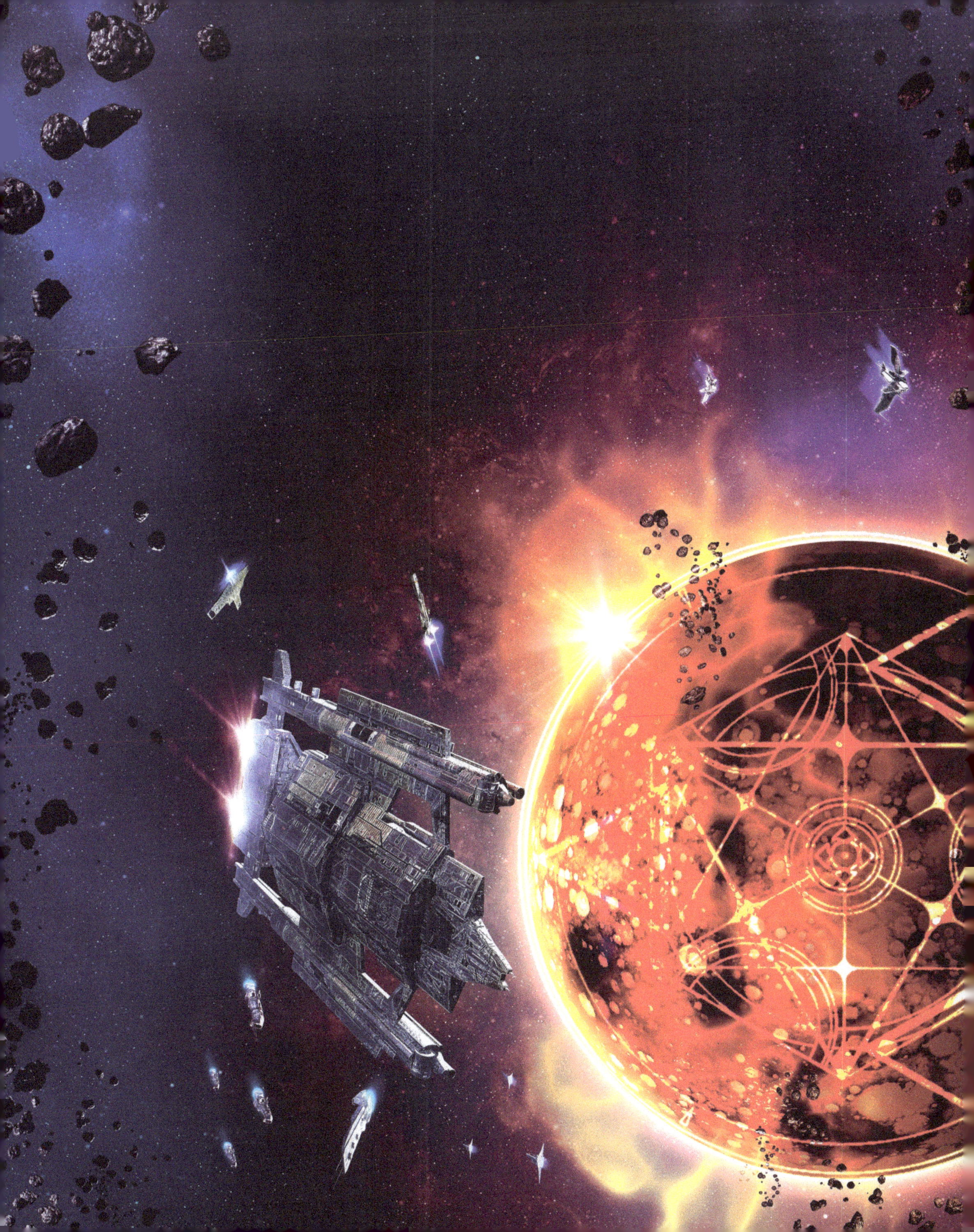

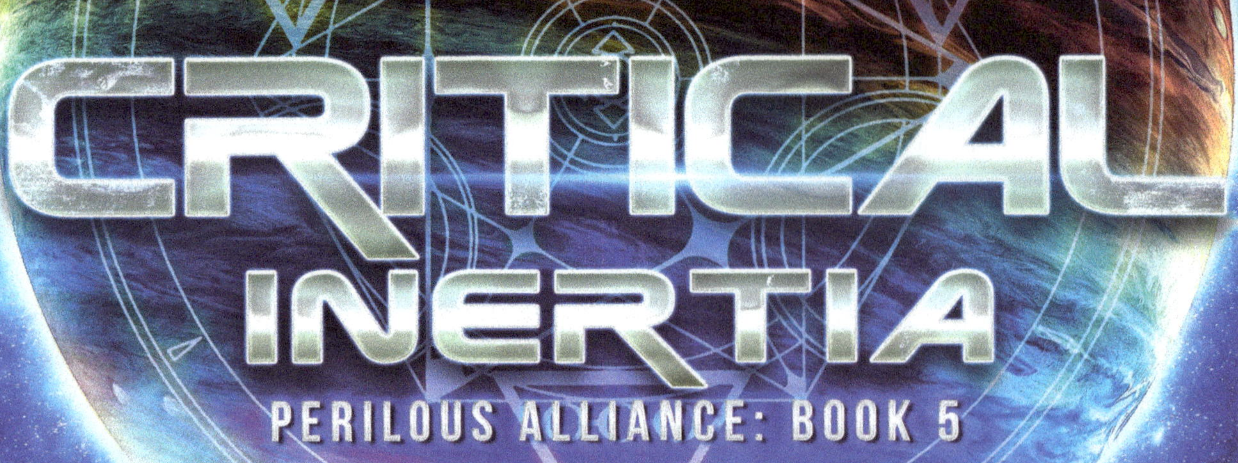

AEON 14
AGE OF THE ORION WAR
CRITICAL
INERTIA
PERILOUS ALLIANCE: BOOK 5

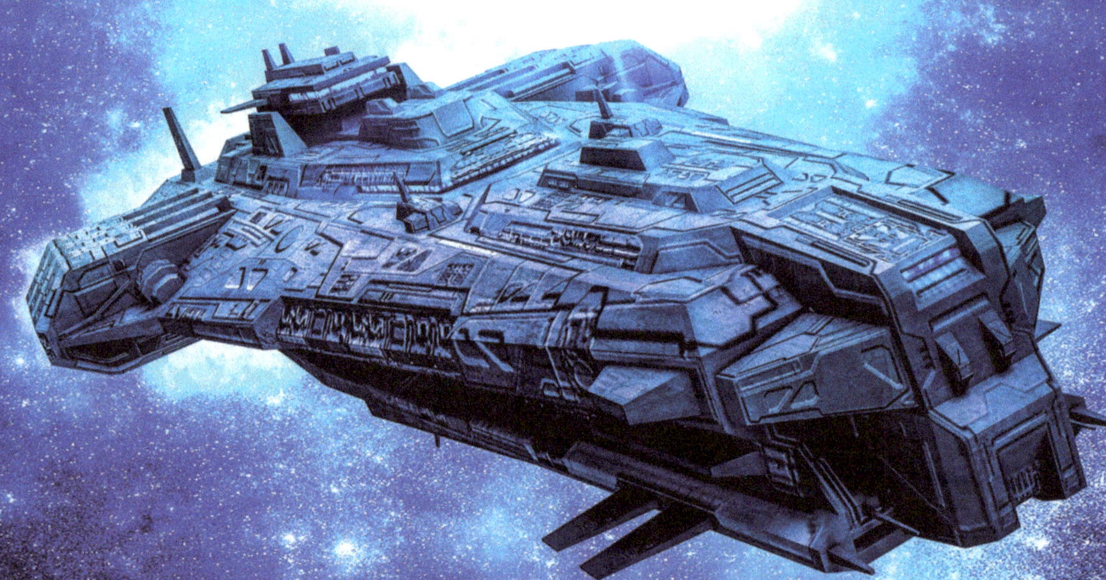

CHRIS J. PIKE &
M. D. COOPER
NEW YORK TIMES BESTSELLING AUTHOR

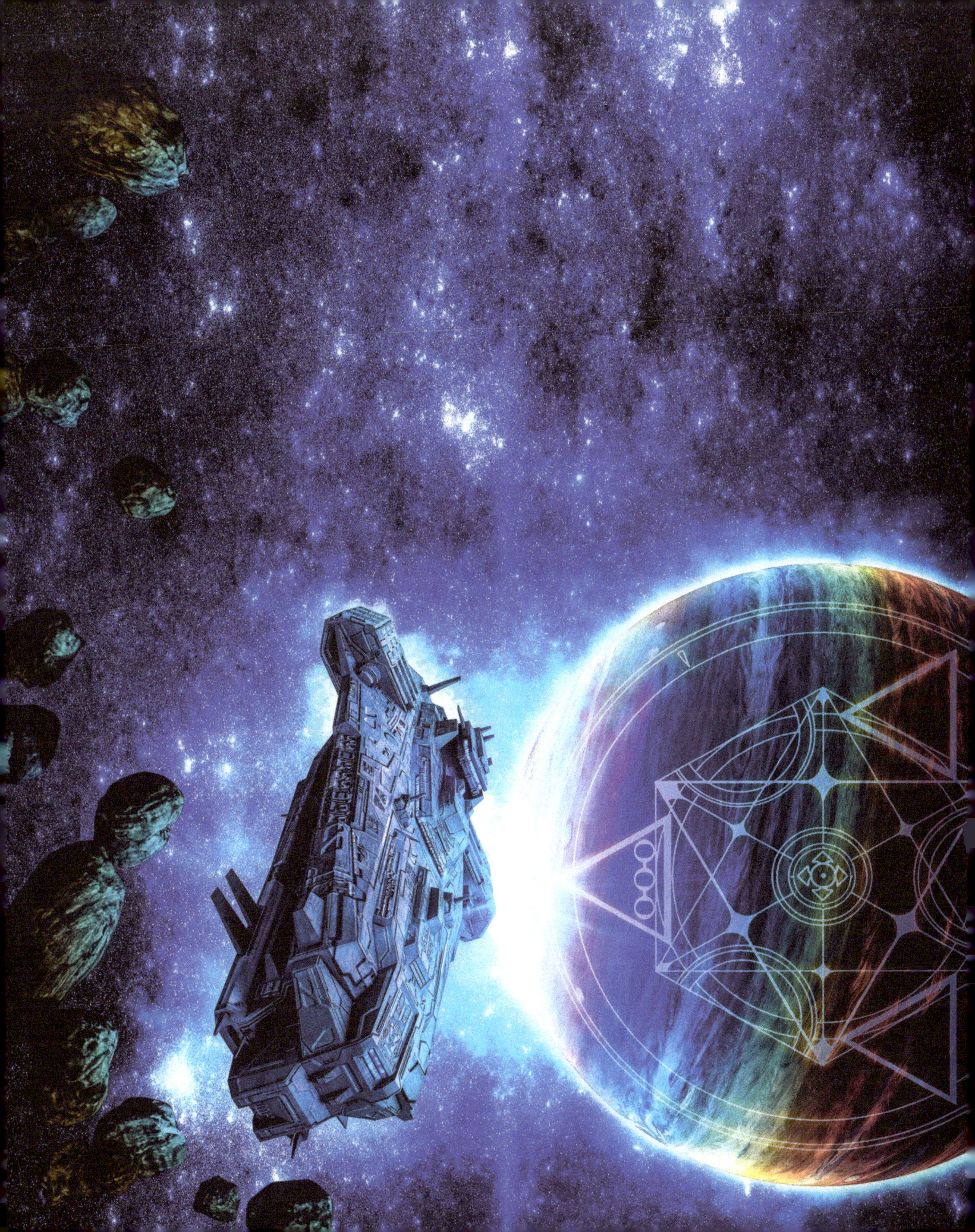

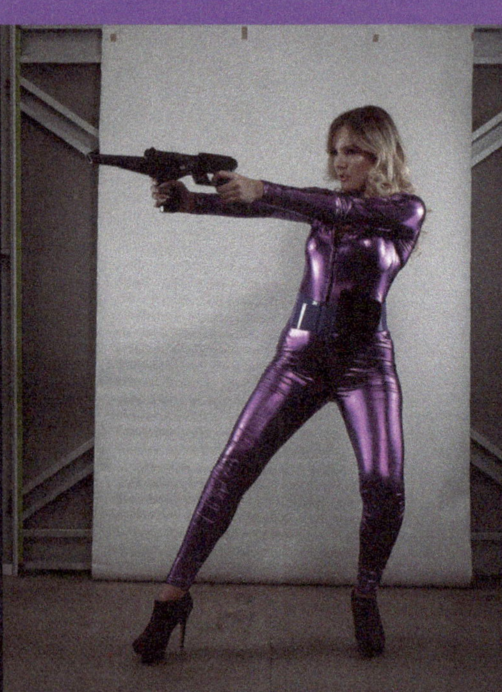

The Perseus Gate covers were the first covers I did with Andrew Dobell. I had planned out the novellas featuring Jessica and the crew of *Sabrina*, but I didn't know how wel they'd do (hint: folks loved them).

Because of that, I was hesitant to sink a lot of money into the covers in case the whole "serial novella" plan didn't pan out. Somehow I went from that to a custom photoshoo

Andrew gave me a great deal, but I'm pretty certain he gave me a deal to get me hooked on custom photoshoots. it doesn't hurt that his art is amazing.

The images from the shoot were fantastic, and when Andrew delivered the first cover I had a moment's worry: I was about to release a book with a pink and purple cover.

I reminded myself that colors are just colors, and pink and purple are great ones. decided that these were covers Jessica would love, and I had determined to always be true to the characters.

Some folks believe these covers are overly sexualized and don't like them as a result. Even so, they've become some of my favorite covers ever, because they are honest in their portrayal of the character, and they don't soft-pedal anything about Jessica.

Opposite: The Gate at the Grey Wolf Star with original typography by Andrew Dobell

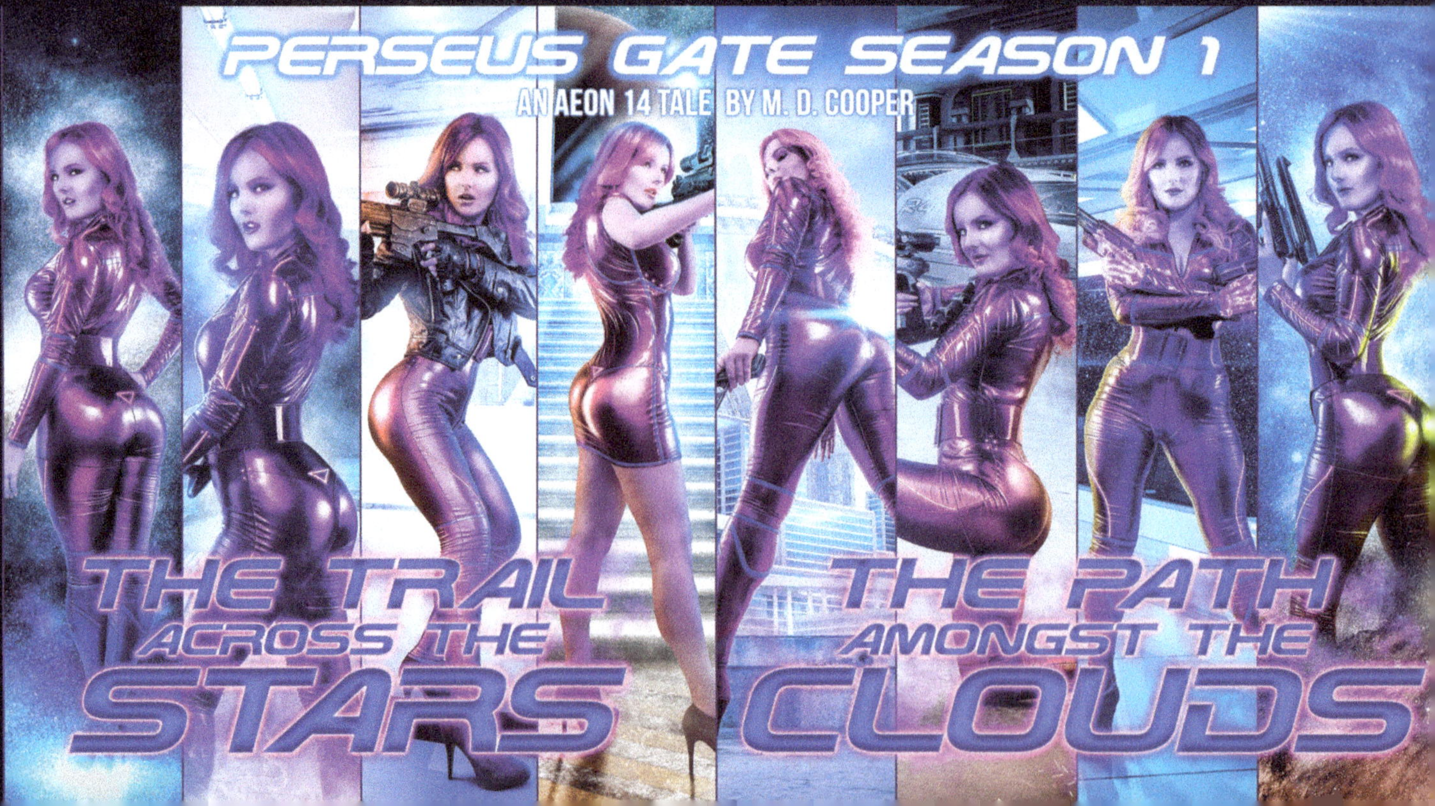

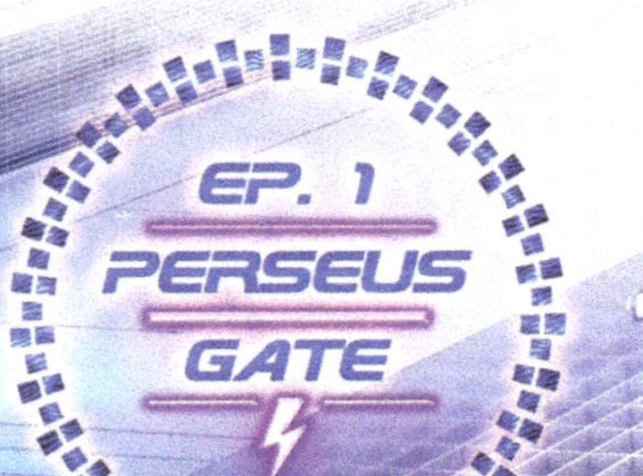

THE GATE AT THE GREY WOLF STAR

Jessica and the crew of Sabrina have finally found Finaeus Tomlinson, brother of the President, after nine long years of searching the Inner Stars.

Now Finaeus has convinced them to take a shortcut through a jump gate—a new technology none of them have ever used before—located at a secret dwarf star mining operation.

But a mysterious group within the Transcend Space Force, known as the Grey Division, has orders to intercept and capture both Jessica and Finaeus.

Trapped at the bottom of a steep gravity well and surrounded by enemies, Jessica and the crew of Sabrina must find a way out of the Grey Wolf System and deliver the crucial information Finaeus carries back to New Eden before even their allies are forced to turn against them.

EP. 1
PERSEUS GATE

THE GATE AT THE GREY WOLF STAR

M. D. COOPER

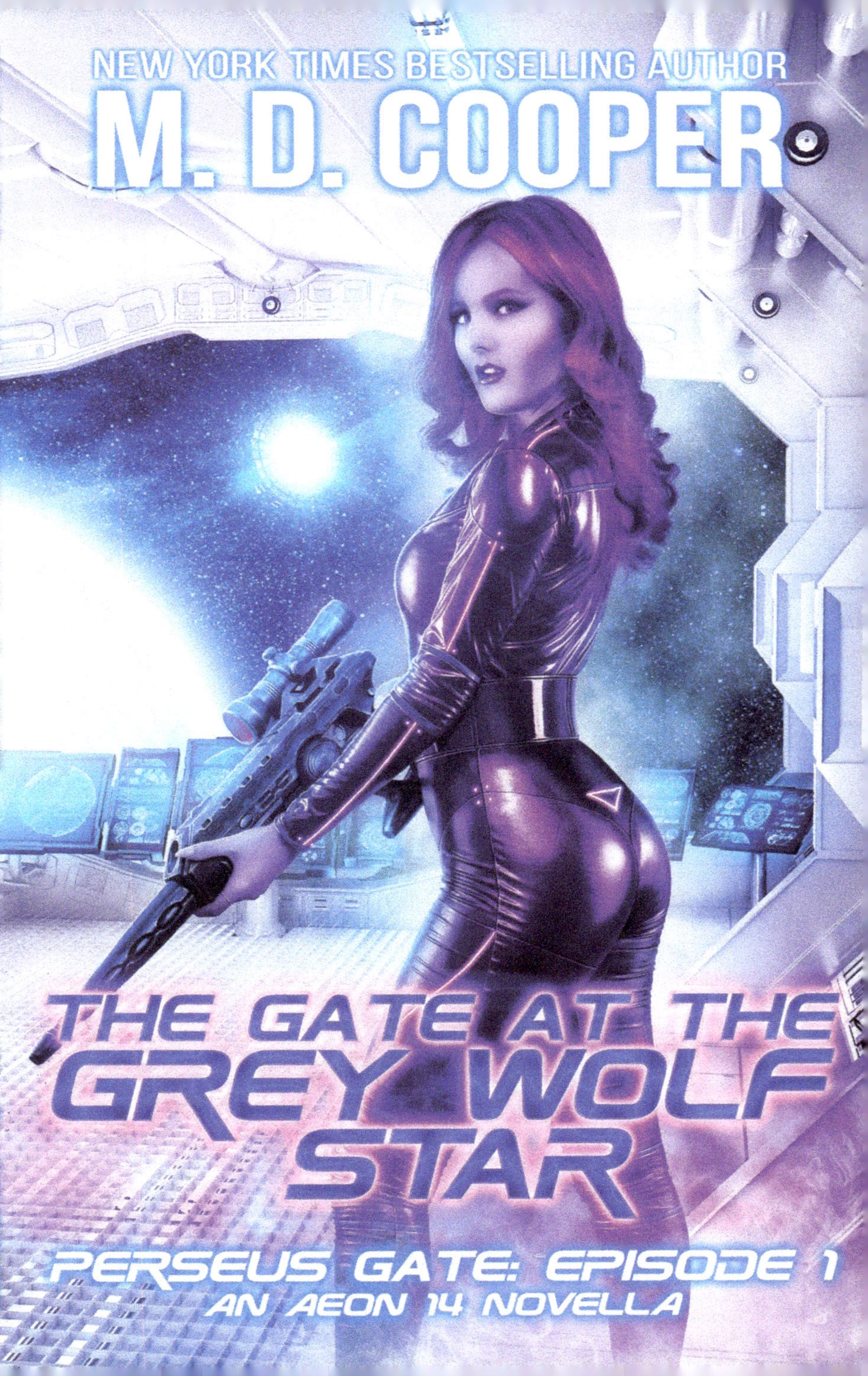

NEW YORK TIMES BESTSELLING AUTHOR

M. D. COOPER

THE GATE AT THE GREY WOLF STAR

PERSEUS GATE: EPISODE 1
AN AEON 14 NOVELLA

AEON 14
AGE OF THE ORION WAR

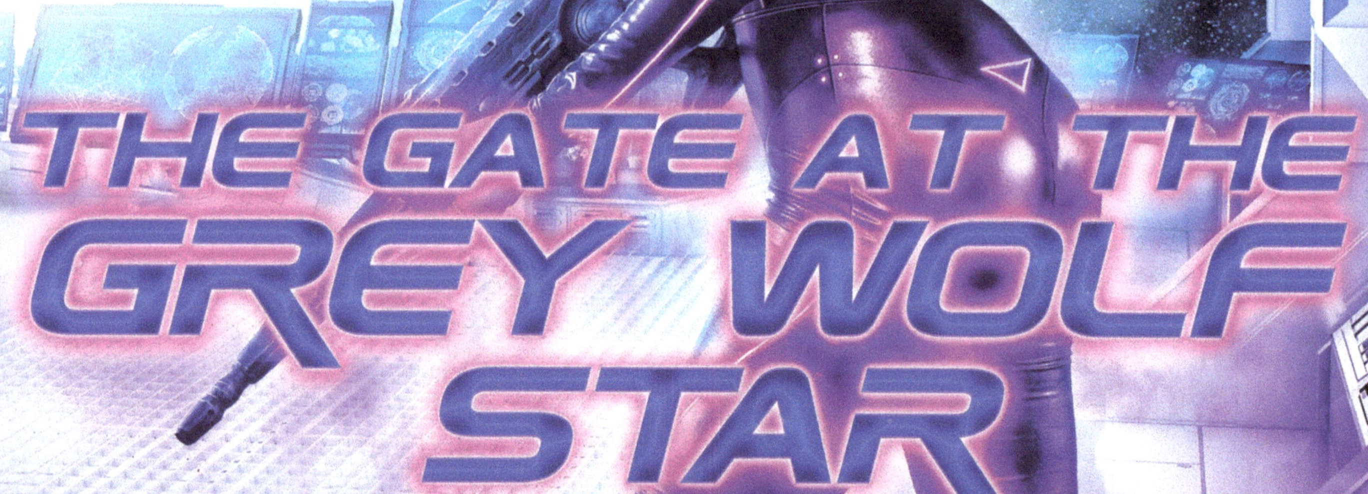

PERSEUS GATE: ORION SPACE
SEASON 1 EPISODE 1
THE GATE AT THE GREY WOLF STAR
M. D. COOPER
NEW YORK TIMES BESTSELLING AUTHOR

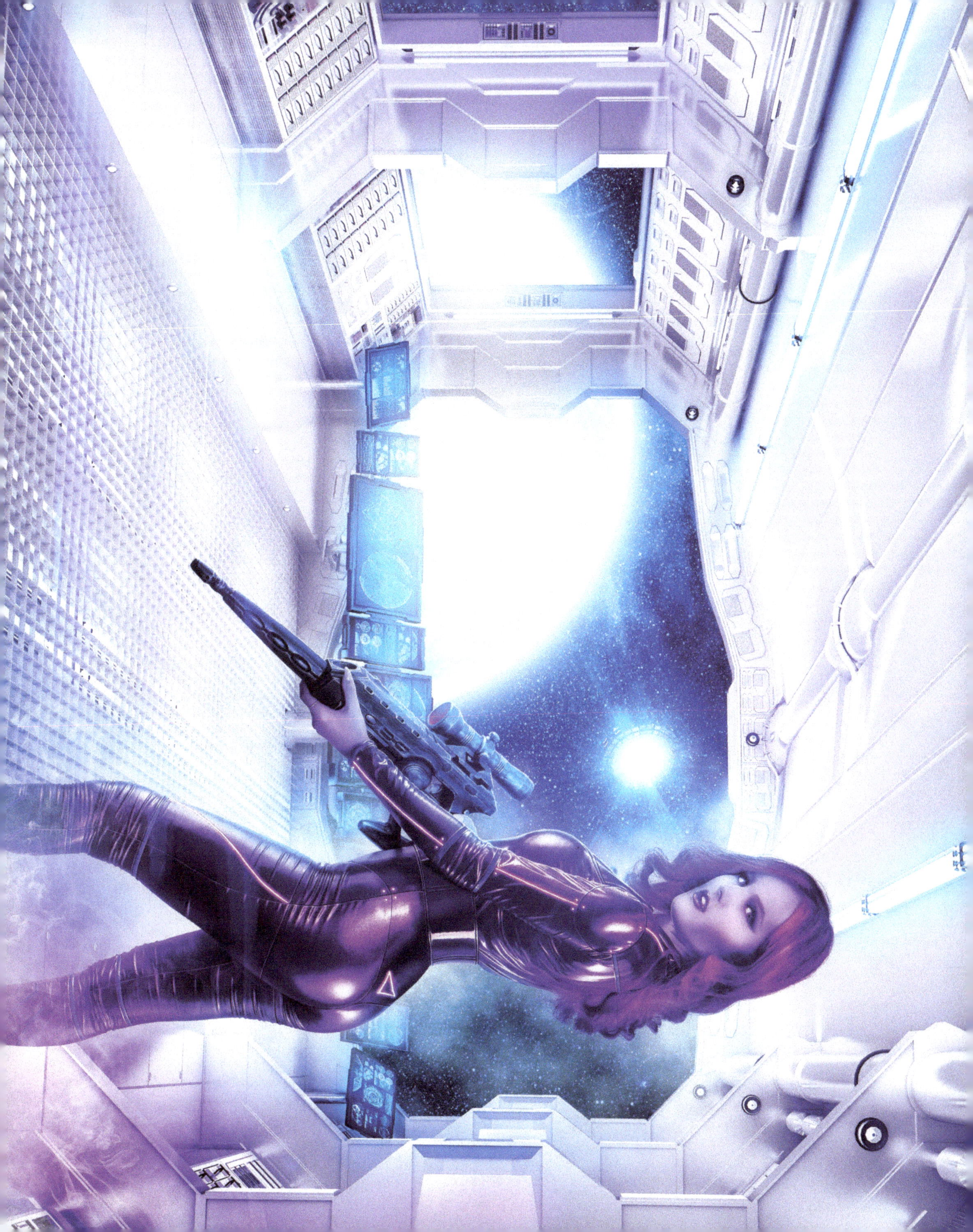

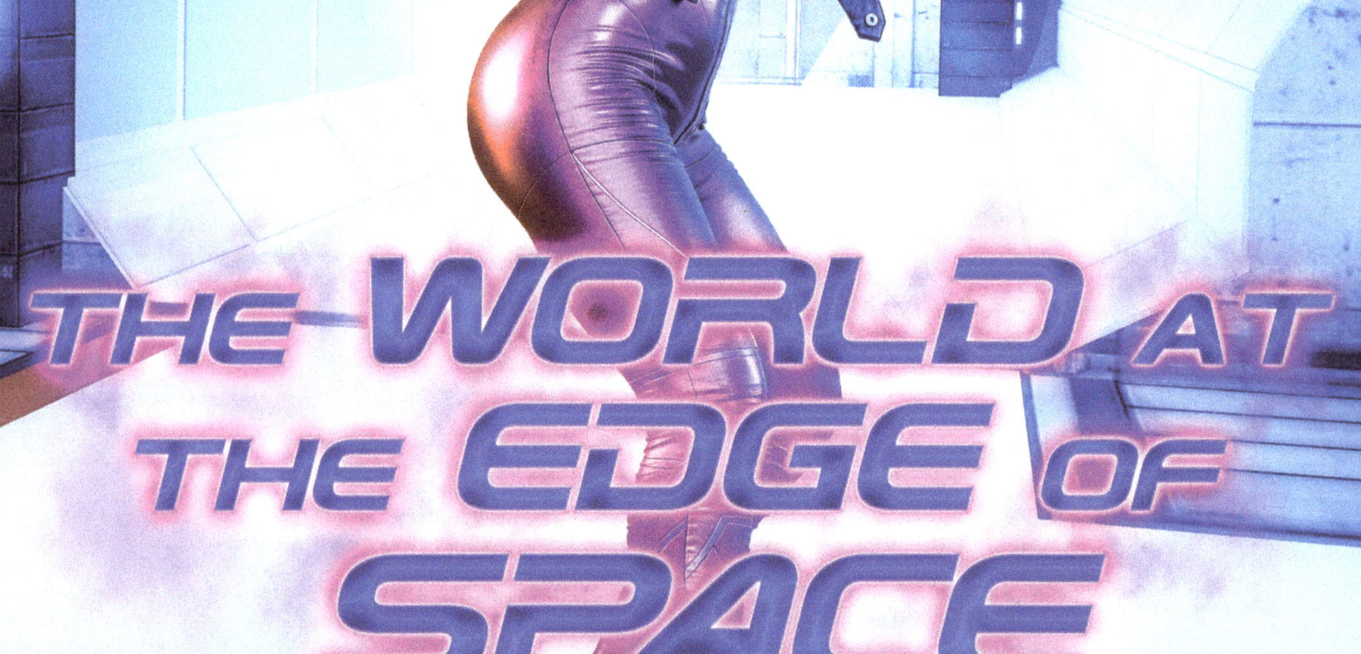

AEON 14
AGE OF THE ORION WAR
PERSEUS GATE: ORION SPACE
SEASON 1 EPISODE 2
THE WORLD AT THE EDGE OF SPACE
M. D. COOPER
NEW YORK TIMES BESTSELLING AUTHOR

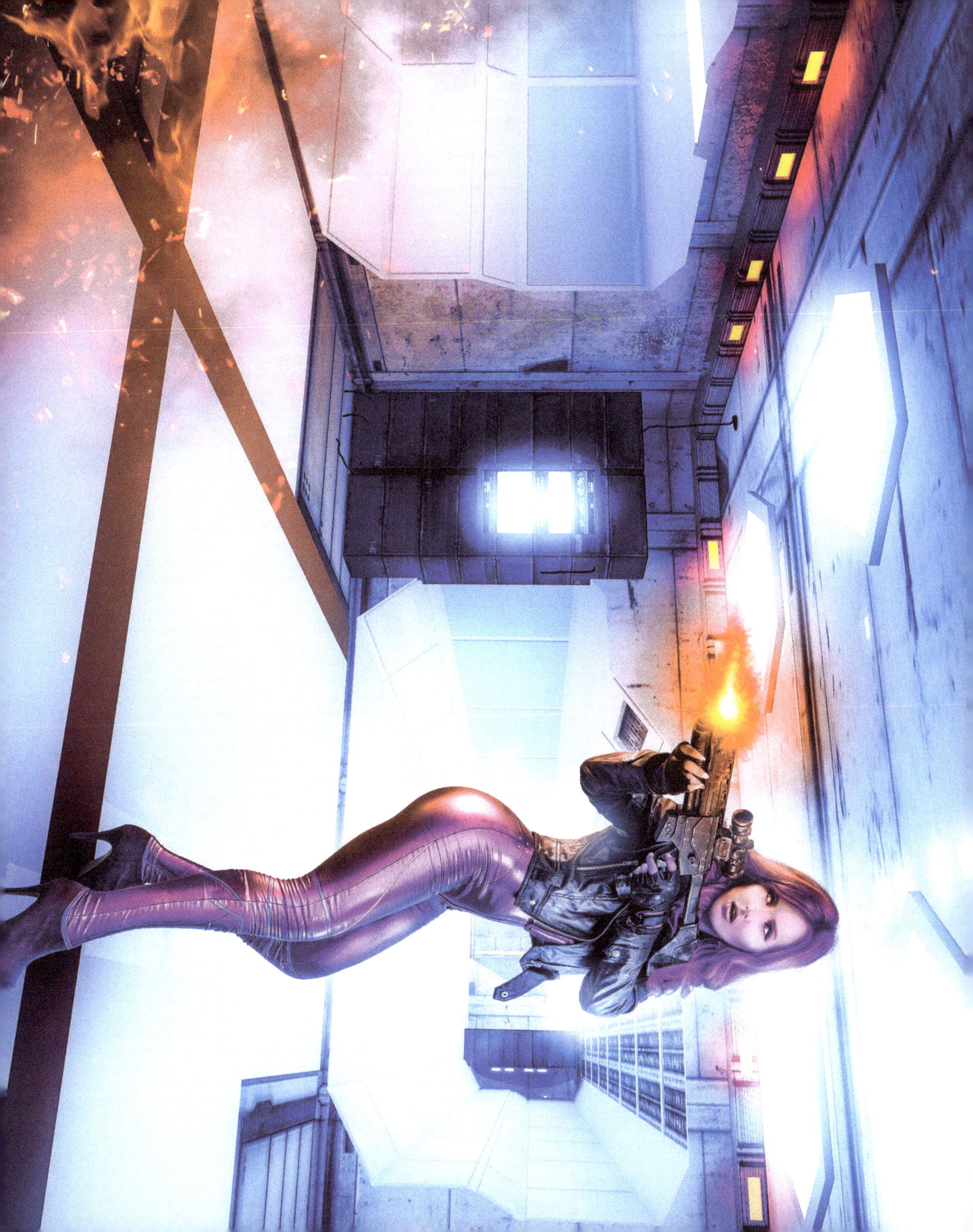

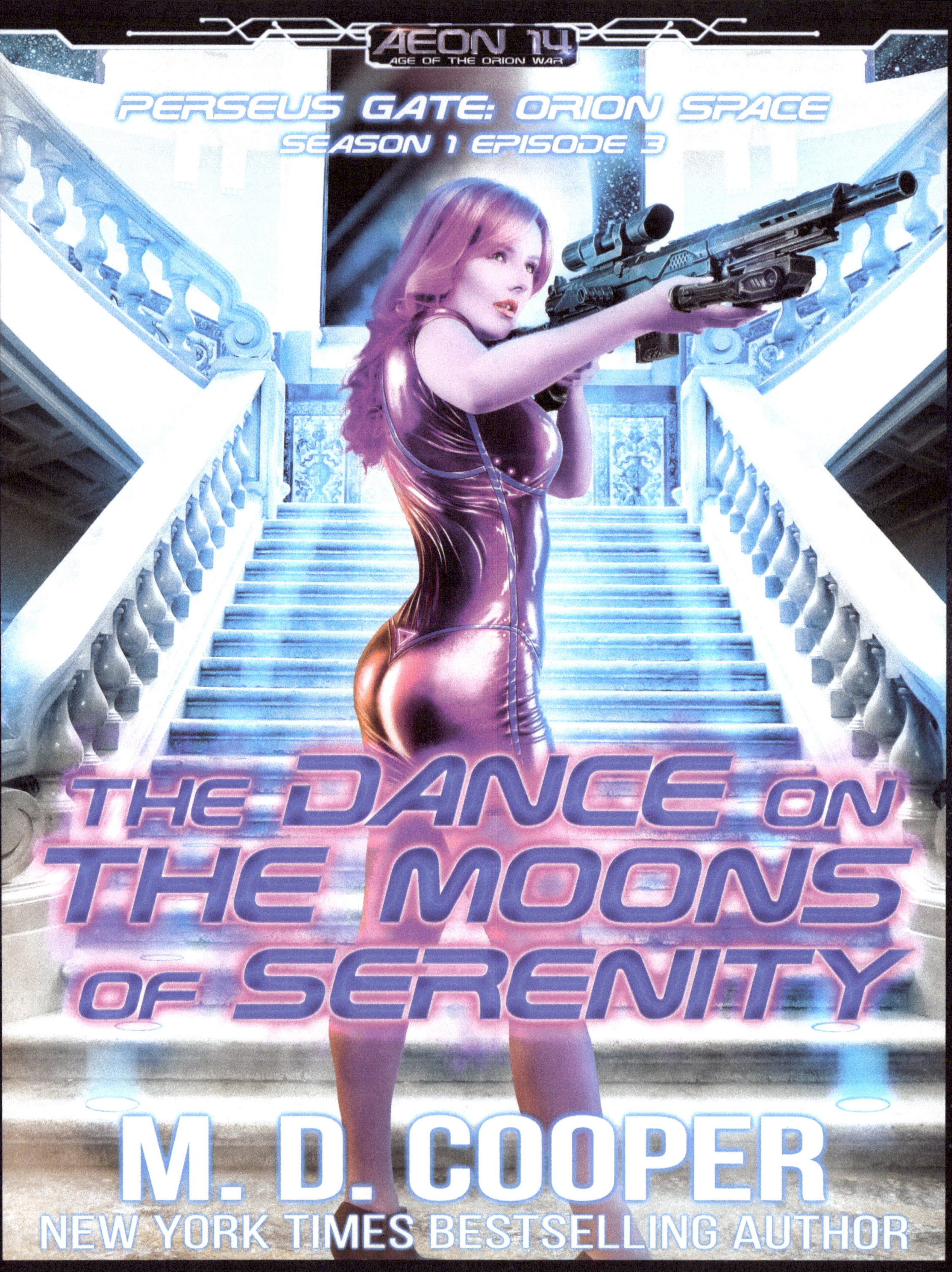

AEON 14
AGE OF THE ORION WAR
PERSEUS GATE: ORION SPACE
SEASON 1 EPISODE 3
THE DANCE ON THE MOONS OF SERENITY
M. D. COOPER
NEW YORK TIMES BESTSELLING AUTHOR

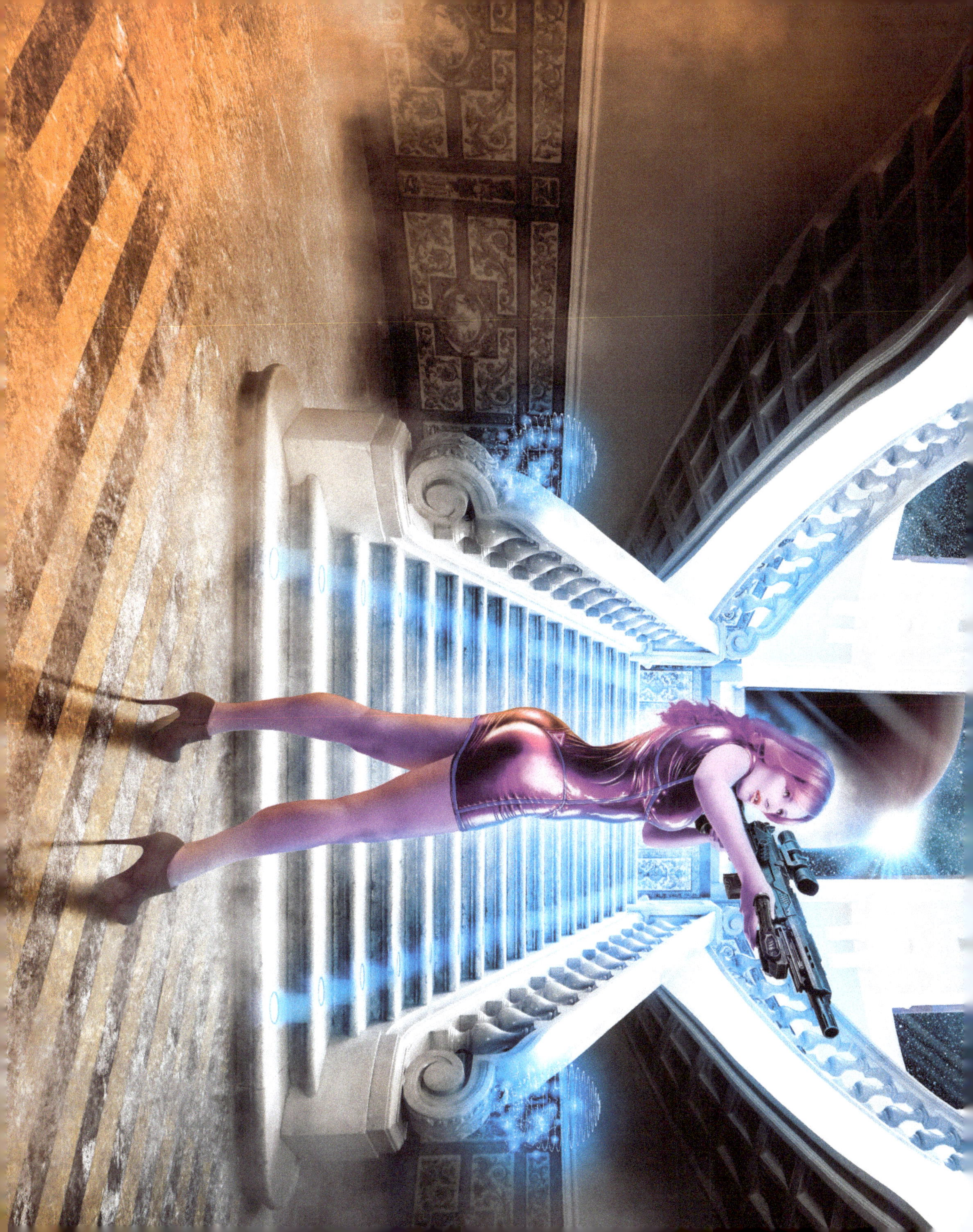

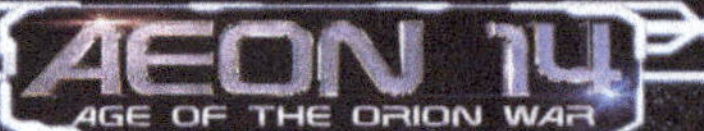

PERSEUS GATE: ORION SPACE
SEASON 1 EPISODE 1 – 3

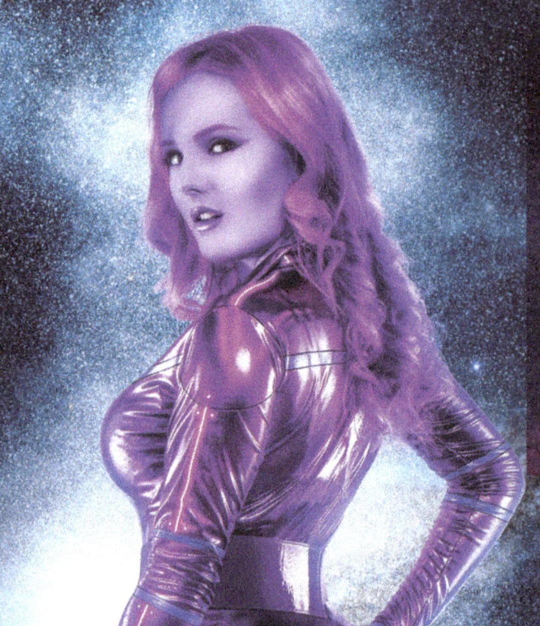

When Andrew first delivered this art to me, I strongly considered releasing the book without any text on the cover at all. The image is just so perfect that I didn't want to mar it with text.

However, the retailers require the book title you provide to match the cover, so that idea never came to fruition.

THE TRAIL THROUGH THE STARS

M. D. COOPER
NEW YORK TIMES BESTSELLING AUTHOR

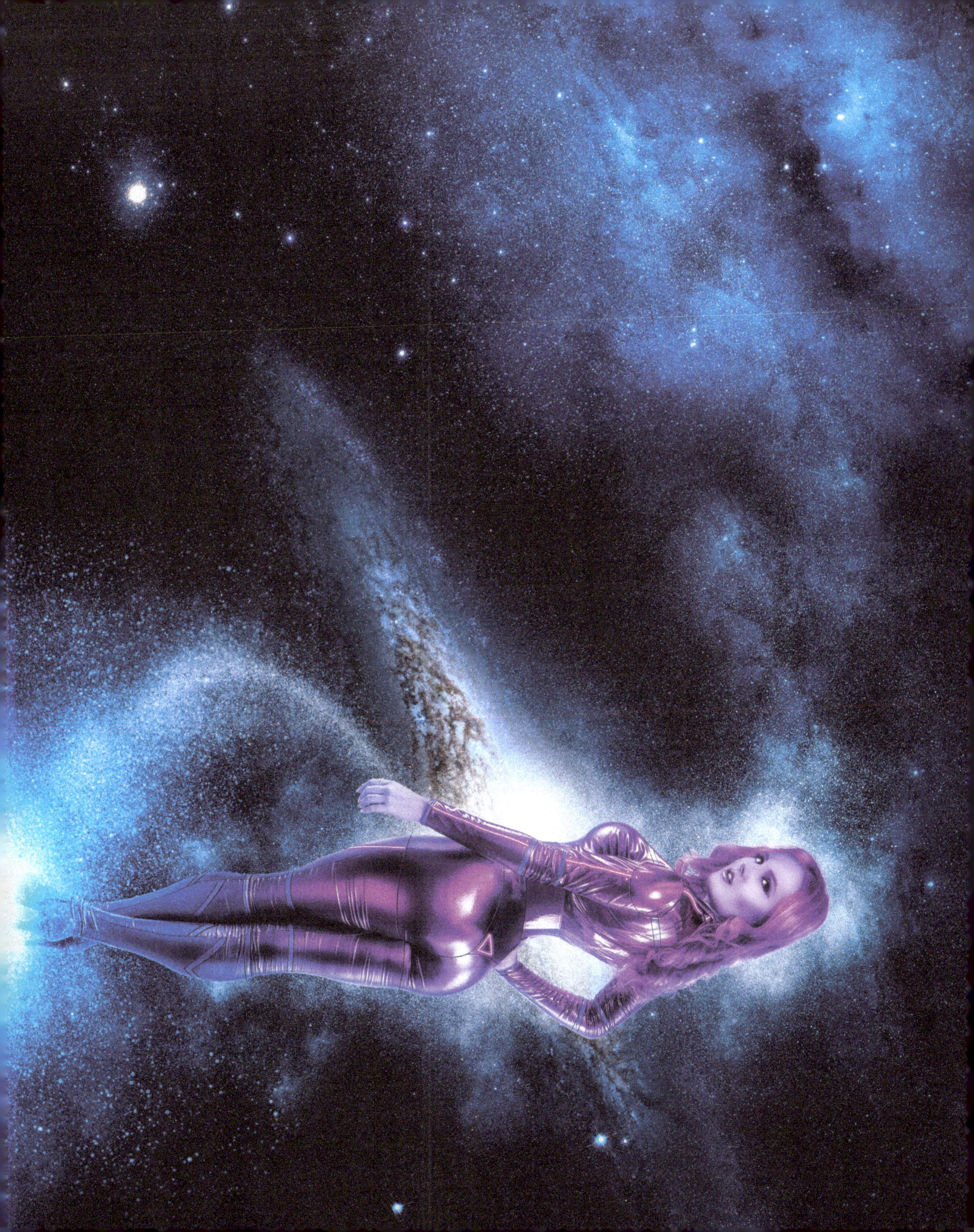

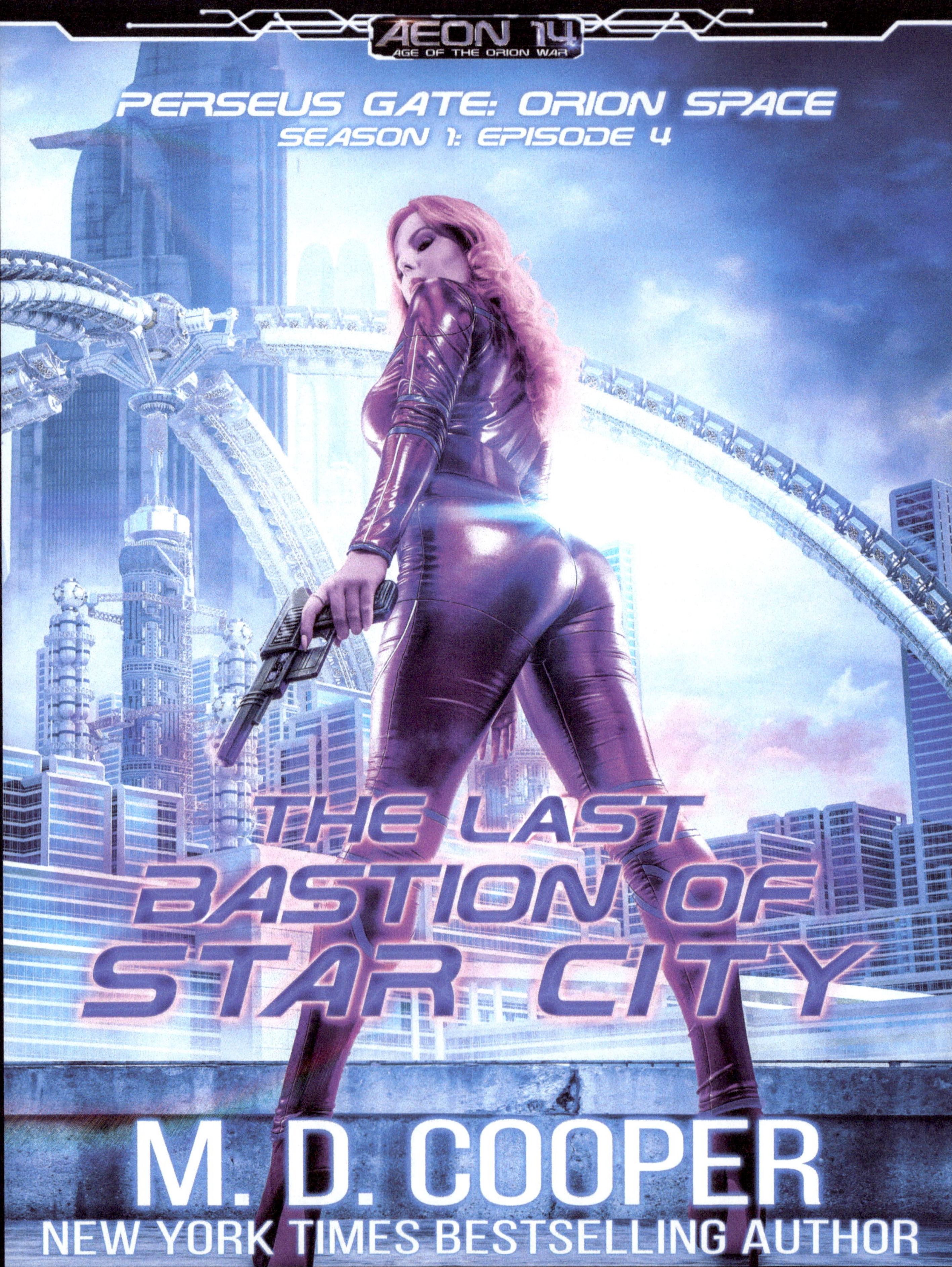

AEON 14
AGE OF THE ORION WAR
PERSEUS GATE: ORION SPACE
SEASON 1: EPISODE 4
THE LAST BASTION OF STAR CITY
M. D. COOPER
NEW YORK TIMES BESTSELLING AUTHOR

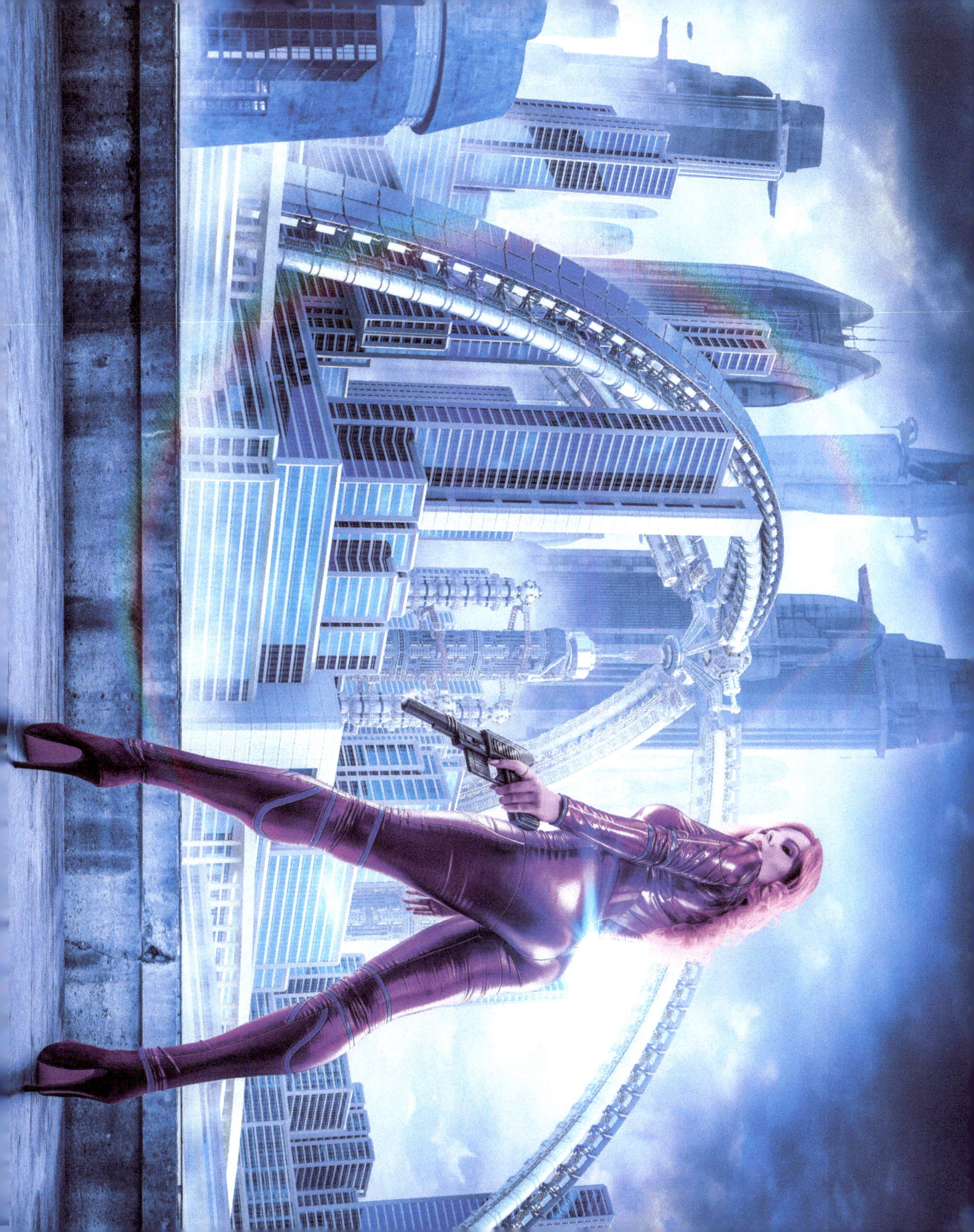

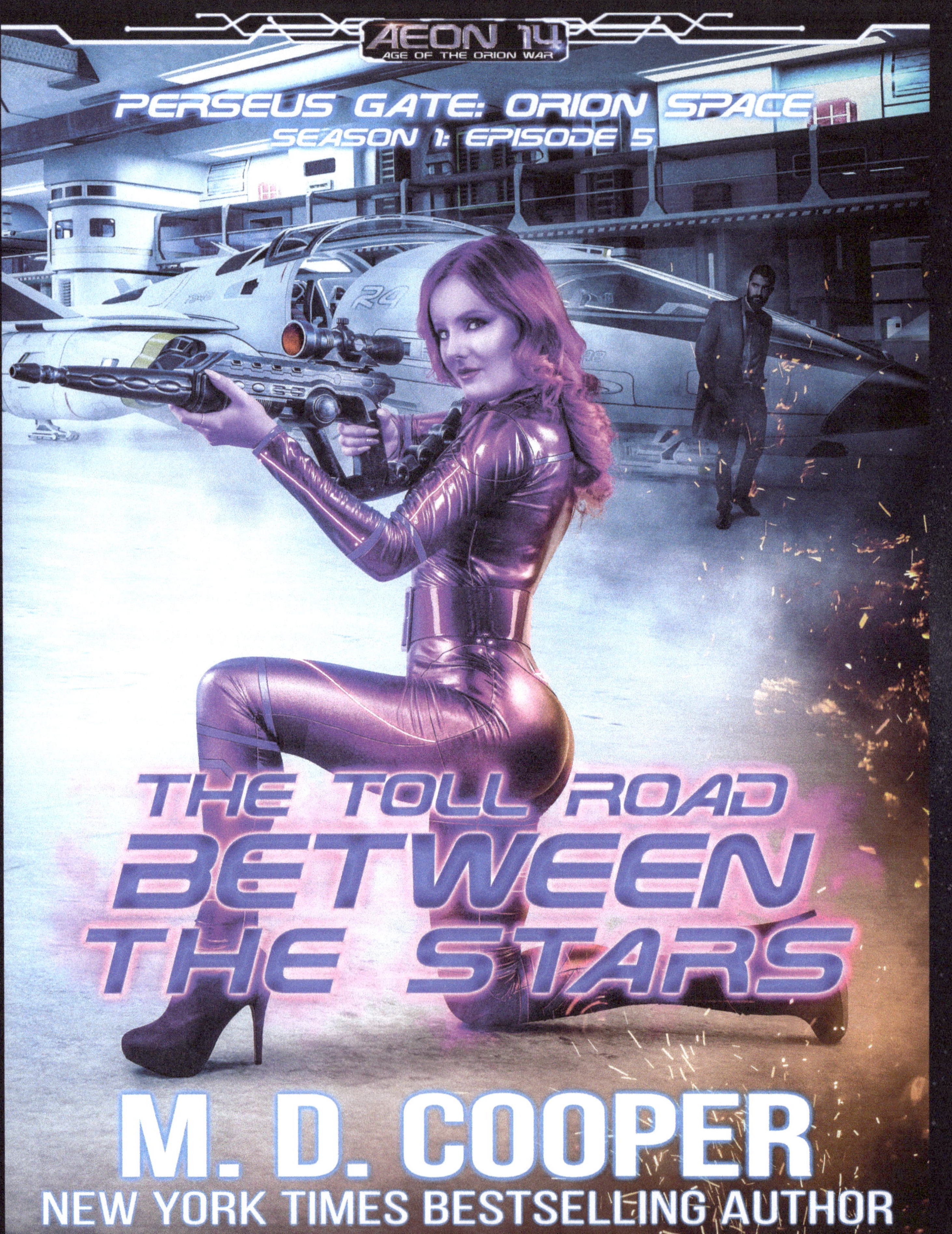

AEON 14
AGE OF THE ORION WAR
PERSEUS GATE: ORION SPACE
SEASON 1: EPISODE 5
THE TOLL ROAD BETWEEN THE STARS
M. D. COOPER
NEW YORK TIMES BESTSELLING AUTHOR

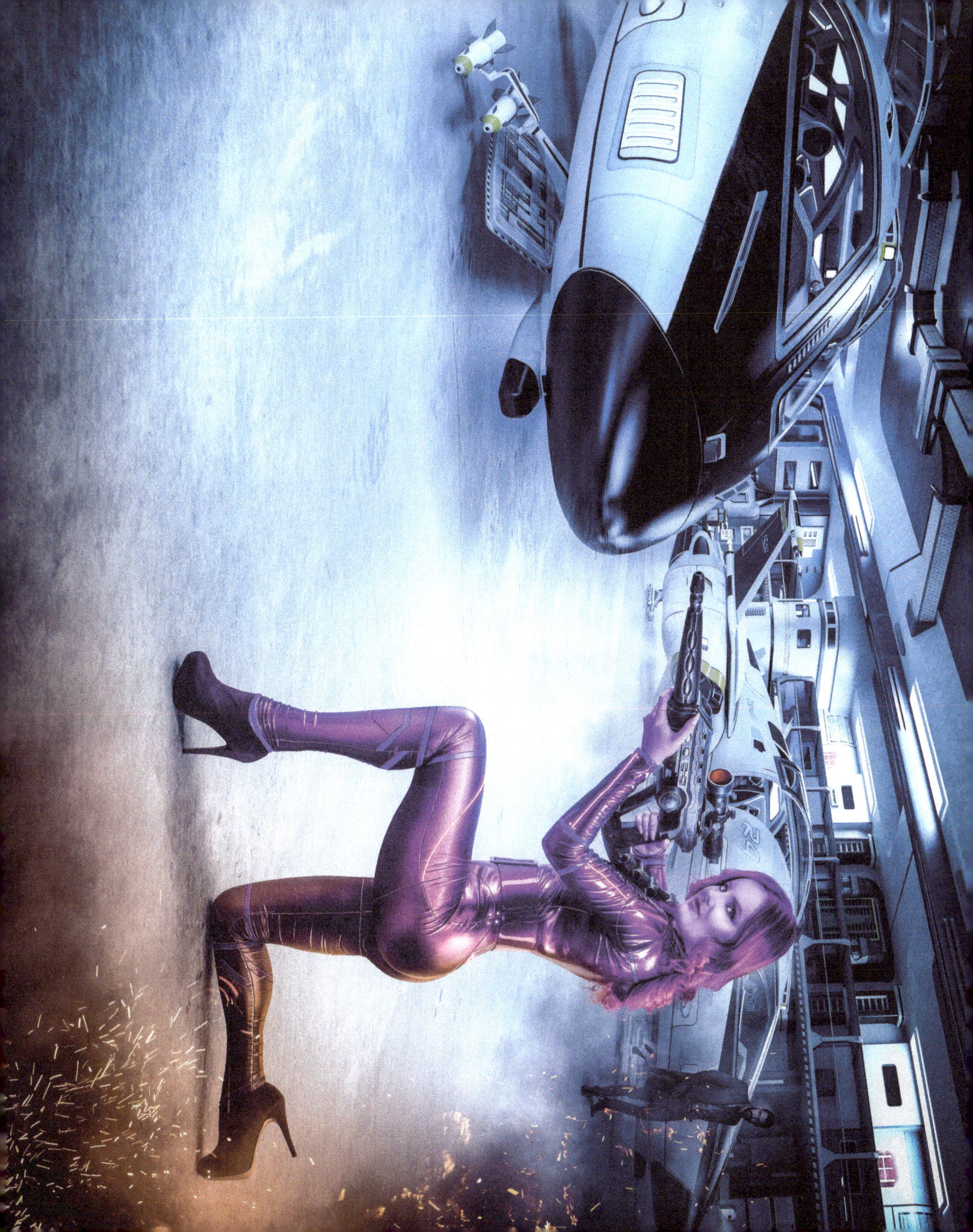

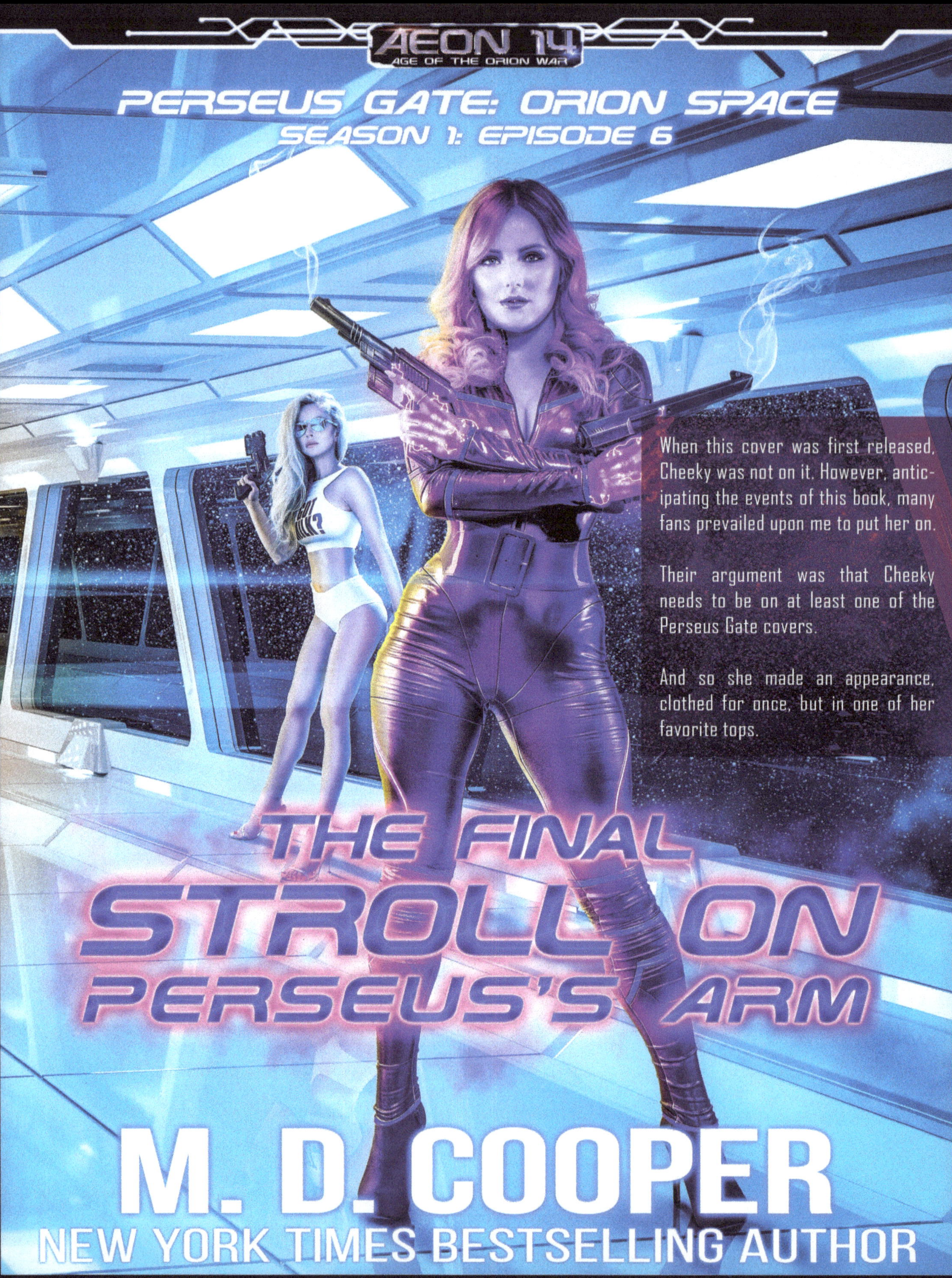

AEON 14
AGE OF THE ORION WAR
PERSEUS GATE: ORION SPACE
SEASON 1: EPISODE 6
When this cover was first released, Cheeky was not on it. However, anticipating the events of this book, many fans prevailed upon me to put her on.
Their argument was that Cheeky needs to be on at least one of the Perseus Gate covers.
And so she made an appearance, clothed for once, but in one of her favorite tops.
THE FINAL
STROLL ON
PERSEUS'S ARM
M. D. COOPER
NEW YORK TIMES BESTSELLING AUTHOR

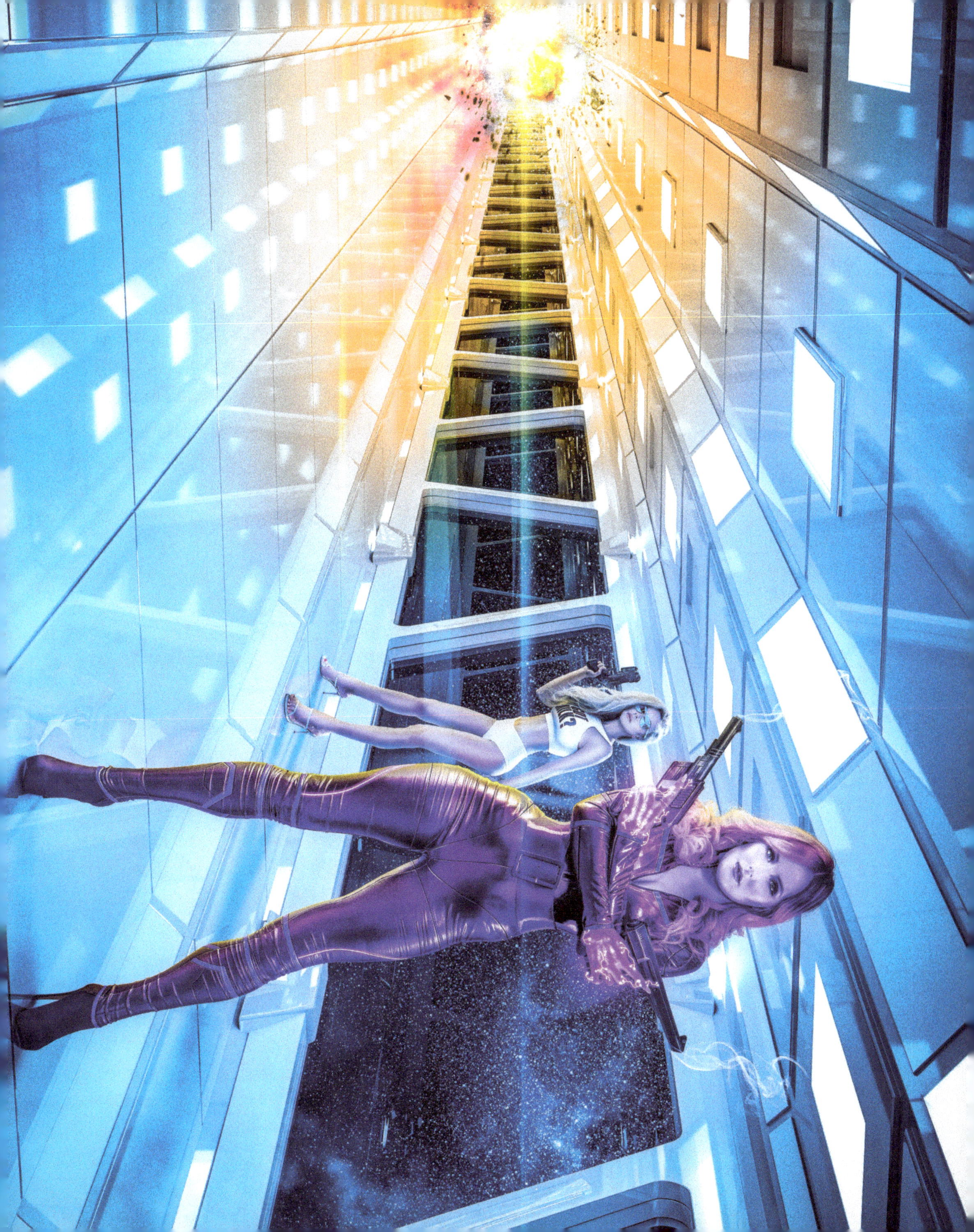

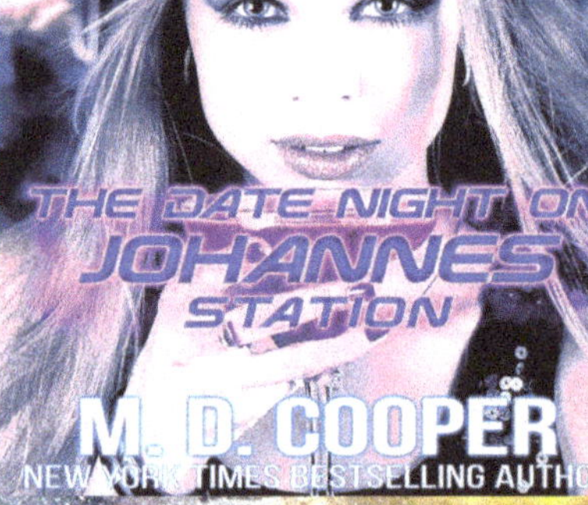

The cover below was only ever made available to JIT readers, and it depicts Cheeky on her date night with Finaeus.

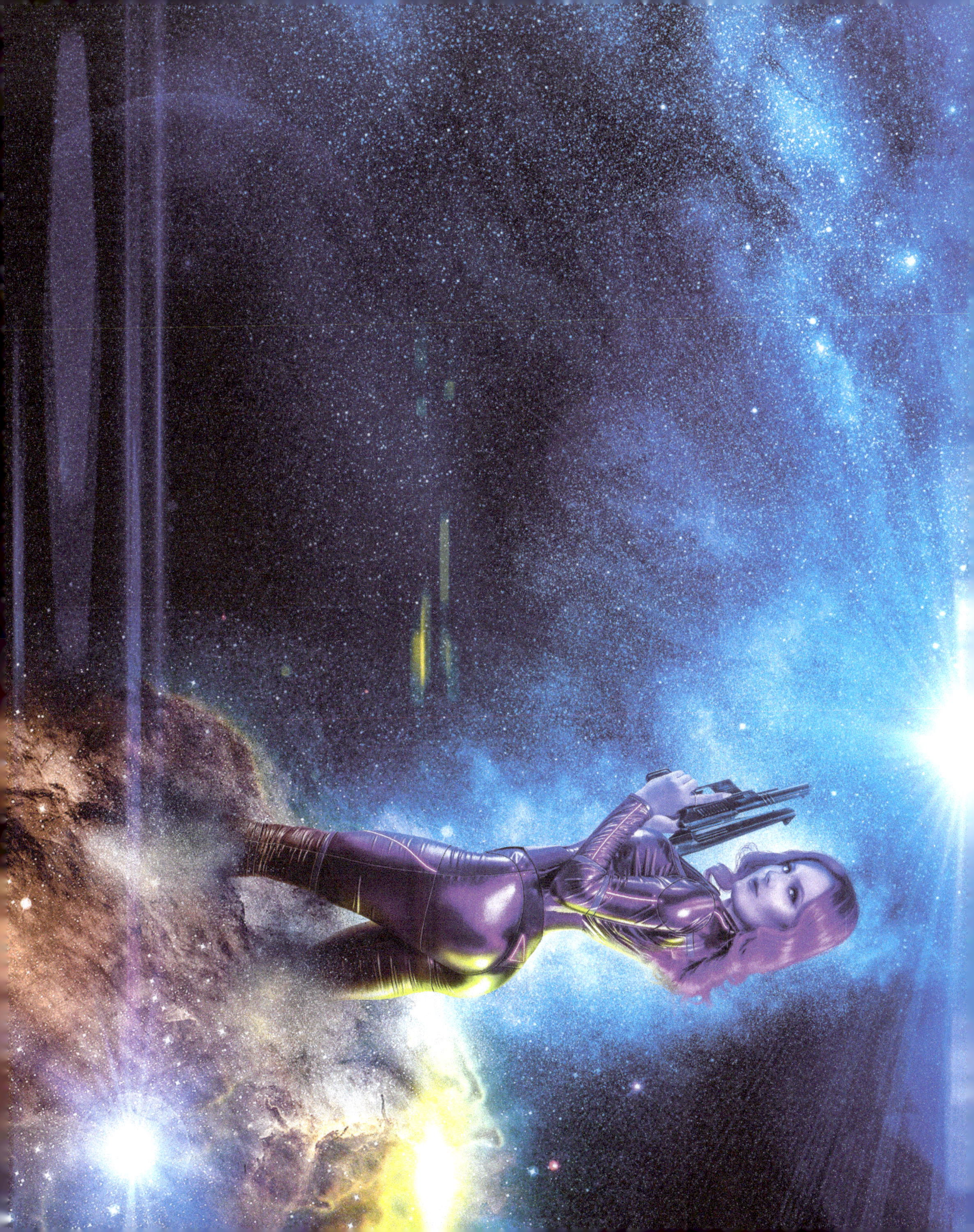

PERSEUS GATE: INNER STARS
SEASON 2 EPISODE 1

A MEETING OF MINDS AND BODIES

M. D. COOPER
NEW YORK TIMES BESTSELLING AUTHOR

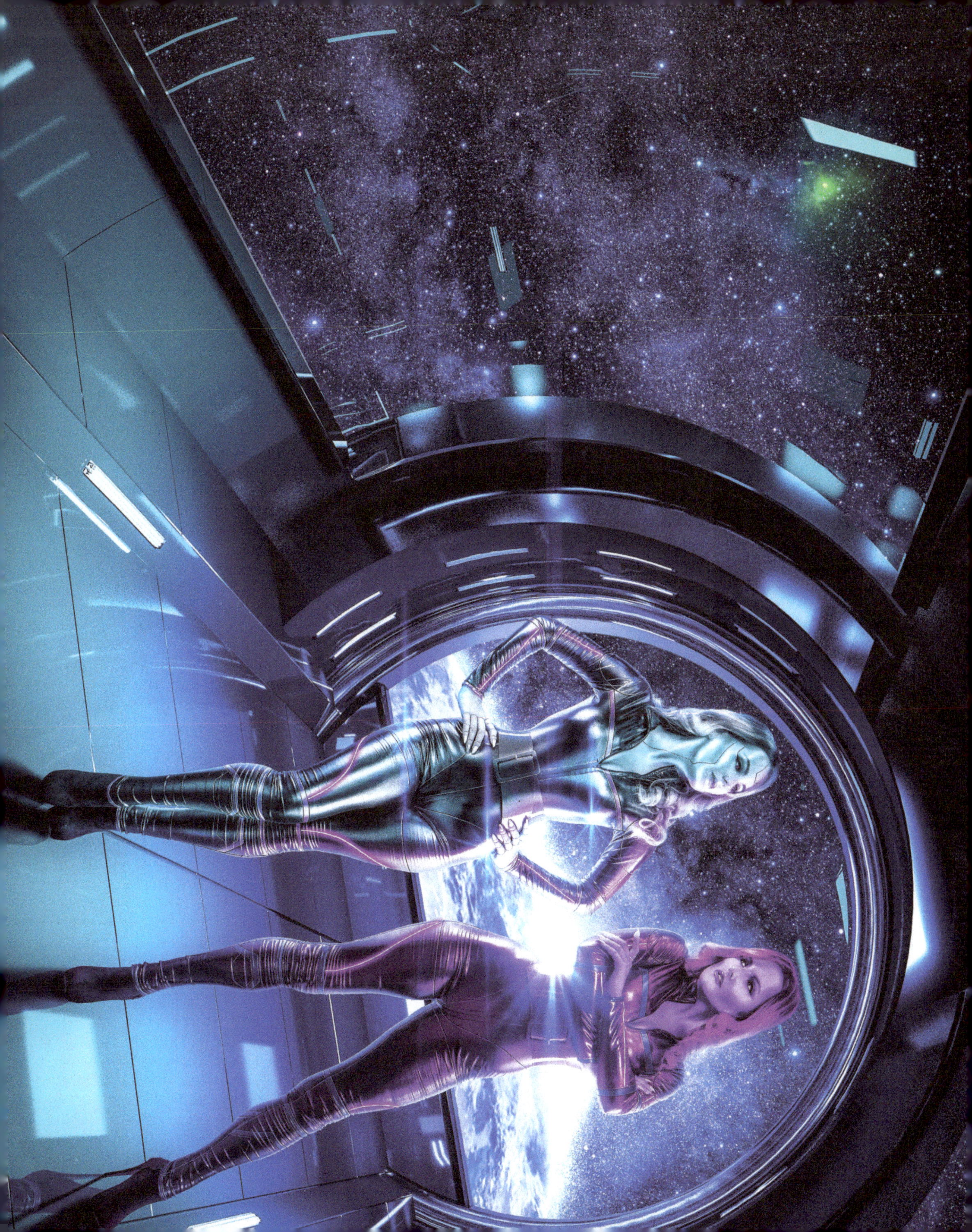

AEON 14
AGE OF THE ORION WAR

PERSEUS GATE: INNER STARS
SEASON 2 EPISODE 2

While writing A Meeting of Minds and Bodies, I realized that I had made a grave mistake: the novel was going to be twice as long as I had anticipated.

That meant there needed to be a new book 2 in the second season of Perseus Gate. In the space of one day, Andrew and I discussed the cover, and he whipped it up, creating one of my favorite covers in very short order.

A DECEPTION AND A PROMISE KEPT

M. D. COOPER

NEW YORK TIMES BESTSELLING AUTHOR

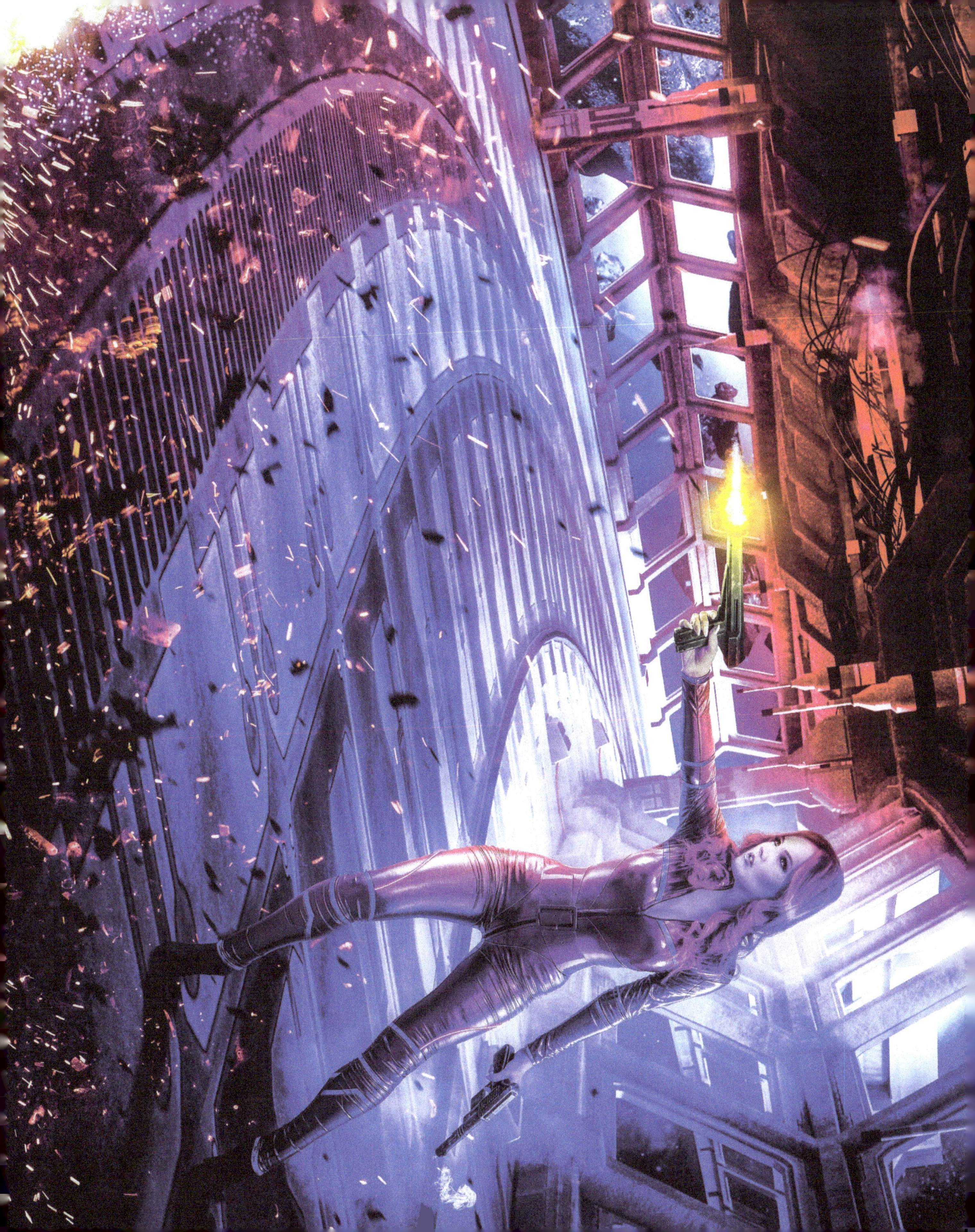

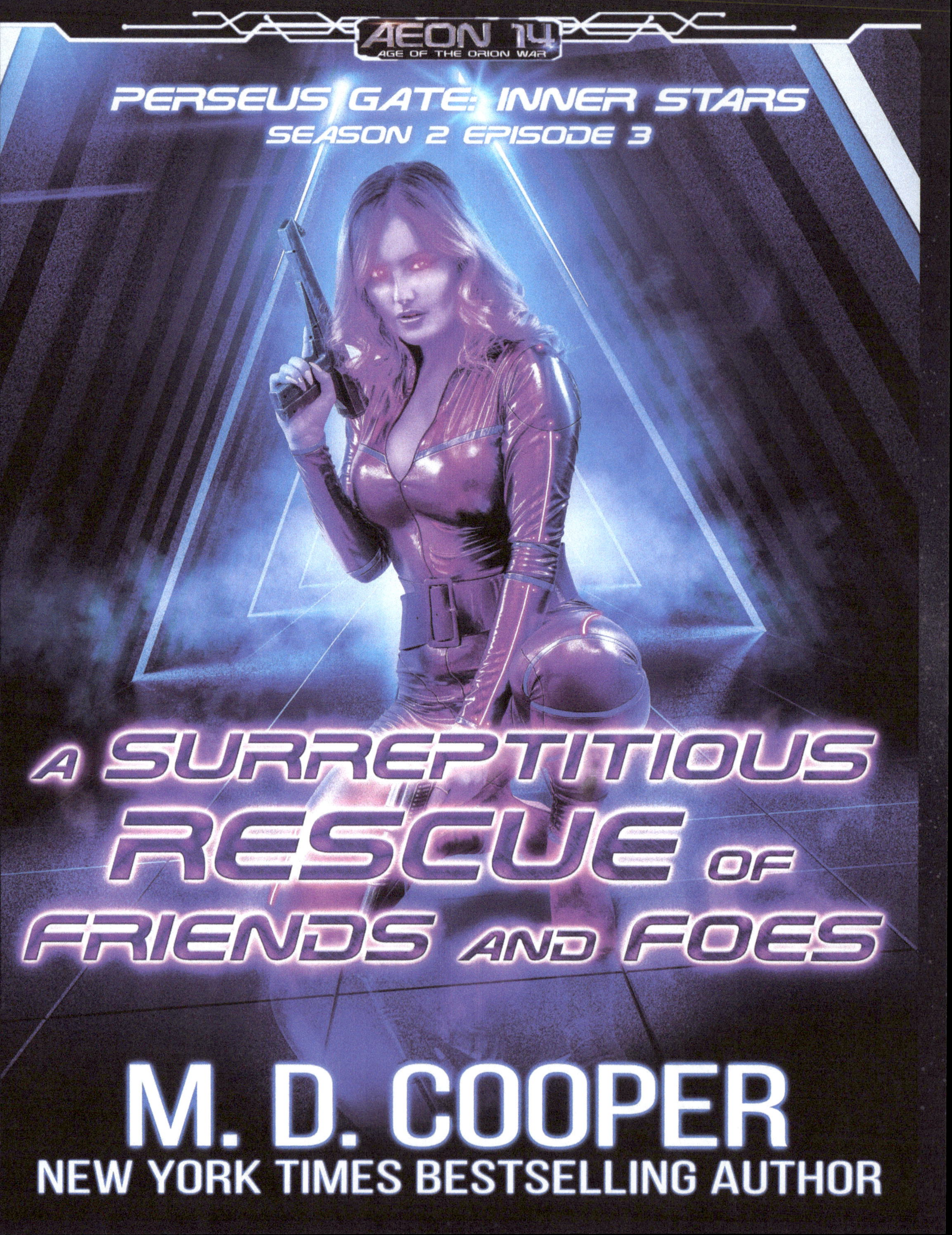

AEON 14
AGE OF THE ORION WAR
PERSEUS GATE: INNER STARS
SEASON 2 EPISODE 3
A SURREPTITIOUS RESCUE OF FRIENDS AND FOES
M. D. COOPER
NEW YORK TIMES BESTSELLING AUTHOR

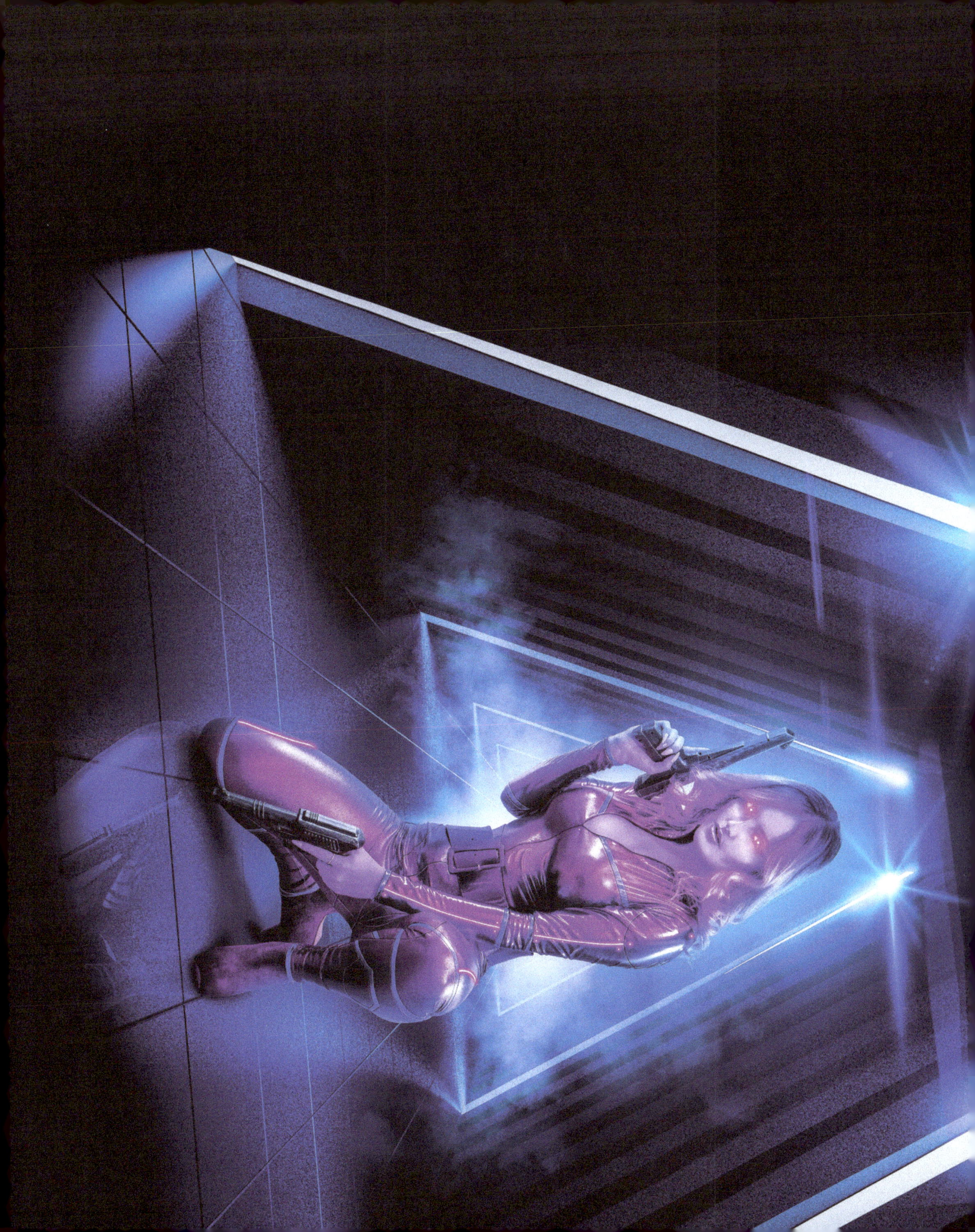

What would be the cover of Airthan Ascendancy, if book covers were wide enough to show a scene such as this. Your eyes do not deceive you, there are three Seras. What should be more concerning, however, is that there are only 2 BLTs.

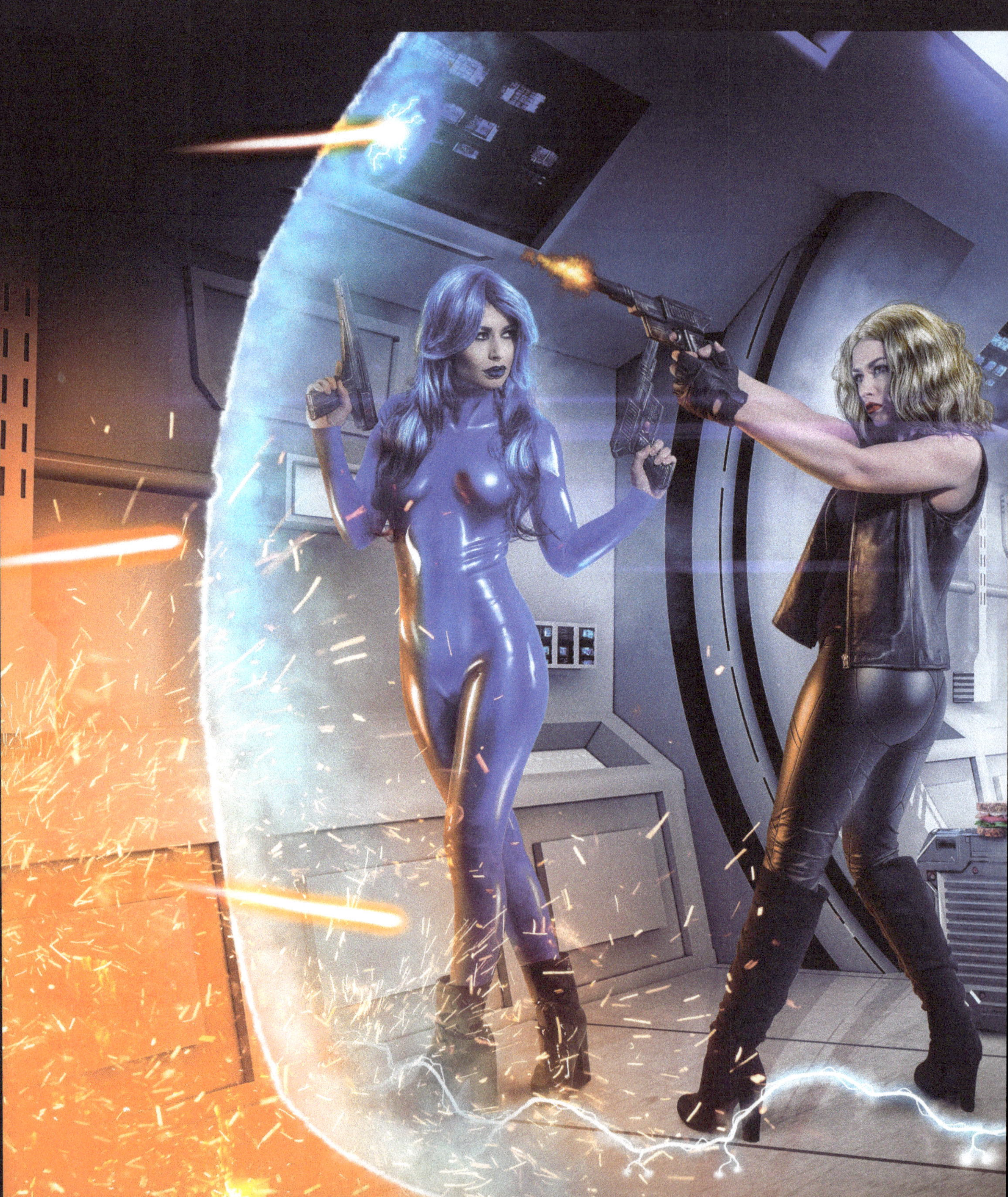

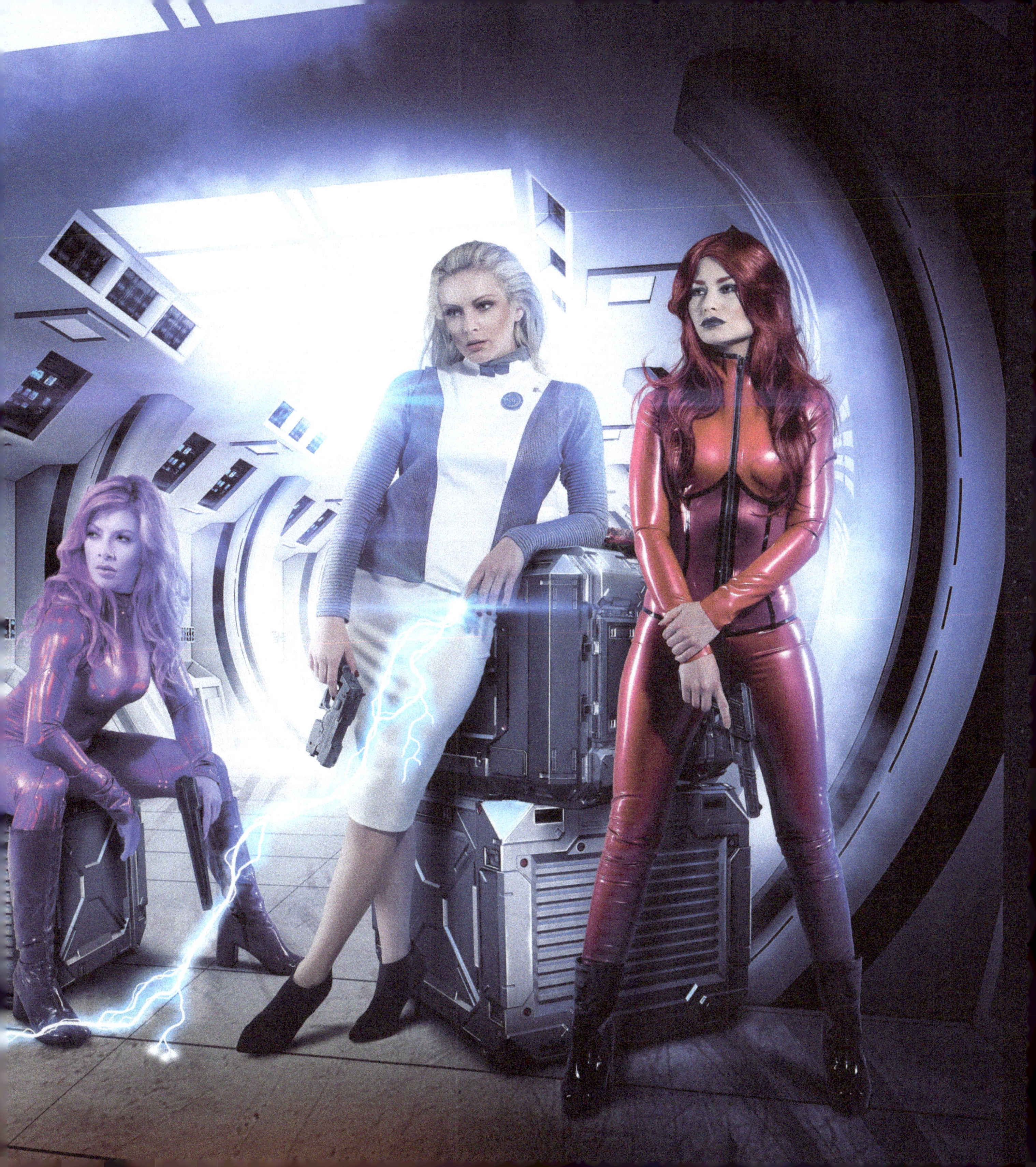

ATTRIBUTION AND CREDITS

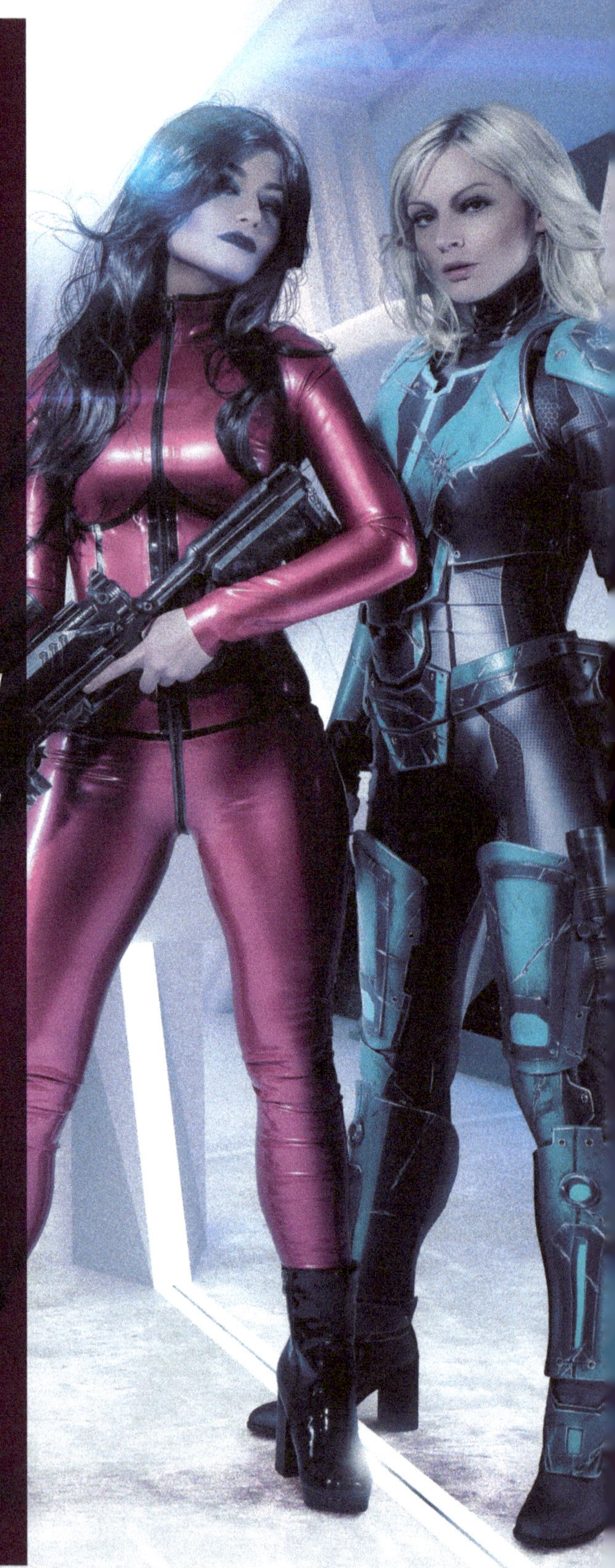

Covers created by Ravven: 2nd & 3rd edition *Outsystem*, 1st edition *A Path in the Darkness*, 1st edition *Destiny Lost*.
Website: www.ravven.com

Covers created by Laércio Messias: 1st edition *New Canaan*, 1st edition *Orion Rising*, 1st edition *The Scipio Alliance*, 1st edition *Attack on Thebes*, *Close Proximity*, *Strike Vector*, *Collision Course*, *Impact Imminent*.
Website: lrcdesigner.wixsite.com/laercioportfolio

Covers created by Ben Ro: 2nd edition *The Complete Intrepid Saga* (print) & ship art used on ebook edition.

Covers created by Adam Burn: *Destiny Rising*.

Covers created by Tom Edwards: 1st edition *Building Victoria*. Rendering of the *Intrepid* also used on: 1st edition *Destiny Lost*, 1st edition *The Complete Intrepid Saga*, 1st edition *New Canaan*.
Website: www.tomedwardsdesign.com

Covers created by Andrew Dobell: 4th edition *Outsystem*, *Special Edition Outsystem*, 2nd edition *A Path in the Darkness*, 2nd edition *Building Victoria*, 2nd edition *Destiny Lost*, 2nd edition *New Canaan*, 2nd edition *Orion Rising*, 2nd edition *The Scipio Alliance*, 2nd edition *Attack on Thebes*, 1st & 2nd edition *War on a Thousand Fronts*, *Fallen Empire*, *Critical Inertia*, all Perseus Gate covers, Fan Fiction Book, *Carthage*.
Website: www.creativeedgestudios.com

Covers by M. D. Cooper: *Set the Galaxy on Fire*, *Ignite the Stars Within*, *To Fly Sabrina*, *Date Night on Johannes Station*.

Version of Intrepid on Fan Fiction book and *Carthage*: Kalishnakov
Tanis's armor: Valkyrie Cosplay (etsy.com/shop/ValkyrieCosplay)
All photoshoots: Andrew Dobell

Art on cover, 1st page, preceding page, this page: Andrew Dobell.

Much of the typography on covers displayed in this book has been altered by, or originally crafted by, M. D. Cooper. Any errors are mine.

Layout, design, typography, and creation of this book: M. D. Cooper. Editing of this book: Jen McDonnell.

All art, photography, stock images, fonts, & creative displayed herein are used with permission and appropriate licenses which are available upon request.